BIORELATIVITY

PLANETARY HEALING TECHNOLOGIES

through David K. Miller

Other Publications by
David K. Miller

BIORELATIVITY

PLANETARY HEALING TECHNOLOGIES

channeled by **DAVID K. MILLER**

3 LIGHT Technology
PUBLISHING

* * *

ISBN-10: 1-891824-98-8
ISBN-13: 978-1-891824-98-2

Published and printed in the United States of America by:

PO Box 3540
Flagstaff, AZ 86003
800-450-0985
www.lighttechnology.com

This book is dedicated to the Group of Forty worldwide meditation group, a group that is utterly devoted to planetary healing.

It would have also been impossible without Gudrun R. Miller and her tireless work in transcribing each channeling. Thanks go out as well to Linda Abell, who prepared the manuscripts and provided initial text composition, and to Bill Spuhler and Kate Sparks, who performed additional pre-editing on each chapter, allowing for a smoother transition from the channeled lecture to the page.

TABLE OF CONTENTS

INTRODUCTION

Biorelativity describes the ability of human beings to telepathically communicate with the spirit of the Earth. The goal of such communication is to influence the outcome of natural Earth events such as storms, volcanoes, and earthquakes. The practice of biorelativity has been ongoing through recorded history and includes such events as Native Americans praying for rain, biblical figures asking for weather changes, and ceremonies such as the Hopi Kachina dance to influence weather conditions for favorable planting and growing seasons.

Yet in our logical modern Western world, practices of biorelativity have not generally been accepted because the Earth is not viewed as a living spirit, and communication with a nonliving body would thus be considered impossible. However, a shift in consciousness has occurred on the planet during the last twenty-five years. Some writers witnessed a major marker of that shift—called the Harmonic Convergence—in August 1987. This harmonic energy convergence marked a new moment in the evolution of humanity's consciousness concerning our relationship to Earth and to the cosmos. We now accept that human beings are interacting with a living planet, and we understand that this living planet also has an energetic relationship to the galaxy.

We have also come to understand that the planet Earth actually has a response mechanism, or feedback-loop system. We live on this beautiful planet, but unfortunately the entire biological and energy system of the planet—the biosphere—is totally dependent on how humans treat the planet, the environment, and other life forms on Earth. Some Earth events such as cyclones, flooding, and strong storms are actually in response to the actions of human beings. Changing humans' thoughts and actions can influence Earth's responses.

PLANETARY CITIES OF LIGHT AND THE TREE OF LIFE CAN HELP WITH EARTH HEALING

I have been working with the concept of biorelativity for more than fifteen years, describing approaches to biorelativity based on my intuitive connection to my spirit guides and teachers, including a fifth-dimensional group of teachers known as the Arcturians. During the last few years, I have received new information and ideas about how to more effectively use biorelativity principles to positively influence the Earth. This new intervention is based on two concepts that the Arcturian guides have offered: the idea of the planetary cities of light and the concept of using the Arcturian Planetary Tree of Life for Earth healing.

Planetary cities of light are areas designated and watched over by planetary healers. These areas are devoted to holding sacred energy in order to preserve the highest, purest, most spiritual energy fields for the area. This means that the areas are committed to environmentally responsible actions, and the people there are living according to higher energetic principles. These energetic principles come from higher energy sources called fifth-dimensional energy. A requirement for activating and becoming a planetary city of light is to have devoted spiritual beings inhabiting the area. These beings must be willing to work with the city's energies, forming energy circles of light around the perimeter of the area. This circle of light can be accomplished by using prayer, crystals, and energetic visualizations. This will help to insure that all activities within the city will be conducted with the highest energy. This includes social, political, and economic business.

The second technology used for planetary intervention, the Arcturian Tree of Life, is based on the Tree of Life that has long been described by the Jewish mystics in the *Kaballah*. The Kaballistic Tree of Life is formed from a unique paradigm of ten spheres interacting with each other and with the Earth plane. These spheres are arranged in triads. Each triad represents a series of energy fields. The bottom sphere represents the Earth and the reality manifested here.

The Arcturians have updated the Tree of Life of the *Kaballah* for the purposes of planetary healing and now refer to its updated form as the Arcturian Planetary Tree of Life. This update includes the addition of two solid spheres of energy to the original Tree of Life, along with twelve areas the Arcturians have designated around the Earth to hold and represent each energetic sphere on the Planetary Tree of Life. These areas are also augmented energetically by downloading etheric crystals into each area. The year 2011 was designated by the Arcturians as the year of planetary healing: These new planetary healing technologies are now ready for implementation.

The following book is a collection of channeled lectures through Arcturian, Native American, and other mystical guides—including Juliano, Chief White

Eagle, Metatron, Sananda, Archangel Michael, and many others—transmitted in sessions from 2009 through early 2011. These lectures describe the exercises and thought developments related to biorelativity, the planetary cities of light, and the Arcturian Tree of Life and can be placed in the general category of newer technology for Earth healing. Although some of these sessions have been printed in previous collections, we have included them here in order to provide a more cohesive and all-encompassing understanding of the nature and recent history of biorelativity in one volume. In this way, you can implement these new planetary healing techniques right now, actively participating in exciting changes as Earth and humanity come together in unity and healing.

CHAPTER 1

TECHNOLOGIES OF BIORELATIVITY

Juliano, the Arcturians, Chief White Eagle, and Sananda

Greetings, I am Juliano. We are the Arcturians. We are focusing our efforts directly on developing and transmitting new spiritual technologies to help transform your planet. Earth is on a path to becoming a fifth-dimensional planet, just as you are on a path to become a fifth-dimensional being. Earth has certain patterns, and there are certain technologies that humans can use to accelerate Earth's transformation. What would a fifth-dimensional Earth look like, and what kind of interactions would Earth have with the Adam species? One of the most powerful traits of a fifth-dimensional planet is that it can interact telepathically with its inhabitants. This is a form of interaction that is based on the technology of biorelativity, a process in which the inhabitants of a planet use their telepathic powers to help create and shape an environment that is in harmony with their own needs and desires.

One of the problems with Earth at this time emerges when we look specifically at the needs of its inhabitants. When well over half of the population of the landmasses on your planet is either directly or indirectly involved in conflict and war, you have a situation that is difficult to accelerate into fifth-dimensional energy. What are the needs of the beings involved in war and conflict? They want more weapons. They want increased ability to destroy their opponents. Ultimately, those in conflict sometimes even have the desire to destroy the country or area in which their opponent lives. From a biorelativity standpoint, you have to think that these inhabitants are sending negative telepathic thought waves to the planet.

Imagine that you are looking at a fifth-dimensional planet, and at the same time, you are also looking at fifth-dimensionally oriented inhabitants on a third-dimensional planet. You would readily agree that the fifth-dimensionally oriented

1

inhabitants are very different from regular third-dimensional inhabitants. They are more interested in unity and harmony, as well as accelerating the transformation that is called the ascension.

In biorelativity, when fifth-dimensional beings are working to transform a third-dimensional planet into a fifth-dimensional planet, then they can use their thought patterns with a certain technology to accelerate and rebalance the planet. That's exactly what the work of the starseeds and the groups of forty on Earth is now. Their task is to work with those groups who desire to be fifth-dimensional, helping them to transform the planet Earth into fifth-dimensional energy.

Causes of Earth's Imbalance

I know many people are debating issues of climate change and global warming. Yes, there is a definite correlation between the Gulf of Mexico oil spill and what is happening with the climate at this time: The Gulf oil spill affected the ocean currents and storms. However, no one seems to be talking about the fact that the conflicts and wars now occurring are also affecting the climate and many global issues in a major way. You have to consider that the war-like, telepathic-energy thought patterns of the people engaged in these conflicts are also major factors in the imbalance that you are seeing.

Biorelativity is based on the needs of human beings in relation to the planet. So why are we using the terms "bio" and "relativity?" From a scientific standpoint, many people would argue that a new balance of Earth is now coming into the forefront. You may even hear people use the argument that Earth changes have been happening periodically for a long time. There have been ice ages before. There has been warming of the planet. Yes, this is all true. However, from the "relativity" standpoint, major Earth changes are not always in the best interest of humanity. Biorelativity describes how people can beneficially influence Earth.

From this perspective, Earth will move to a balance that is agreeable both to itself and humanity alike, in which humanity's relative needs are balanced with the needs of the biosphere. That is what we are saying when we use the word biorelativity—humanity's needs are seen in relation to the needs of the biosphere and all the inhabitants of the planet at that moment. It is not in the best or highest good of the inhabitants to experience another ice age or another cyclone, for example. Relatively speaking, these drastic events can create chaos and do not help. Of course, Earth changes could be rebalancing Earth in the long term. But you have to ask yourself: Is there a less complex and less destructive way to achieve the balance? There has to be a more harmonious way. Look at all the energies on Earth now that must be rebalanced, such as atmospheric pollution, the oceans, and negative auric energy created by wars and conflicts.

You are going to be called on many times in the near future to perform biorelativity exercises. You will be needed by many different countries and used in many different areas to help alleviate the force of coming Earth changes that are currently just below the threshold of manifestation. In this lecture, we want to focus specifically on the technologies of biorelativity you will need, explaining some newer techniques and newer terms that will be useful in your biorelativity work.

MEASURING THE STRENGTH OF THOUGHT WAVES AND AMPLIFYING ARCAN ENERGY

The first technological term I want to introduce is the term "arcan." An arcan is a unit of measurement that we on Arcturus use to describe the strength of a thought vibration. On Earth, you might use terms like watts or volts or amperage to designate or describe the characteristics of electric energy or current. You might also use certain units to measure the strength of electromagnetic rays or electromagnetic energy. We know that the thought wave is an electromagnetic energy, but it is of such a faint nature that humanity does not have the instruments to measure its strength; there is therefore no reliable instrumentation on Earth now to measure the strength of a thought wave.

You might ask, "Why would we want to measure a thought wave?" When you are using biorelativity, you want to increase the power of thought waves and accelerate the arcan energy to the highest level possible. The reason you would want to do this is that you are seeking to overcome so many other thoughts, so many other patterns, that are unknowingly downloaded into Earth. To effect change, you need be able to produce a stronger thought wave. It is therefore helpful in biorelativity work to have a measurement of the power of the thought wave.

You have some interesting demonstrations of thought strength on Earth. One that comes to mind is the psychic Uri Geller, who demonstrated that he could bend spoons with his mind. There were some discussions about whether this was a hoax, but we are not going to discuss the pros and cons of that issue. We will say that trying to bend a spoon with thought is an example of how one could measure the arcan output of a thought. A higher output or higher arcan thought would manifest a change such as the bending of a spoon. We are interested in how we could increase the thought patterns that starseeds are emitting to rebalance Earth so that there would be less storm strength, fewer hurricanes, and fewer earthquakes.

The second concept I would like to address relates to how we can amplify the arcan energy of thoughts. There are several different methods to accomplish this.

The first method requires that you understand the direction of a thought. Many people like to visualize thought energy flowing in a straight line. If you were going to visualize the electromagnetic wave, you would see or perhaps think that it is flowing in a straight line. Yet in actuality, the most direct path is measured and seen more as an arc. That is why we use the term "arcan" as the measurement of thought energy.

When you are visualizing the transmission of a thought wave in biorelativity exercises, we suggest that you visualize the thought traveling in a curve or a slight arc. Because of the sensitivity of thought waves, how you visualize the thought directly correlates to the strength of that thought wave as it travels through the ethers. The power of the thought is increased by visualizing the thought transferring or traveling as a slight arc.

Bringing Earth into the Fifth Dimension

We know of the value of the amplification of thought waves. We have established our Arcturian temples as places to help amplify thought with many crystals around those who are meditating. We have selected special people to serve as full-time meditators who continually send out positive thought patterns to our planet. This enables us to maintain a beautiful planetary homeostasis. On our fifth-dimensional planet and other fifth-dimensional planets we have visited, there are no storms, hurricanes, or volcanic eruptions. There are no surprise events that can be catastrophic. With the help of our meditators and our spiritual work, we have evolved Arcturus so that a new feedback-loop system has been achieved that helps maintain homeostasis. This is how the fifth-dimensional Earth could look. It would be in a higher state of harmony, so you would not see the current level of volcanic eruptions or storms. You would see a balancing that some would refer to as a Garden of Eden; this would allow the development of beautiful cities of light.

The goal of bringing Earth into the fifth dimension is to balance the planet. Fifth-dimensional planets achieve a harmony of spiritual vibrations that also allows them to interact with higher beings on other planets. Earth is capable of achieving such fifth-dimensional harmony. Yet from our perspective, Earth is still at a somewhat primitive and elementary level of development because there has not been an intense effort to use biorelativity to stabilize the environment. The beautiful advantage you now have is that there are starseeds like yourselves on Earth who are ready to participate in the restabilization of the energy fields of the planet. This will set the foundation for Earth to move into the fifth dimension.

Hold a beautiful vision of the fifth-dimensional Earth in your mind. Envision how, using biorelativity, Earth will exist in harmony with the fifth-dimensional starseeds working on it. In order for a planet to move into the fifth dimension, it must have fifth-dimensional starseeds to activate and accelerate this transformation. Visualize and hold the image of the fifth-dimensional transformations that are going to occur on Earth. They are occurring on Earth now, for there are many starseeds holding and working with these transformative fifth-dimensional images.

Obviously, we are focused on the intensity of the thought, and that is why we introduced the measuring device of the arcan. Let us say that you want to send your thought patterns of harmonization to a person as a healing. In the first stage, you would send the healing thought energy directly to their cosmic-egg field, or aura. Then you would send the healing as a vibrational thought that would perhaps be received by the person at the top of their cosmic eggs. Some people would call that top area the crown chakra. After being received, the thought vibration would disseminate through the recipient's whole vibrational field, including their entire cosmic egg.

Let us use the same analogy with Earth. If you are having a catastrophic event in a particular area on the planet, general healing starts by first sending energy to the Earth's aura or energy field—which extends far above the entire Earth—and then to the problem area. The first foundational biorelativity exercise would therefore be sending energy to Earth. At that first level, you might ask, "How would I do that? Would I send it to Inner Earth and the whole Earth? What image should I use?" These questions also relate to different discussions about meridians and ley lines.

To answer the last question first, it might help to know we call Earth the Blue Jewel. The beautiful images taken of Earth from your satellites and spaceships have given you this perspective of Earth's energy field. To be able to send energy to the entire aura of the Earth, you need to hold a perspective image of Earth from about fifty or sixty miles above the planet's surface or even more. This perspective places you in a geocentric or geostationary orbit that could be as much as 18,000 miles above Earth. Visualize such a point above Earth to start the exercise.

For the purpose of identifying the geocentric or geostationary orbit, we have placed a marker above Earth that we call the Iskalia mirror. We have aligned the Iskalia mirror in a geocentric, geostationary orbit above the etheric energy field of Earth and directly over the center of the North Pole. That point corresponds to a person's crown chakra. The first level of biorelativity is to send that kind of higher fifth-dimensional energy through the top of the Iskalia mirror and into Earth. This allows that energy to be redistributed in a balancing way. In this way, you can send light and healing energy to the top of the Iskalia mirror and then distribute it to the whole planet. We would say that this is a powerful thought-healing exercise for Earth.

Amplifying Your Thought Waves

Remember that I said you would want to send the healing thought with the highest strength. How many arcans of thought or light can you send alone? One person by him- or herself can send perhaps ten arcans of light that could be distributed to the highest point of Earth. This is why we have said that you need to amplify the thought patterns, and the way to do this is to use the etheric crystals. In our Arcturian temple, thought energy is amplified by special etheric crystals placed around our meditators. In this way, the thought patterns and the energy can be increased in strength by ten or fifteen times. This is a significant increase.

Many people believe that increased thought power is dependent on having a certain number of people. It is true that the number of people do influence the arcan power of a thought, but I do want to point out that one person or being can hold a powerful thought for humanity and can even overcome many other people's thoughts and their lower energies—the thought that Jesus-Sananda demonstrated is a good example of this. Don't think that it is always necessary to have thousands and thousands of people.

In general, it is preferable that you have large groups, though. We have noticed that the key number of starseeds or lightworkers needed to have the highest arcan energy in thought patterns for biorelativity is 1,600, or forty groups of forty. We have also said that when you are doing individual groups, forty people in a group would also be a significant number. And when you are doing a biorelativity exercise for a specific event such as a cyclone, it is also most powerful and effective if you can have forty people working together, focusing their energy and their thoughts.

There is a second aspect of this exercise: Once you do the general biorelativity activity from the top of Earth as I have described, then you can directly go from the top to that point on Earth that specifically needs balancing, sending rays of balancing light to that needed area. It is also important to work with the radar images on the Earth. We love the weather radar technology of your planet. When you are coordinating the biorelativity with the Iskalia mirror during a large storm, send the light from the mirror to the visualized weather radar image and visualize that the storm patterns are diminishing. This is also effective.

The third aspect of this exercise is that your thought waves can be accelerated and the arcan healing energy from your thoughts can be amplified by using the etheric crystals. If on a particular day you are powerful enough to produce ten arcans of thought energy, then you can multiply that by fifty if you send your thought energy through the etheric crystals. If you sent a five-arcan healing thought wave into the etheric crystal, then that etheric crystal is an amplifier and that amplification can be tenfold. As an extra boost, the healing thought can also reach the Iskalia mirror and come back down into Earth even more powerfully. You can even use more than one crystal for this amplification—although if you use more than two crystals, then we recommend at this point that you use them in triangular formulations if possible. You might take any three crystals that you feel closest to and create a different triangle of energy, or a triangle of healing light. From that triangle of light, you can send up almost fifty arcans of thought energy.

THE IMPORTANCE OF MERIDIAN LEY-LINE PATTERNS

The meridian ley-line patterns are also an important aspect in downloading thought energies for biorelativity. We suggest that one of the Arcturian Group of Forty members obtain a map or a globe for a visualization of Earth. Draw the ocean flows and currents on the globe and then use that visual image for a biorelativity exercise to moderate the ocean flow. The ocean flow has a direct feedback loop into the core of Earth to help create a homeostatic balance. Those ocean currents represent meridian lines. Other meridian lines that are helpful for biorelativity exercises have to do with the Ring of Fire in the Pacific Ocean, the ley lines going across the equator, and the ley line that runs from the North to the South Pole. Surprisingly, the twenty-four-hour international time-zone measurement is also representative of a type of meridian. This meridian system has been superimposed on the planet, but it still has validity as a system.

In discussing the meridian lines, we have introduced and have been using the ring of ascension. This represents an etheric ley line around the cosmic egg energy field of Earth. Let us visualize again that we are above Earth, and we see Earth's energy field as a cosmic-egg shape. We are in a geocentric, geostationary orbit above Earth above the North Pole, near the Iskalia mirror. We are sitting in an etheric energy state around that mirror. We are multidimensional: We have our fifth-dimensional bodies there and our third-dimensional bodies on Earth. Hold that image for a moment.

Connect your third eye with a thought and send that thought to the etheric crystal that you are closest to in your heart. It could be the Grose Valley crystal in Australia; it could be the Mount Shasta crystal in Mount Shasta, California; or it could be the crystal in Montserrat, Spain. Send that thought of the healing and rebalancing of Earth and the greater harmony of humanity to the crystal. From the crystal, that thought is amplified. Since you are in a higher state, you are sending that thought in at five arcans, and it will come out from the crystal at fifty arcans.

The thought moves from your third eye to the crystal, and from the crystal it goes directly up to your fifth-dimensional body above the Iskalia mirror and then through it. As you sit above the Earth by the Iskalia mirror, you can take that energy from the etheric crystals and send it through the mirror. It is then amplified again and downloaded directly into the energy field of Earth. Hold that pattern now. As you do so, the energy is downloaded into the cosmic egg of Earth and distributed to many different sources and places. This includes many different ocean currents and rifts in the aura of Earth.

As we hold this energy, I want to point out some other factors for increasing the arcan power of these thoughts. Any time you are able to place an alignment in this type of biorelativity work, you also amplify the thought-field energy. The thoughts are not restricted by space. You can also send or receive thought patterns from the Central Sun. Because you are connecting your thought with the Central Sun, you are able to amplify your thoughts from that energy source as well. Many of you are able to work with the star Arcturus, especially when it is up at night in your location; this is another powerful alignment that will be helpful for you.

It is also helpful to remember that these alignments exist not only in space but also in time. The 11–11–11 date marked a powerful alignment, for example, providing an opportunity to increase the arcan power of your telepathic thought so that greater and more effective biorelativity exercises can be accomplished. Of course, the alignments on 12–12–12 and December 22, 2012, are also powerful periods that have great potential for increased arcan thought energy.

We are just about finished with this thought exercise, and so I would like you to rematerialize yourself from the fifth-dimensional body above Earth next to the Iskalia mirror and come back down into the physical body. Know that this flow of energy and light will continue for at least the next two hours. You may visit the Iskalia mirror at any time during the next two hours.

I would now like Chief White Eagle to speak with you about other methods of increasing the telepathic powers for planetary healing, and how you can increase the arcan energy power of your thoughts. I am Juliano. Good day.

THE POWER OF THE MEDICINE WHEEL

Greetings, I am Chief White Eagle. *Hey ya ho ya hey! Hey ya ho ya hey! Hey ya hoooohhh.* All my words are sacred. I honor each of you because I know of your commitment to the planetary healing. I know that many of you have come back into this incarnation now to experience yourselves as planetary healers and contribute your skills and heart energy to the transformation of Earth.

Juliano has introduced an important and powerful idea. In order for the planet to transform into the fifth dimension, it must have fifth-dimensional starseeds working on the planet. The planet cannot enter the fifth dimension without the work of the starseeds. That is why many of you are so committed that you want to stay on Earth beyond the first ascension, or the first wave; you want to stay here until Earth herself is ascended. I honor this commitment. I honor and understand your feelings. But you must also understand that your ascending contributes to the further development of the higher thought waves so that Earth can ascend. It is a great advancement for the planet when the people on it ascend. It is all recorded in Earth's energy field and Earth's aura. Your work on the development of the transformation of Earth is not lost when you ascend.

Speaking from the native people's perspective, I can tell you that we use the medicine wheel to increase the arcan energy of our thoughts. We know that the medicine wheel has great power to accelerate thinking. It is difficult for me to formulate a quantitative measurement the way Juliano has done. I would have a hard time saying, "Go into the medicine wheel and you will increase your power of your thoughts ten times." We don't think in scientific terms. We just know that the medicine wheel is a sacred tool that comes from higher galactic sources.

When we meditate and speak to the Mother Earth in our medicine wheels, our thought patterns and energy are greatly accelerated and amplified. That is why we use our medicine wheel in ceremonies—both for personal and planetary healing. We use the wheel in many different ways to accelerate the power of our thoughts: at night for the full moon, at dawn, and in the evening time. We use it when there are certain stars overhead. We also use it in prayers and prayer circles. Think about this: The medicine wheel is built on Earth—right on Earth, my friends. We feel that having the medicine wheel is helping us in our planetary healing by giving us direct access to Earth's feedback-loop system.

We spend great time and effort building the medicine wheel with the most beautiful stones and the most beautiful crystals we can find. All of the work that we commit contributes to the power of that medicine wheel so that it can amplify our thoughts to their greatest ability. Group of Forty starseeds, create forty medicine wheels around the planet and you will be able to amplify your thought powers for healing Earth. I know that you will respond. If you have everyone work in your medicine wheel at the same time and coordinate the times with all of the group members around the world, you will all be most impressed with the power of your planetary work.

People have said, "Chief White Eagle, what about talking and praying as a form of biorelativity? Instead of visualizing, you also talk to Earth." In some ways, we are like the ancient *Kaballah* masters in Jewish mysticism. We believe in power speaking by using the purity of words. We know that the choosing of the words is just like the choosing of the right thoughts. When we are creating the powerful medicine wheel, we know that each word spoken in that medicine-wheel environment is sacred. Each word spoken there can go directly to the right place on Earth to bring change and create a newer higher balance that can be helpful to humankind.

Mother Earth, we pray to you now in our etheric medicine wheel that Earth can be rebalanced in a new feedback-loop system. We pray that this new process will descend on Earth and bring her into a higher alignment that will make all Earth transitions more harmonious. I, Chief White Eagle, call on the medicine wheel to align with the Central Sun.

We use chanting and dancing because we also know that when we get ourselves into a trance, we transcend our normal level of consciousness. We enter a realm from which we are really able to increase the power of our thoughts—or to use the language of Juliano, the arcan energy of our thoughts. This approach to chanting is similar to what the Kaballists do when they pray: They seek to increase the power of their thoughts. I hope that all of you will work in your medicine wheels in the days and weeks ahead. I will be with each of you when you enter your medicine wheel. Now, I ask for a brief comment from Sananda. I am Chief White Eagle. Ho!

LADDERS OF ASCENSION HOLD THE LIGHT

Greetings, I am Sananda. I am so pleased and impressed with your work with the ladder of ascension over Jerusalem and over the Temple Mount. I open my heart to each of you who have done this powerful work. I want to announce that the next ladder of ascension will be downloaded in Sedona, Arizona. Know that this will be a special moment in the spring of 2011 (autumn if you are in South America). At the equinox transition time, I will be present to help you download the second ladder of ascension into Sedona, Arizona.

I know that each of you wants to contribute to the ascension. Even if you do not ascend in the first wave, know that the creation of these ladders of ascension is the key to downloading fifth-dimensional light. A planet needs ladders of ascension to hold the light and connections to the fifth dimension, and the groundwork is now being laid for the next ladder of ascension. These two ladders of ascension will be a great foundational energy to hold and download fifth-dimensional light.

Remember the ladder of Jacob and how the angels and other higher beings were going up and coming down. Ascending is going to a higher dimension; descending is downloading, bringing energy down into a particular place. Know that there will be other activations, from Sedona to Lago Pueblo and to other powerful cities of light. We will be working to create this sacred, powerful energy. A new balance is coming to this Earth. You will be pleased at its power and effectiveness. Let the Tree of Life also be known as *Eretz ha Aur*, the tree of light, for it is the goal of the Tree of Life to spread light throughout the planet and this dimension. I am Sananda. Good day.

CHAPTER 2

THE LADDER OF ASCENSION OVER JERUSALEM

Juliano, the Arcturians, Sananda, and Archangel Michael

Greetings, I am Juliano. We are the Arcturians. We are pleased and excited that we have been able participate with your work. With your cooperation, this work focused on downloading the heavenly ladder of ascension over the Dome of the Rock in central Jerusalem. This event is a key factor in your ascension work. Ascension into the fifth dimension requires many different connections and completions of tasks. You have to understand the complexity of the ascension and the many different circumstances that must come into perfect alignment in order for you to ascend.

Many of these have to do with the planetary alignments. We have noted, for example, the importance of alignment with the Central Sun on December 21 and 22, 2012. We have also noted the alignments related to the precession of Earth, which is on a cycle between 26,000 and 27,000 years long. There are also many other activations in the galaxy. We know that Earth and this section of the galaxy is a spiritually active and spiritually open area. You remember that we have talked before about eclipses—how wonderful they are and how sometimes people will travel to different parts of the world just to experience them. An eclipse may be visible in Australia but not in Ohio, for example. From a galactic perspective, this analogy could be used in talking about the Central Sun. This could mean that there is a position of the planet Earth in the galaxy that would have a unique, important, and key role in the upcoming alignments with the Central Sun. Imagine, consider, and visualize that Earth is close to this powerful alignment that is coming very soon.

Now, many different aspects of the 2012 alignment have been discussed, including Earth-change aspects and end-time aspects. Our position is that the

December 21 and 22, 2012, alignment covers a multidimensional, multifaceted shift. Some of that shifting has to do with what we have called the "turning point." This means that things must come into fruition, which in turn sets other events into motion. Shifts and changes must be set into motion, because at the turning point, there will not be an opportunity to reset the energy. This is another way of saying that the changes are not inevitable. These are not the end times. Instead, what is key is that all of the starseeds, all of the lightworkers, and all of those who want to ascend—including all of the planetary healers—must give their full efforts to their spiritual work.

What is set in motion now will be accelerated and activated tremendously in 2012 and especially in December of 2012. Whatever is set in motion will be activated. Those who are in darkness, those who are in a state of polarization, those who are working for greed and domination, and those who are working to abuse the environment will possibly continue that path. But—and this is the big "but"—the consequences of whatever path you are choosing will be accelerated greatly at the 2012 December turning point.

Spiritual Effects of the Central Sun Eclipse

Those who are doing spiritual work like you will find a great acceleration and a great opportunity during this time. When you think of alignments, think of eclipses. Let us talk for a moment about a lunar eclipse. You know that a total lunar eclipse may take three to four hours to occur. The actual full eclipse could last for three or four minutes. Three hours before the full eclipse, you might notice that a shadow is already beginning to form on the Moon. A third of the eclipse would occur after another hour. An hour beyond that, the Moon would be half in shadow. By the third-hour mark, the full lunar eclipse—or total eclipse—would be activated. Then it might take another hour to return to two-thirds and another two hours to go to one-third of an eclipse. The total eclipse may only last for several minutes.

The same is true of the solar eclipse. You know that at the point of the full solar eclipse, there is a total shift of the electromagnetic energy and light rays reaching Earth. This goes both for the lunar and the solar eclipses, but the electromagnetic changes are stronger during the total solar eclipse. Certain biophysical and cosmological light experiments can be done only during the solar eclipses. In fact, it was during a solar eclipse that Einstein's theories of light and relativity were actually proven, thanks to special conditions that are only available during the solar eclipse.

I want to compare the eclipse to the idea of the transition alignment on December 22, 2012. There will be a total eclipse with your Sun and the Central Sun during this time—a total alignment of such powerful energy, such beautiful light, and such spirituality. It will last for a day—maybe as long as thirty-six hours. We are talking about an alignment or an eclipse that is many, many light years away. The Sun is about 96,000,000 miles away, but we could not even give you the figure of how far the Central Sun is from Earth because we are talking about thousands of light years.

Remember that one light year is measured by the distance light travels in one year. The speed of light is 186,000 miles per second. Multiply that by sixty minutes, then multiply that total by twenty-four hours, and then multiply that total by 365 days. Now you get an idea of the amount of Earth miles that just one light year is. It is almost inconceivable in human terms to measure the alignment distance. I can say that this eclipse with the Central Sun is going to last for twenty-four to thirty-six hours. I also can tell you that we already began this eclipse in 2011; we are now at approximately a 10-percent eclipse with the Central Sun.

Many of you have already felt this shift. Remember that there is a key point about eclipses, especially relating to solar eclipses. You know that if there is a total solar eclipse—say between 12:00 noon and 1:00PM—there is darkness on Earth at the moment of total eclipse. The birds and the animals become confused; they begin to see it as night. Sometimes there has been great fear during such moments, because people—especially in earlier times—had no understanding of eclipses. They had no understanding of what was happening from an astronomical position. People would act erratically; they would act in irrational ways because the stabilization of the light energy from the Sun was disrupted.

Now I want you to use this idea in trying to understand what is going on as we are moving into the eclipse energy of December 2012. Even at a 10-percent eclipse, you have already noticed and seen that people can become more irrational. When you look at the confused response of the animals and birds during a solar eclipse, you understand that this reaction occurs on an animalistic level. What the Kaballist calls the lower self can become more confused energetically during the eclipse time. As we move past the 10-percent eclipse time forward toward 20 or 30 percent, you can expect that there could be an increase in confusion.

Everyone is susceptible to confusion. Even though you are a lightworker working on the fifth dimension, you still have your animalistic self, your lower self. Much of the work of ascension has to do controlling your animal self and transforming that energy into higher energy and your higher self. For some of you, that is one of your soul lessons. When the animal self becomes confused, this can sometimes activate the spiritual self, the scientific self, and the explorer self. Remember how I explained that the scientists were able to prove the theory of relativity at the time of a solar eclipse? This is another way of saying that high intellectual accomplishments, high spiritual achievements, and high spiritual perceptions become possible during an eclipse.

What would be considered a high spiritual achievement? Of course the jackpot is the ascension. The entire period before, during, and after the eclipse is a time when a higher spiritual sensitivity is available and high spiritual accomplishments are more possible. From the spirituality standpoint, this is very exciting; it is magnificent for spiritual seekers and as soul workers. Right now is a perfect opportunity to be on Earth for these purposes. This is the perfect set of circumstances for participating in an ascension.

We have made new spiritual technologies available for Earth. All of these technologies focus on one main goal: bringing down fifth-dimensional energy into Earth's energetic realm. We are able to accelerate a spiritual sensitivity and spiritual achievement by doing this, especially because we are in the light of the eclipse of the 2012 energy field. This means that you also are able to activate to the highest level of your spiritual sensitivities. Your spiritual abilities are only going to get stronger during this eclipse because you have been focusing and working with us.

One of the new spiritual technologies that we have been able to offer only became available recently. With the help of many of the Group of Forty members, we were able to activate a ladder of ascension over Jerusalem. This provides a new access point for the ascension energies. For an explanation of this, I am going to ask Sananda to speak with you more, as well as Archangel Metatron. I can tell you that we, the Arcturians, have been working with many advanced planets, including some that have actually gone through the ascension.

One of the big spiritual technologies for a planetary ascension is the establishment of the heavenly ladders of ascension. We want to place, at a minimum, three or four more ladders of ascension around the planet. We believe that we can do this with your assistance. Some may ask, "Why would you need more than one?" I can only say that with the mass population and with the high number of starseeds, it is possible and helpful to have several more ladders of ascension. Those other ladders are still in the planning stages. At this point, we are very proud of the activation of the ladder of ascension over Jerusalem. Sananda will now speak to you. I am Juliano.

CLIMBING THE LADDER OF ASCENSION

Blessings and greetings. I am Sananda. I open my heart to you and send you my blessings as well as the blessings of my father and all of the ascended masters. You know how important Jerusalem is to our work, and you know the spiritual energy that is there. The ladder of ascension that was activated was actually a renewal of an ascension ladder that has been available throughout the many centuries in Jerusalem. I could say that in many ways it was easier to reactivate an old ladder of ascension than to create a completely new one.

We are living in a different time from that of your forefathers or your ancestors. It is a time of great polarization and conflict but also of high spirituality and spiritual light. For the first time, there is a great awakening and a great opportunity for a large ascension that will include thousands and thousands of people. Never before in the history of this planet have so many potential starseeds and lightworkers had the opportunity for such a mass ascension.

You may ask, "How would I use the ladder of ascension, Sananda?" There are several important points that I will tell you about this ladder of ascension. First, you must be filled with love and unity to approach the ladder and be admitted to its energy field. You must be filled with oneness that can only be expressed through your foreknowledge of the fifth dimension. You must approach the ladder of ascension with unity consciousness, with your highest consciousness, and with your ability to perceive the unities of the polarizations. You must be able to perceive the perfection of the divine plan that is right before your eyes. You can hold this perception, even though you may not see exactly how everything is proceeding at normal levels of lower consciousness.

Remember that at the ladder's entry point—right by its first step—you will interact with its energy and enter a higher state of consciousness. Do not worry if you do not feel that energy pull or energy opening. Just know that your intent, your spiritual studies, and your meditations have given you the foundation to activate the energy and bring yourself into a higher state of consciousness. Then the rest of the ladder can appear. In the beginning, you will only see a few steps. As you get closer and begin to climb and look up, you will see many steps.

The second thing of great importance is that you do not have to be in Jerusalem to reach the ladder. Juliano has taught you many techniques of thought projection. Yes, it would be preferable to be there in Jerusalem at the moment when the ascension energy is at its highest, at the moment you can ascend. But at the same time, know that the ascension ladder and the mass ascension occurring at this point above the Temple of the Rock will have a positive effect of untold magnitude on the entire planet.

It is one thing for an ascension to occur in remote areas like Lago Puelo, Argentina, where only a few people would actually witness it. But it is quite another matter when the skies open up, the ladder of ascension appears, and thousands of people begin to ascend over Jerusalem. You know how everyone watches Jerusalem. You know how the news of that area travels with lightning speed around the planet. Even if you cannot be there personally, you can thought-project yourself there. Now we have a Group of Forty member there to hold and anchor the light of ascension and the ladder of ascension for the starseeds and lightworkers.

The third aspect of this ladder is that is that as you meditate, visualize, and transport yourself etherically to the heavenly ladder of ascension, you will experience a magnificent feeling of ecstasy and joy. I can assure you from my own personal experience that nothing can compare to the joy and the ecstasy of an ascension. No experience on Earth can even come close. You will grasp all of the pains, sorrows, trials, and tribulations that you have gone through during all of your lifetimes on Earth and you will receive them all with love and joy at that moment.

You will know that all of the work you have done and all of your experiences have brought you here and prepared you for this ascension. At the time these circumstances occurred, you may not have understood why you were going through this particular problem or why this particular circumstance came upon you, but it will become so very clear the moment you approach and go up the ladder. You will understand that this was part of the process and preparation for your ascension. I know from personal experience that a cruel and painful death will not be a barrier in any way to your ascension. That has been proven. It has been experienced. It has been shown to the world. This does not mean that you must or will have such a death, but it does show and teach that all Earth experiences will be put into the right perspective at the ascension. *Kadosh, Kadosh, Kadosh, Adonai Tzevaoth.*

We are going to work with Juliano to establish three more ascension ladders on this planet. I will be with Juliano and Archangel Metatron when they reveal the locations of those ladders. We must anchor and hold the energies of the ladder of ascension over the Temple Rock for at least the next thirty days, and then we can begin to point to the next one. Remember to use thought projections. Send yourself to this area and to this ascension ladder. Use the etheric crystals that Juliano and the Arcturians brought down—they can serve as a spiritual particle accelerator. Juliano was talking about physics and cosmology, and we can use this analogy for increasing spiritual energies. So if you want to spiritually project yourself to the ladder of ascension over the Dome of the Rock—the Temple of the Mount—then you could use the etheric crystals as a spiritual accelerator.

Go now to your favorite etheric crystal, as Juliano instructed you. I am sending my light and energy directly to Montserrat, where that beautiful etheric crystal is. Send your light and energy to Montserrat near Barcelona, Spain, if you want to join me. The light of Montserrat is being projected to the ladder of ascension now. Now project yourself from the Montserrat etheric crystal to the base of the ladder of ascension over Jerusalem. I am there at the base of the ladder to greet you. As we stand at the base of the ladder, look up with me to the higher rungs. Look upward to the fifth dimension. You cannot climb the ladder now, but I have opened the doorway. I have opened the ladder's energy field. Look up with me and see the angelic hosts. There is my son, Archangel Michael. Let him speak to you now from the sixth rung of the ladder. He is at the sixth rung, floating in etheric light. I am Sananda.

SHIMMERING UP THE LADDER OF ASCENSION

Greetings, I am Archangel Michael. I welcome you all to this beautiful ladder of ascension. You can feel the interaction of all of the prophets, the great sages, and the great religious leaders who have been at this place over the centuries. I am helping to bring a new activation, along with the renewed activation from all of the fathers. That is the new activation of the star families, the star brotherhood and sisterhood, and the fifth-dimensional masters.

The fifth-dimensional light is beaming down the ladder from the Central Sun. I am helping to bathe and direct that light to each of you. Receive this light now. It will help you to better climb the rungs and steps of the ladders—the ladders of ascension. As you approach the ladder and the steps of ascension, become aware that your body is like a coat. All you have to do is take off the coat, and you are in your soul light; you are in your soul energy field. *Nefesh Ha Ya. Nefesh Ha Tov. Neshamah. Neshamah.*

The light of your higher self is radiating as you move closer to the ladders of ascension and to the steps of ascension. The Neshamah is your higher self. Juliano has talked to you about shimmering, a process that connects you with your fifth-dimensional self. Visualize at this moment that your fifth-dimensional self is at the top of the ladder and that you are now in a heightened state with your third-dimensional self. You are in such a heightened state that you could take the coat of your lower self off and shimmer yourself to the top of the ladder. Your fifth-dimensional self is there waiting for you at the top of the ladder of ascension. At the count of three, I ask you to shimmer yourself up to the top. Your physical body will remain down here. Shimmer to the top of the ladder now!

We are now in a beautiful etheric garden with high-frequency light. You are released temporarily from the burden of your third-dimensional body as you sit here in a great circle with me—Archangel Michael—Sananda, and Juliano. I will enter into silence and meditation while you experience this great light. [. . .] It is so good to be with friends in this circle of light. It is great to be in this great circle of light with your starseed friends. I wanted each of you to know that. You are in a circle of friendship; you are in a circle of brotherhood and sisterhood. We are called the White Brotherhood and Sisterhood. We are a soul group. We are a soul family devoted to the highest light possible. Shimmer back to your third-dimensional body on Earth now!

We are back at the base of the ladder of ascension. You have shimmered yourself back with a huge new spiritual light quotient, a new spiritual energy field. You have helped us to reactivate the ladder of ascension in Jerusalem in a deeper way. Return back to the etheric crystal that you started from—in many cases, it will be Montserrat. Then travel back to your physical body, to wherever you started from. Reenter in perfect alignment. Place your right hand over your heart and—if you feel it—state the affirmation: "I feel my heart energy connected to this ladder of ascension over Jerusalem."

You may remove your hand. Remember that Juliano has told you that we are only 10 percent into the eclipse energy. Look what we can already accomplish with 10 percent. Imagine what higher energy and spiritual light you can experience as we move closer to the total eclipse of the 2012 time. I feel tears of joy for you because I know how hard it is to be on Earth. At the same time, I know how joyful and how loving it is to join us when you go up this ladder. To the best of your ability, try to love your life and what you are doing; try to bring the highest amount of your soul energy into this body.

Know that this connection to the ladder of ascension goes deep into the magnetic energy field of Earth. At the same time as it is going up to the fifth dimension, this ladder of ascension is also bringing down fifth-dimensional light into the core of Earth. It is spreading this light throughout all the grids and magnetic fields of the planet. It is sending this light to all of the high sacred spots on the planet—all of the acupuncture points. Know that this is a planetary healing light. The ladder of ascension is connecting the fifth dimension to the third-dimensional Earth at this moment. I am Archangel Michael. Good day.

CHAPTER 3

KABALLAH, ASCENSION, AND THE TREE OF LIFE

Nabur

Greetings, I am Nabur. We want to discuss the Tree of Life and its accessibility and expansion. In this time that you are living in, I can assure you that the Tree of Life is more accessible than it has been during any other period on the planet Earth. The original downloading of the Tree of Life was given and expressed through a select few higher beings. Now the information and the blueprint for the Tree of Life and what it represents are being transmitted throughout the planet. This is a positive development. The original Tree of Life and its expansion represents a galactic spiritual knowledge that was given throughout the galaxy and the universe. This is the reason why it is so special, because it represents the multidimensional nature of reality and manifestation.

The Tree of Life demonstrates the existence of other dimensions. It starts with the idea that manifestation on Earth is at the bottom part of the tree but that Earth can only manifest through work done in the higher spheres or higher dimensions. This means that the reality of Earth and the third dimension is based on work that is occurring in other spheres and in other dimensions. What you experience on Earth is only an aspect of your multidimensional nature, and what you see on Earth is only one aspect of the many different interactive and dimensional forces that are occurring. These forces have led to the manifestation of the third dimension and Earth.

The first obvious understanding of the Tree of Life has to do with duality. The tree has three columns. The nature of the tree has to do with the essence of the right and the left columns and how a balance can be found through the middle column, as well as with the top and the bottom energy of the columns. The top, which is known as *Kether*, or the crown, represents undifferentiated, unmanifested light that comes from the Creator. It is the driving force, but it is undifferentiated. Undifferentiated energy means that it is not useable and not comprehendible in a human's mind.

This undifferentiated energy follows a downward path to manifestation. On the path to manifestation, the undifferentiated energy must go through dualities: It must go through the right and the left columns and eventually into the center. The center represents the balance. In order for manifestation to occur on the multidimensional higher spheres, balance and harmony occur in the upper levels. This means that for humankind, there is a possible energy of perfect balance, even though that energy of perfect balance may be in the higher sphere, or higher realm. You can therefore understand that there is a higher balance despite the polarities, despite the conflicts that you see now on this planet.

The second understanding of the Tree of Life has to do with the nature of the Tree itself, as well as the nature of the ten spheres. These are all dynamic spheres, dynamic energy fields that are representative of the creation and the process of creation. Therefore, our knowledge of this process is increasing as humankind is expanding its consciousness. What was unknowable about the Tree of Life in AD 1400 is now more knowable. There is new information, knowledge, and ability for humanity to understand. That is why we say that this Tree of Life is more accessible than ever to humankind. The tree represents how both consciousness and beings are manifested.

Most importantly, this is a dynamic Tree of Life, which means that there is a changing aspect to each element. Humankind could not have known this undifferentiated energy 600 years ago. Now humankind has a higher ability, a higher energy, and a higher awareness through which it can comprehend the undifferentiated energy. I am not saying that humanity can totally grasp undifferentiated energy, but there is a new understanding of the Tree of Life to be grasped. The crown, for example, can also be understood from the integrations of the Tao into the Tree of Life. The new ideas that are now available have to do with the unities that are now occurring in some religious thinking and with some religious mystical unities. New mystical insights offer humanity a greater ability to comprehend the Tree of Life and undifferentiated energy. Modern people can comprehend the forces and harmony that can exist to balance polarities.

THE PERFECTION OF GOD

Another insight into the Tree of Life is that the bottom influences the top as much as the top influences the bottom. That is a confusing issue to some people, because many would say that only the higher energies influence the manifested Earth. How is it possible that the manifested Earth can influence the higher spheres?

The new understanding of the Tree of Life is going to show that not only does the energy come down from the top through all the spheres and manifest, but there is also a backflow of energy. This backflow has to do with the nature of climbing, or ascending, the Tree of Life. This is very similar to climbing Jacob's Ladder. The Tree of Life is going to bring people closer to the concepts of ascension because, essentially, ascension is using your higher energy to climb the Tree of Life into higher spheres and multidimensionality.

There are safeguards so that a total collapse, or a total destruction, on the third dimension would not harm the higher realms, yet the higher realms are interactive with the lower realms. In order for that interaction to occur, there must be an interdimensional exchange. This concept that I describe leads to the conclusion that *Kether*, the higher crown, is affected by what is going on in the lower realms. This seems to be in contradiction to the idea that God is perfect, because being perfect, God would not be affected by what is going on in the world. Yet this overlooks a key point—any characteristic or any feature that humankind can have or manifest is also a feature of the Godhead energy. In other words, God can also have that trait, which means that God is affected by what is going on in the lower realms by people. It is a characteristic of God, so God is affected, but this does not diminish God's perfection. This is the paradox.

In order for the truth of *Kaballah* to be manifested, an integration of all higher consciousness with the third dimension must occur. One must understand the nature of this interaction of the higher and lower realms. The truth is that God is a personal God as well as an undifferentiated energy beyond the comprehension of humankind. People have the ability to be affected by higher and lower energies. That is a characteristic that would be included in God's energy field as well. The contradiction is that God is still in a state of perfection even though affected by his creation. Why should God not be affected by his creation? That is why God sends messengers. That is why God sends angels. That is why God sends emissaries such as Sananda to Earth to foster unity that will effect a higher evolution. This means that the nature of the Tree of Life is an expression of how one gets closer to God. One doesn't directly interact with God; one must follow a pattern of energetic emanations. This is what the Tree of Life represents.

HIGHER ENERGY

It may be helpful to discuss balancing mercy versus judgment as another aspect that is represented on the two pillars on the Tree of Life. It is well known that there were worlds before this world in which mercy reigned. But mercy was so out of balance that devastation resulted from too much kindness. Therefore, kindness is now being counterbalanced by judgment, but judgment can also be too strong. This new balance is now being manifested in the world.

You know that too much understanding and too much kindness will allow certain groups who have evil intentions to gain control of resources and planetary ideals. They may have evil intentions; therefore, one of the lessons now on the planet has to do with understanding the nature of kindness or mercy versus judgment. This lesson is going to be manifested in many other aspects in terms of how people are going to deal with Earth and Earth changes.

Hidden knowledge, which is known in Hebrew as *D'aat*, is now going to be manifested because it no longer needs to be a hidden sphere. A new sphere, the sphere of manifestation between the third and the fifth energy, is being downloaded into the Tree of Life to accommodate the energy for ascension. This new sphere is directly above *Malchut*, or the Kingdom.

We want to point out that while the Tree of Life is the core of the *Kaballah*, it is not the sole aspect of the *Kaballah*. There are many related theories and ideas that form the basis of the *Kaballah* and, in particular, relate *Kaballah* to the energy of modern-day ascension. The first concept and energy in *Kaballah* relating to ascension is reincarnation. It is well known by many Kaballist masters, teachers, and rabbis that this life is not our only life. You have had multiple lives. In fact, many of the Kaballist rabbis, including the *Baal Shem Tov*, were able to read and see your past lives by looking either at your hands and reading palms or by looking at your foreheads. The basic idea of reincarnation relates to the concept that, in order to ascend, you must be able to complete your life lessons and your soul lessons.

In the *Kaballah*, ascension was offered to several Biblical figures. The raising of the chariots by Elijah and also the ascending of the etheric ladder by Jacob are two examples. These were examples of how the people were able to transcend the concept of waking consciousness and go to the higher realms. Most impressive and most important in all of the Biblical and ancient histories is the ascension of Enoch. "Enoch walked with God; then he was no more, because God took him away" [Genesis 5:24, New International Version]. This means that Enoch ascended, transformed, and became Metatron. The point is that in order to ascend, you have to be of a higher energy. Enoch was already of a higher energy, as were Eliahyu and Elijah. Elijah used the energy of the merkava, or the etheric energy of the chariots, to ascend.

THE UNIFICATION OF THE REALMS

The *Kaballah* also offers the directions for completing soul lessons. The diagram, or the blueprint, for completing the soul lessons is offered in the Tree of Life, where there are twenty-two paths. Those twenty-two paths are often correlated to the major arcana in the Tarot cards. These paths are based on the concept of duality and integration of duality, which is one of the key lessons in the *Kaballah*. In the ascension, one needs the ability to integrate and unify duality. A key concept in the *Kaballah* is the work of unifying the upper and lower realms. One talks about unifying the energy on the third dimension with the higher energy as a way to raise the sparks and raise lower energies. When we talk about ascension, we talk first about raising the third-dimensional energy to the energy of the fifth dimension.

Kaballistic interpretations of the traditional stories in the Old Testament also reveal the existence of the other dimensions. In these interpretations, the Garden of Eden is actually a description of the fifth dimension. The fall of Adam and Eve from the Garden is, in fact, a metaphor for leaving the fifth-dimensional realm, leaving the realm for unity to the realm of duality in the third dimension. It is in the duality of the third dimension that the energies must be reunified.

Unlocking the codes of ascension is another important Kaballistic concept for the ascension. The key concept here is that higher consciousness needs to be unlocked. Normal consciousness needs to be transcended so that one can perceive the higher realms. The perceptions of the higher realms enable one to ascend: You have to have a preconceived notion that there are other realms. Not only that, you have to practice going to these other realms. These higher realms are often referred to in the Hebrew lessons of *Kaballah* as the *Olam Habah*, or the world to come. The world to come is really the fifth-dimensional world. It is not the astral world but the higher world to come.

Using the sacred codes to unlock the energies of ascension means that you are to unlock your perceptual field, your perceptual awareness, so that you can perceive and direct your ascension. This is the key: You perceive and direct your ascension. You notice that in Jacob's Ladder, Jacob sees the ladder going upward. Enoch experienced a higher energy, and he immediately disappeared from Earth and ascended. Enoch represents the ascension in total; in the ascension you seem to disappear from Earth but actually transform into your fifth-dimensional self.

You can unlock the codes of ascension using the sacred words: Holy, holy, holy is the Lord of Hosts. This also demonstrates a key Kaballistic idea for the ascension. This key concept is the power of the Hebrew sound and the power of the word. In this case, *Kadosh, Kadosh, Kadosh, Adonai Tzevaoth*, chanted with intention and the right enunciation of power, opens the inner sanctuary in the mind to unlock the keys of ascension. This will then allow the ascension to occur. Again, you must unlock the codes of ascension for yourselves to ascend, and the key is speaking these sacred words or sounds. One of the basic concepts of the *Kaballah* is that sound has healing power and energy.

In the modern ascension, a sound will be enunciated at the start. This sound will be heard by those who are the starseeds and higher beings. That sound will also unlock the codes of ascension and signify the beginning of the ascension. Remember, there will be a sound that you will hear at the ascension. You can unlock your personal codes of ascension through sounds and sacred words, but the ascension energy itself will occur and be announced through a sacred sound that has not yet been emitted. It may be similar to the sound of the *Shofar* (Hebrew for Ram's horn).

The Sphere of *Tiferet*

The Tree of Life is holographic. By holographic, I mean that there are trees within trees. One aspect of one sphere has all ten spheres in it, and then you ascend in that sphere so that you can go up to another sphere. The concept I want to introduce now is the center of the Tree. After you cross the center sphere, which is called the sphere of the *Tiferet*, you can touch all other spheres. This center is a sphere of harmony that has often been referred to as the sphere of Sananda. One goes up the ladder, so to speak, so that one can ascend.

After transcending the center sphere, the sphere of *Tiferet*, you then reach a point where you no longer need to return to the third dimension. You do not need to reincarnate back on Earth. In other words, in modern-day ascension and in ascending the Tree of Life, you reach a point at which you do not have to return to Earth, because you have reached the higher-dimensional world.

This is another key concept in the *Kaballah*: There are other higher-dimensional worlds. Therefore, you can reach a higher plane. Once you reach higher planes, there is no need to return to the lower world, which is the third dimension. The *Kaballah* offers a powerful tool for self-work. That tool of self-work means that working the spheres helps you to understand and complete the lessons of this incarnation. When the lessons are completed, then you are able to ascend. I know that you may not complete all lessons 100 percent in this lifetime, and so we have the concept of grace. Grace originates in the *Kaballah*. It originates in the sphere of kindness, or mercy. There is mercy when the soul offers you grace so that you can take advantage of this opportunity for ascension.

Kaballah means to receive, and this beautiful message of the Tree of Life needs to be received and processed. The energies of the *Kaballah* point to the

Tree of Life as a blueprint not only for personal ascension but also for planetary ascension. These concepts contained in the spheres are also keys for planetary work. There are codes and instructions within the Tree of Life through which the planet and the interaction of the planet with higher beings can be activated for a planetary ascension.

In the *Kaballah*, the master of ascension, the key leader of ascension, is Archangel Metatron. Enoch is the first recorded higher being who was able to ascend. He became Metatron, and Metatron is overseeing the ascension for many people. The angelic world is cooperating and working to assist all of you in ascension. Archangel Michael is also involved in the ascension and, of course, is a great Kaballistic leader and teacher. Your cords of attachment can be cut with the assistance of Archangel Michael. It is hard for all of you, no matter how much energy work you do, to eventually release yourselves from the Earth world alone, so call on the angelic presence. Call on Archangel Michael and Archangel Metatron, and they will assist you on all levels for your ascension. I am Nabur.

CHAPTER 4

BIORELATIVITY AND THE IMMUNE SYSTEM

Juliano, the Arcturians, and Archangel Metatron

Greetings, I am Juliano, and we are the Arcturians. We are aware of the importance of the human immune system as Earth's energy changes. The human immune system is often unable to keep up with the evolutionary changes necessary to keep it intact. When we look at evolution, we look at the different systems that have to change in order for people to adapt to the new energy and the new situation on the planet. We consider ourselves students of planetary evolvement and planetary ascension, and so as we travel to many different planets in our galaxy and even beyond, we are always investigating the processes that a species goes through in order to survive and adapt.

The evolutionary process is an intriguing one, and it is not linear. Perhaps you might think of evolution as being linear because of the work of Charles Darwin and other evolutionary theorists. There is a lot of truth, of course, to their concepts of evolution—that there is a progression on a timeline focused on natural selection and the survival of the fittest. This certainly does seem logical. However, there are quantum energies and quantum leaps in the evolutionary process. Sometimes a quantum leap is necessary in order for a species to survive on a planet. This means that the normal linear processes would not totally add up and would not provide the next necessary impetus for the shift that must occur in order for the species to survive. Quantum energy brings in extradimensional energies that transcend the normal linear process. This transcendence and integration allows a species to make the necessary evolutionary leaps to survive.

The planets that we have visited and studied present a mixed picture of evolution. Some of the intelligent species who have consciousness like you were able to make the evolutionary leap and integrate quantum energy, while others were

29

not. We want to understand what the difference is. Why do some species seem to adapt while others don't? The difference has to do with the beautiful concept of biorelativity; the species and conscious beings on planets that survive have embraced biorelativity.

BIORELATIVITY, EARTH'S AURA, AND CHI

Biorelativity involves telepathically communicating with the planet in order for the planet to make shifts that are in alignment with the needs of the species. We can explain this process using Native American spirituality as an example. Within Native American traditions, one is able to pray to Mother Earth and talk to winds, weather patterns, and waterways, for example. There is also a feedback loop in biorelativity that involves the energy of Earth interacting with the systems of the species on it. This is a way of explaining how biorelativity can engage Earth's energies to help humanity—and specifically, the human immune system—to evolve: The energies from Earth can be dispersed through the energy field of the human aura.

To understand this more clearly, it is helpful to study the energies of the aura and to understand how the aura reflects problems in the immune system. I have often spoken about damage to the human aura from nuclear radiation. Our analysis shows that the use of nuclear energy and the explosion of nuclear bombs on the surface of the planet and in the planet itself have created holes in Earth's aura. These holes, then, can drain the energies of Earth. Likewise, your own auras can have holes. If your aura had deficiencies in it from extensive drug use, for example, then your aura would be leaking energy. The leaking of that energy would eventually create problems for your immune system and your energy field.

Generally, people do not consider that Earth has an aura in the same way that a man or woman has an aura, but it does. Earth's aura contains universal energy that is necessary for the survival of humanity on Earth, and humanity's energy field interacts with Earth's energy field. This interaction needs to be appreciated and understood. The Chinese have realized this concept and have tried to explain it. The ancient Chinese described what they called the universal energy as "chi." Chi is the life-force energy. When there is a great deal of chi in the energy field of a person, then that person is very vibrant and active. When there is a leakage of chi, then that person can easily become sick.

Understanding this, the Chinese have developed creative methods of gathering chi energy. Chi energy is all around this planet and all around the universe, and now some people are even learning to bring down chi energy from outside of the solar system. The chi energy can now even be brought down from the Central Sun, which contains a different life-force energy. The chi energy field and Earth's aura energy field overlap. We are seeking to gather people to receive and download more chi life-force energy into Earth.

Chi is an energy that you cannot see or touch, but it is an energy that you can feel. As we said earlier, there is an interactive relationship between the aura of Earth and humanity. When Earth's aura is leaking energy, then the chi energy is not as powerful for humanity, and humanity isn't able to gather and hold as much life-force energy. We can say without a doubt that the life-force energy on Earth is not as powerful as it needs to be because of these leaks. When the life-force energy is weaker on Earth, then humanity's immune system can also become weaker.

STRENGTHENING THE IMMUNE SYSTEM

We need to discuss with you how to seal those leaks. We must also discuss an important aspect of the immune system having to do with understanding the viral outbreaks that so many people on this planet are concerned about. The basic method and process of a virus is that it tries to attach to and shift the DNA. Through the shifting of your DNA, the virus is able to replicate itself in your immune system. It produces an illness based on its ability to self-replicate using the DNA energy that is in your system. There is fear pervading the planet right now about viruses. The H1N1 virus currently known as the "swine flu," for example, is not lethal, but it is a type of virus that can expand dramatically and rapidly on a planet. An aberrant virus of this type could begin to replicate itself by attaching to people's DNA structures and then creating havoc.

This may be the first of several waves of viruses that are going to come to this planet. When a species is in as much stress as humankind is right now, then these kinds of viruses are usually not alone. There are waves of viruses. Some people even think there might be two or three or maybe even five different waves of viruses that can go through the population. Just protecting yourself from a single virus is not going to be enough, because you have to protect yourself in terms of the whole process. So how do you work with your DNA systems so that you will be protected? We will look at and discuss this from the vector of ascension. But first, we will look again at the evolution of the immune system.

The immune system has not generally kept up with the rapid changes that have occurred on this planet. From an evolutionary standpoint, we could say that people should be able to evolve and help their immune systems adjust in order to survive in a new environment. Some of the environmental problems humanity faces include: an intensely polluted atmosphere, polluted waterway systems, and holes in Earth's energy field due to nuclear radiation and the high density of extra radiation coming from outside the solar system through the Sun to the planet.

These environmental problems are resulting in the depletion of the chi energy field on the planet. However, to counter this energy depletion, a new life-force energy is coming to Earth through the Central Sun.

All of these things must be taken into consideration concerning your immune system. There are exercises to activate your DNA system so that it will not respond to aberrant viruses that may make it into your energy system. This means that your DNA system will not allow itself to replicate negative energy from a virus. The first step in this process is to accelerate your own DNA energy. You need to regain conscious control of the DNA process. Your immune system will not allow itself to be wrongly replicated. This new process is open for you because you have used a similar process in your evolvement when you have unlocked the codes of ascension.

In the earliest lectures and discussions of ascension, we brought through a great deal of information about the codes of ascension. We discussed the idea that there were certain core rules and core sounds that represented the codes of ascension. These codes could be toned or sounded. By sounding the coded words, the DNA within your energy system would be activated for the shifts necessary to allow your ascension. This has several important basic ideas. The first is that to ascend requires a shift in your DNA. This is different from the shift in DNA we are talking about with viruses. In that case, a virus replicates itself within your energy system to create an illness. The opposite is true of the DNA shift in ascension.

We are opening up positive evolutionary codes through certain tones and sounds that will allow your brain and your energy systems to unlock the codes of ascension. This will allow a major evolutionary change in your energy systems. The tones and sounds for unlocking the codes of ascension were brought through Archangel Metatron and Archangel Michael. The tones are the Hebrew words *Kadosh, Kadosh, Kadosh, Adonai Tzevaoth*—holy, holy, holy is the Lord of Hosts. These are ancient Hebrew words, but they have galactic origins. The tones and sounds of these words resonate with the internal DNA that controls your ascension. With the right toning, you can unlock the codes of ascension so that your DNA will activate and allow you to make the evolutionary changes for your ascension. These changes include changes in your belief system, in your physical structure, and in your energy system. Remember, your body has to "disappear" in ascension—that is, the body has to vibrate at a higher and higher speed so that it disappears.

EXERCISE: EVOLVE YOUR IMMUNE SYSTEM

We have talked about the energy of shimmering as a prelude to ascension. The shimmering energy is one of the exercises people have asked for that is necessary for unlocking the codes of ascension. You also need to do corresponding work to keep the ascension energy developing in your body and to help evolve the other systems of your body—the belief system, the emotional system, the physical body, and the spiritual body—to prepare for the shift.

We recommend a two-part exercise process to develop conscious control of your DNA. The first exercise includes the use of sounds and tones to activate the energy within your DNA to strengthen your immune system, and the second exercise includes the use of affirmations. The ideal outcome with these exercises would be that, even if you did get in contact with the virus, the virus would not be able to replicate itself and work with your DNA. The first tone or sound for accelerating the consciousness and the relationship of your consciousness to your DNA is a very high-pitched sound. We will try to produce this sound for you as best we can through the channel. [Tones.]

This sound is a tone that announces a clearing to the immune system and that you are coming to cleanse and to clear. If your immune system were exposed to a virus or to some intrusive energy, then the first step would be to try and use this tone to pierce it and obliterate it. Use a higher tone if the virus is in your system and is trying to access the DNA. However, once the virus accesses your DNA, then it will try to do what it wants.

In that case, go into the next sound, using the following words: "Let the healing light enter my immune system." As the healing light enters your immune system, there is an acceleration of the evolution of the immune system so that you can next say, "I unlock the codes of healing light within my DNA." As you say those words, the immune system and its DNA are accelerated to a higher vibration. In the acceleration of the immune system, the vibrational energy of the immune system goes to a level of energy that is higher. The lower-energy virus cannot parasitically attach to your energy system and begin to replicate because the immune-system energy is vibrating at a higher level that will overcome the virus.

This exercise goes into the concepts of vibrational healing medicine. Vibrational healing medicine is based on the energetic principle that vibration is the key to all healing. In fact, when a person is ill, his or her vibrational energy field becomes slower. The vibrational healing happens when there is an increase in the energy field, particularly in the immune system. Then we can unlock the healing codes. You have within your energy system the ability to unlock the codes for a fifth-dimensional healing of your immune system. When you hear these beautiful tones and sounds, you can unlock the codes that will be necessary to accelerate your fifth-dimensional immune system codes that will accelerate and advance the DNA in your immune system. For this part, I will turn things over to Archangel Metatron, who will guide you through these words, then I will return. This is Juliano.

Access DNA through Healing Light

Greetings, I am Archangel Metatron. You have the ability to have advanced immune systems and advanced DNA work. When you read stories of miraculous healings, you may wonder how this happens. The way it happens is that the healer is able to send energy and light into the DNA of the healee's immune system. That DNA begins to unlock the energy of the person so that he or she is healed. What is important to understand about this type of healing is that the DNA energy is unlocked. When a healer knows how to access the DNA through healing light, this is the most effective healing.

At this time you want the most advanced and vibrationally high immune system possible, because you want to be able to fend off the lower-vibrational viruses that may come into your immune system. The idea of placing higher energy into cellular structures has been demonstrated by the beautiful idea of sending love energy to water. You may have seen these beautiful images by a Japanese man who has shown how the molecular structure of water changes based on the love energy that is sent to the water molecules. We can unlock the codes of the immune system through these tones and sounds, and it will put you in such a high vibrational state that if you come in contact with lower-vibrational microbes, bacteria, or viruses, they will not be able to enter. If the viruses do enter, then their instructions to your DNA on a cellular level will not be effective.

You have heard the tones and sounds that we are going to use, and we are going to send them together. The first one will unlock the codes of ascension again. The tones for the codes of ascension can also be used to unlock the codes for your immune system. Then we will also use special codes for unlocking the immune system. Even though your codes of ascension have already been unlocked, remember that it is a process that needs to be updated and repeated, partially because there is a general density and slow energy on the third dimension. [Tones.] *Kadosh, Kadosh, Kadosh, Adonai Tzevaoth.* I, Archangel Metatron, call on the healing light to unlock the codes of ascension for everyone who is hearing or reading these words. In particular, I send this healing energy to the country of Mexico, which has experienced the central energy of this virus. The country of Mexico will now be more in alignment with the opening of the codes of ascension for the planet.

Now focus on your immune system. We will use the famous Hebrew phrases that you have heard before: *El Na Refa Na La* . This is also a code for unlocking the immune system so that the changes can occur. You can say this affirmation: "This is my intention. My higher energy will unlock my higher codes in my immune system so that my immune system will raise a higher vibration. *El Na Refa Na La.*" Let your immune system go to a higher-vibrational energy field now! *El*

Na Refa Na La. Now feel your energy system and feel your immune system. They have jumped in a quantum way to a higher vibrational frequency. If you feel that there is a lower energy trying to come into your immune system, then say this affirmation: "Only higher vibrational energy can come through my immune system. Lower vibrational energy cannot come through. I seal my aura."

Each country has an immune system energy field. I, Archangel Metatron, am looking at the immune-system energy field of the entire country of Mexico. It is true that there is a leak in the immune system of that country. There is a collective interaction on the immune systems. The immune system responds to lower vibrations. It responds to fear. There is a necessity to raise the vibrational field of the entire country of Mexico and its relationship to its energetic immune system. In this meditation, focus now on Mexico and listen to my words: "*El Na Refa Na La,* Mexico."

I, Archangel Metatron, bring down a golden corridor of light through the center of Mexico City. This golden corridor of light is connected with the energy field of the Central Sun. A new chi life-force energy from the Central Sun is being downloaded into the center of Mexico City now. That chi energy field is expanding over the whole city. It is expanding over the whole country, and there is an enhanced chi life-force energy. This chi life-force energy is filling up the depleted chi energy field in Mexico. There was a depletion of chi energy field around Mexico, and it was trying to spread throughout the planet.

As we go around the planet Earth, we fill up all of the leaks and we hold a higher vibration. *El Na Refa Na La.* So I ask you to say, "I am able to hold this newer vibrational field in my immune system. I am able to hold this higher vibrational field in my immune system. Lower energies cannot attach themselves to my immune system and use my DNA. My DNA will only be used for ascension and acceleration into higher energy fields. My DNA will only be used for accelerating my ascension and higher energy fields." Hold this light. Hold this thought now in a brief meditation. *Kadosh, Kadosh, Kadosh, Adonai Tzevaoth. El Na Refa Na La.* The energy light of Archangel Raphael is filling your immune system now with golden light, unlocking the codes for a highly advanced immune system. Archangel Raphael is the great healer and his light is now going into each of you to advance your immune systems. I, Archangel Metatron, am sending the healing light of Archangel Raphael to Mexico to raise the energy level of the immune system of the whole country.

Juliano has talked about the relationship between biorelativity, Earth, and how Earth's energy can help accelerate your own healing. This process needs to begin with connecting to the chi life-force energy of the Central Sun. The second part is that you need to work through your divine meditations to seal Earth's energy field. I recommend that you seal the aura of Earth using the ring of ascension. It is difficult for even a large group of people to work on sealing Earth's aura because it is so large and there are so many deviations. The ring of ascension is already in place. It is like a halo, and you can project your energies into the ring of ascension and this will propagate a healing and a sealing of Earth's aura. Finally, focus on Earth's power spots. The power spots are where higher-vibrational energy resides. Connect with that higher-vibrational energy from Earth. These power spots contain special energetic boosts to your immune systems. I am Archangel Metatron. I return you to Juliano.

PULSING EXERCISE TO CLEANSE THE AURA

Greetings, I am Juliano. We will conclude with a pulsing exercise. Visualize your aura and see that it is in the shape of the cosmic egg, blue and pulsing. See that it contracts on my command now. As the aura contracts, it goes into the center of your stomach, the solar plexus, as a small ball. As it expands, it pushes out all lower-vibrational organisms, bacteria, and viruses out of your system. They are thrown out of your aura. Now your energy field begins to pulse and at a much more rapid rate. As it is pulsing at the rapid rate, that pulsing will prevent lower-energy viruses and bacteria to enter. It is pulsing at this speed [rapidly tones]: *tat, tat, tat, tat, tat.* As it is pulsing, feel that the pulsing increases to a point that you begin to shimmer.

As you shimmer, you connect to your fifth-dimensional body and your fifth-dimensional immune system. You can access quantum light and quantum energy from there. We need a core number of people in Mexico to activate their fifth-dimensional immune systems. When a core group of people begin to activate their immune systems to a higher frequency, then the country's immune system will increase. You can represent the newer wave of fifth-dimensional, lightholding beings that have higher immune systems. The acceleration of your immune energy will be a trigger for the whole country to fight off any virus.

This exercise will raise the vibration of the whole country's immune system. You can also go to other countries and do this—even to the whole planet. A light from the ring of ascension will help you in a quantum way to accelerate your immune energy. The biorelativity process can attract fifth-dimensional energy through the ring of ascension and bring that fifth-dimensional energy into the Earth and then into the whole country. This will begin an acceleration and beautiful healing. I am Juliano. Good day.

CHAPTER 5

CELLULAR AND COSMIC MEMORY

Juliano, the Arcturians, Archangel Metatron, and Chief White Eagle

Greetings, I am Juliano, and we are the Arcturians. We want to look at the topic of homeostasis from the perspective of cellular memory. Cellular memory transcends lifetimes and even different eras. It is carried with you from many ancient times. The cellular memories that you have from your childhood are still dramatically affecting you. Many have looked at reincarnation as the great clearing, believing that when you die and go into the intermediary realms, it is from that position you are able to be reborn. This belief is that there is a cleansing of the cellular memory, and therefore you come back into this lifetime with a "clean slate."

From the Arcturian perspective and from our studies of your cellular biology and evolution, however, we have noted that while reincarnation does mean that all cellular memory is erased, it does not necessarily mean that there is a total clearing. When we look at other galactic civilizations, we have found that mistakes are often repeated. We have noted that some civilizations on some planets, despite the best intentions of many of their higher beings, seem to repeat patterns that end in their destruction. A psychologist in Europe named Sigmund Freud even postulated the idea of repetition compulsion, which states in a very simplified way that people tend to repeat earlier incidents based on their memories of them.

Your cellular memory actually transcends a lifetime, and what you are bringing into this lifetime is often based on what happened in a previous lifetime. That could be a positive thing, though it could often be a negative thing. Some of you have very high talents from previous lifetimes, and so you may now have penchants for the understanding of languages or music that were likely brought with you to this lifetime from a previous incarnation. Those cellular memories are now enabling you to access and work with those traits. That aspect of cellular memory certainly seems to be very positive.

On the other hand, you know that there have been particular problems in this lifetime that each of you has faced. Some of those problems are health problems, some are relationship problems, and some are even financial and career problems. It has often been the case that those cellular memories from previous lifetimes have been reloaded into your mind and into your genetic codes. The energies in this lifetime will bring you into situations that are in correspondence or in resonance with your cellular memories. These renewed situations—coming from the resonance of your previous lifetime cellular memories—occur for a specific purpose. This specific purpose has to do in part with your evolution and in part also with your need to complete certain lessons. Cellular memory does seem to have some logic when we are speaking of it in terms of reincarnation.

The Cellular and Cosmic Memory of Earth

When we look at a planet, we can also say that cellular memory is operating on a planetary basis. When we look at cellular memory and the million—and even billions—of souls that are now incarnated on this planet, then we can also say that cellular memory is playing a major role in some of these conflicts, tragedies, and upheavals that you are seeing. Cellular memory plays an important role in cosmic justice, or what I would prefer to call "cosmic memory." "Cosmic justice" is a term that has been used to describe the rectification of events from other lifetimes or even from other planetary systems. It is an attempt to describe karma on a cosmic basis. It is a term that describes karma in a way that takes into consideration people's energies and experiences from other planetary systems and from other galaxies. We, the Arcturians, believe that the concept of cosmic justice is a useful tool.

In our discussion of cellular memory, we also want to introduce the concept of cosmic memory. Cosmic memory is a more encompassing concept that states that the energies and events that people are attracted to are related to their previous experiences and are locked into their cellular structure; therefore, these people are attracting or bringing that energy together. This can become complicated when you are looking at a planet like Earth that has six or seven billion people. If you consider that many of those people who now inhabit the planet are bringing in cosmic memories from many parts of this galaxy and many lifetimes from other planets, you might be overwhelmed trying to understand everything that is occurring now on Earth. I know that each of you seeks answers to understand the many complicated events that are occurring as we speak. These Earth events may seem without logic and without reason, yet they do have an energy relating to cosmic memory.

The evolution of a planet has to take into consideration the cellular cosmic memories of its inhabitants. The concept of cosmic memory relates to the fact that these memories influence DNA, essentially allowing extraplanetary influences on the Adam species. As you know, the influences I am referring to here are other civilizations from extraterrestrial sources, as well as other beings, such as those called the "Gray beings," the Orion people from that planetary star system known as Sirius, and influences from earlier conflicts on stars distant from Earth where civilizations inhabited remote star systems. Remember that there were star civilizations in existence for centuries and millennia before you even appeared on Earth. These star systems and planetary systems went through many advanced stages technologically and spiritually. They also went through some disastrous and catastrophic energies. Those energies and conflicts from those earlier star systems in some cases led to severe destruction of a planetary system. I know that some of you have cellular memories of these catastrophes. The energies and memories from these civilizations—which occurred millions of years earlier—are embedded in the cosmic memory of many people on Earth.

Why is there such diversity of beings on this planet who have different religious views or different perspectives? Remember, Earth is a freewill zone, and because of that energy of free will, many people and species have been attracted to come to the Earth for the rectification of certain cellular cosmic issues. Earth now is re-creating or has re-created a situation that is similar to earlier planets that were in a state of evolution comparable to what is now occurring on Earth. Earlier planetary civilizations have reached this point before. This point can also be called the point of evolution, and it has also been referred to as the point of catastrophe. Other terms used to describe this current situation are the "point of enhancement," the "point of transcendence," or the "point of implosion."

Become aware of your own cosmic memories. Expand this idea of cosmic memory to include cosmic justice and cosmic karma. Use this perspective to understand what is going on now on Earth. What appears so confusing on the Earth now is actually a reenactment of earlier dramas that have occurred on other planets. You, as starseeds, also have that cosmic memory of these events and are thus attracted to Earth at this time. Some of the starseeds are returning to observe this cosmic drama again. The cosmic drama that is unfolding can only exist in a certain environment, and that is the freewill environment. That environment also has to do with the energies of ascension and of 2012. There is this tremendous spiritual freedom and energy that is also paralleling the cosmic drama that you are seeing played out on Earth.

CELLULAR CLEANSING WITH EACH INCARNATION

I want to now introduce this new concept called cellular cleansing. There is a particular German word that can be used for this cellular cleansing: *Reinigung*. This is a beautiful descriptive word that includes the concept of cleansing and clearing at the same time. In the Arcturian spiritual system, we look for this cleansing, or this *Reinigung*, in several different ways. The first is the way that I described earlier. A cleansing and a clearing can include memories and traumas from earlier reincarnations. We also know that a clearing and a cleansing happens as you are reborn, but while everything may be lost in your conscious memory, the imprints of previous events from past lives still remain deep in your DNA memories. In other words, your energy and knowledge and mistakes from those past times remain as imprints. You do not come back into the incarnation with the conscious benefit from that experience, but you may come back with the energy and the resonance to attract yourself to a similar situation so that you can reenact it, so that you can replay the drama in a way that can lead to a resolution and a transcendence of any unlearned lessons and dramas.

There are, of course, pitfalls in trying to learn lessons during your incarnational cycle. Some of those pitfalls have to do with the concept I mentioned to you called repetition compulsion. In the theory of cellular memory, you tend to attract those situations that were important to your soul development, whether or not they are positive or negative from your perspective. You need to repeat experiences so that you can correctly choose that which enables you to transcend and move on to other places that contribute to your soul evolution, and there is a tendency to compulsively repeat them until you learn the lesson from that experience. We know that in describing the term repetition compulsion, the word "compulsion" in the English language has a strong connotation. According to our review of the channel's memory cells in language, the idea of compulsion implies force: One is forced—compelled—to do something if there is a compulsion to do it. So when we say that cellular memory can come through with a compulsion for repetition, we are saying that it is a pretty strong force—a force that will require huge effort to overcome.

These principles also work on the planetary level. People can return to a planet and come together on a planetary level in order to bring forth new energy and newer choices. The choice now on Earth is between the transcendence of polarization versus a catastrophic implosion due to an inability to resolve those polarities. Having those choices then offers the opportunity for the possibility of evolution.

SHIELD POSITIVE MEMORIES

We always look for new spiritual technology, and one of our missions is to provide and access new spiritual energy. We have studied the entire situation we described, and now we understand that you can have a cellular memory clearing while you are still in an incarnation. In fact, to uplift and maintain your spirituality to the highest level, especially in these times of cosmic unfolding and cosmic manifestation of karma, the ability to work on a cellular level and do the cleansing while you are in this incarnation becomes paramount. Let me review this again: Memory cleansing or clearing can occur in *this* incarnation.

This means that you can have the complete removal of your own memory compulsions, your earlier memory programs, and also the memory programs from other planetary systems or other situations and other incarnations. However, this must take into consideration a very important fact—namely, there are also many positive memories. I'll use the example of languages. You do not necessarily want to remove your memories of other languages that you had or the talents that you had as healers from other lifetimes. But maybe you would like to remove the cellular memories of illness and their manifestations.

Maybe you would like to remove the cellular memories of overattachment to the cosmic drama on the planet. Maybe you would like to remove the cellular memories of violent energies that you might be carrying with you—which also might include your wish to see the destruction of certain people who are harming the planet. Maybe you would wish to remove the memories of your time in Atlantis, where some of you might have been contributing to the energy of high technological weaponry. If that was the case for you, you believed at the time that the high technological weaponry was the way to balance the planet against the polarized energies within it. Now you see that building weaponry was not the way to do it.

These are examples of memories you would like to cleanse, but with the knowledge and awareness of consciousness in this incarnation and while also preserving the positive part. This is the same method as self-protection. For example, many of you are familiar with the white-light technique through which you place a white band of light around your aura. We have talked about using the white band of light around you. As in the placement of other shields, you want that shield to have a certain permeability. That permeability means that the shield would allow light, Christ love, higher Kaballistic energy, and energy from 2012, the Arcturians, and other angelic beings to come through. On the other hand, you would not want the energy of discarnate spirits who are of lower vibration to pass through it. In other words, that band of light allows positive light and energy in, but no one who has negative thoughts or negative energy toward you will be able to penetrate that wall.

In the clearing of cellular memory, you want a similar type of shielding to be in place. That shielding would protect and allow the positive memories to come through, but not the negative memories. Remember, we are talking about memories from other lifetimes as well, which are of a lower vibration, have a certain compulsion for repetition, and a certain power within your system for programming these events. Those would be cleared. That would give you a fresh start and a fresh perspective, enabling you to be in a far more powerful position mentally, physically, emotionally, and spiritually on this planet. In some ways, this clearing would be a true spiritual cleansing, a spiritual healing that would allow you to be free of these lower programs and memories that still could be affecting and influencing you.

A Meditation for Clearing and Cleansing

Bring yourself to the highest vibrational energy now, as we embark on cleansing and clearing. Bring yourself to your highest light frequency and blend and bond with all who are participating now in this exercise so that you will gain an energetic upliftment in your vibratory light. You will now be able to participate to the fullest extent possible in this exercise. Feel a blue corridor of light above each of you. This blue corridor of light is connecting you and your energy to the fifth dimension. Your spirit body is lifting out of your physical body and lifting out from the crown chakra. As your spirit body, which we also will refer to as the "spirit astral body," is lifting out of your body, it will carry the imprints and memories in your emotional, physical, and mental body.

All of those memories and imprints are now coming with your spirit astral body. Even those memories that may not be in your awareness now are still being called on to come into this journey. Your spirit astral self rises out of your physical body and follows the blue corridor of light. You travel through the blue corridor of light to the starship Athena. As you connect with the starship Athena, you enter our huge healing room. In the healing room, there are holographic healing chambers. You may enter your own personal chamber that we have set aside and programmed for you. Each chamber has an appearance somewhat like a telephone booth with a comfortable chair and a computer screen and other advanced spiritual technologies. Enter your own holographic booth.

Become aware of all of the cellular memories that are in your four bodies. You can energetically project these memories into our holographic computer and on to the holographic computer screen. These are cellular memories, so they are directed by your thought projection and your commands. As they are projected on to the screen, notice that many memories and images are going through the screen simultaneously—or at least in nanoseconds of each other. You look at them with intense interest. You process them with lightning-like speed. Take a moment to allow this fantastic energetic light from your cellular memories to pass through the screen. Some of these images are from other planetary systems. Some of these images are from other lifetimes that you may not even remember participating in. You are, for the most part, old souls.

Rest assured that all of these memories are now in the computer, and I, Juliano, am bringing down a beautiful light, a cleansing energy, into your crown chakra. This cleansing energy in your crown chakra is tied into all of the cellular memories that you have projected on to the screen. The older negative patterns, the compulsions that lead to lower vibrations and lower energies, can now be cleaned and cleansed. I want to explain this: It does not mean that they are removed or forgotten—rather, the compulsion energy to repeat them in any way is now neutralized. The energy of wisdom and transcendence that would come from that memory is enhanced and integrated with this light that I send down to you now as you sit in your holographic chamber.

You have all received and integrated this energy of cleansing and your memories. The cosmic ones that are of a lower vibration are neutralized and cleansed. Now, as you look at the screen, only those higher images, those higher vibrations and those transcendent energies, now come to the forefront. Perhaps some of you who are knowledgeable with computers know of the energy called "defragmentation," where the computer attempts to put together certain files and certain patterns. This defragmentation image would be one possible image that you could use now to understand that all the positive images, all the positive memories, all the positive experiences are now defragmented and placed together into this beautiful pattern of light.

The other memories that are of lower vibration and have some compulsion for repetition are now moved into another section of the screen that doesn't have any power. This allows you to be in the highest vibrational state. If there were a necessity for you to recall those memories, you can still do that. There is no need at this point to do that, because you have gathered all of the knowledge, all of the higher perspective, from these previous events. Now your whole computer screen is filled with these positive memories. Hold that vision now.

Now you have integrated and balanced all of this beautiful energy from the cleansing, and you have done it while you are still in this incarnation! This brings you a step closer to a higher evolution through what we have called the Reinigung, the cleansing. Prepare to step out of the holographic chamber. As you step out, you feel the light and energy of our healing chamber from our fifth-dimensional ship Athena. You will take with you this memory of being in the fifth-dimensional spaceship. You will take with you this energy of being in the healing chambers.

Follow me as we leave the starship. Come down through the corridor, following the blue light. Then travel through a corridor back to Earth and come to a place above your body. You are about twenty feet above your body. We will do a realignment, a recalibration, so that you will come into your physical body in the correct perfected alignment. Remember, as you come in, all of the higher energies and higher memories are now coming back, giving you new healing energies, new healing abilities for yourself and others. You have a greater perspective and greater protection. Do a perfect alignment now into your physical body and then rebalance and download and come back into your physical body now. It will take several days for all of this energy to go through your system and upgrade everything through spiritual osmosis. In cellular memory, the higher vibration transcends the lower vibration. All of the memories in your structures are now being updated from the beautiful work we have done in the holographic healing chamber.

In working with cosmic justice and cosmic memory, we could make the argument that you are returning to complete your positive karma for your ascension. There are peculiar circumstances in this ascension energy. First, there is the energy of potential catastrophic implosion of a planet. Yet at the same time, there is also the doorway to ascension. You are planetary healers as well. The exercise that we just did for your personal benefit can also be used to cleanse the planet and the planetary memory. Planetary cleansing is more complicated because there are so many different sources and so many different energies intermingling on the Earth.

You have heard before that some of the other extraterrestrial beings that came to Earth engaged in DNA tampering. This tampering created impurities; your DNA has energies from other planetary systems. This tampering helps us understand why there is so much upheaval on the Earth now. Earth is in a tremendous upheaval on all levels. Earth life would be a lot simpler if there was just the energy of the one Adam species and the original programming had not been tampered with. To deal with just that one system would actually be relatively easy compared with the complexities that are now facing this planet. Earth now has multiple influences that are often contradictory and polarized. They can be harmonized, they can be transcended, but the effort and the energy needed to overcome polarizations requires quite an effort. I will turn the next part of this lecture over to Metatron. I am your beloved friend and teacher, Juliano.

LET HOLY LIGHT FILL YOUR CELLS

Greetings, I am Archangel Metatron. You know that the DNA is a sacred code. You know that the codes of ascension contain sacred codes. When you are working with cellular memory and energies and you are uplifting them and reconfiguring them for higher light, then it must be approached from an attitude of sacredness and holiness. You have done some powerful shifting, and I want to help you now to create the energy field of the sacredness so that you can hold this. You can shift the DNA and the code. Cellular memory has to do with DNA codes because cellular memory is also part of a program. Anytime you look at or shift a program, then you want to approach this task with the highest light, the highest vibration. You want it to be surrounded with the right holiness.

I, Archangel Metatron, am now going to bring in that light of holiness to each of you through these sacred sounds. [Tones.] *Kadosh, Kadosh, Kadosh, Adonai Tzevaoth.* Repeat them twice more. Let the light of *Kadosh*—the holy light—fill your cells. Let the memories that are of the higher holy light, the *Aur Hakadosh*, fill you now. Let the holy light stand in your presence and be projected from your present self to your future self on Earth so that you will walk in the holy light, and you will be able to send holy light to the planet. Each of the ten etheric crystals downloaded into Earth are now being filled with the energy of this holy light, an aspect of the golden harmonic balls of light.

In this way, the sacred holy light and the awareness of that light can become part of the activation of your cellular memories and of the cellular memories of the planet. The planetary energy is now being filled through these etheric crystals with holy light. Pure light, pure energy, cleanses and purifies the cosmic and the cellular memories. Blessed is the Holy One, and may each of you be blessed. You are beings of holy light. I await you on the fifth dimension. I am Archangel Metatron. *Kadosh, Kadosh, Kadosh*—holy, holy, holy. *Shalom.*

BRING OUT YOUR SACRED SHIELDS

Greetings, I am Chief White Eagle. [Tones.] *Hey ya ho ya hey!* All my words are sacred, my brothers and sisters! We bind our light and love together. Know that it is time to bring out your sacred shields. It is time to bring out the energy of the shields that we have talked about many times. Do not neglect your etheric shields, those powerful shields some of you made in the past. Shields are a necessary part of the shaman and of working on the third dimension in spiritual transformation. They are a necessary tool in cleansings and in protecting you from the many different negative energies that are erupting on this planet now.

If you do not have a shield in your mind, then visualize a new shield. If you can't, then find someone who could help you make a shield or draw a shield. If you already have a shield, visualize it now in front of your physical aura here on the third dimension, and let it be reinvigorated. Let that shield stand as a guardian of you as a lightbeing at this sacred time, at this sacred place. You must have a shield in place; it is just part of your expansion.

Yes, you can have many different shields. You do not have to use the same shield each time. Some of you spirit workers are also shamans. Shamans use different shields and have many different ideas of shields. Use the image of the shield that sings with your heart and that you know is right for you at this time. When you are in resonance with your spirit shield, then you are impenetrable to lower vibration and lower energy. Even the lowest of the spirits cannot touch and go through the shield. I, Chief White Eagle, at this moment, activate and empower each of your shields now so when you pick them up, you will feel a new sense of protection and spiritual resonance. *Ho!* I am Chief White Eagle.

CHAPTER 6

THE SPIRITUAL TECHNOLOGY OF ASCENSION

Juliano, the Arcturians, and Archangel Metatron

Greetings, I am Juliano, and we are the Arcturians. The ascension and its energy are flooding the energy field of Earth now. There has been a new and powerful influx of ascension energy that has had a dramatic effect on the starseeds and has also created huge perceptual openings. By "perceptual openings," I mean that many of you are able to see and experience higher realities and higher energy fields and that you have also experienced an increase in your sensitivity.

At this point, I would like to offer further insights about the ascension as well as information about the spiritual technology of ascension. I am aware that many people have described the ascension in different ways. For example, some people have said that the ascension is actually in place; therefore, you will ascend within your Earth body but stay on the Earth. This is one interpretation of ascension, but ascending and staying in place on Earth is not our interpretation. Although the expectation remains among some that the ascension will be an upliftment in place while you remain in your Earth body on Earth, we still maintain that this event will occur as I have described it before. In fact, we believe that many of you also have a different expectation of the ascension. In this understanding of ascension, you will raise your frequency. Your vibration then will move to such a high point that you will disappear from this realm and reappear in the fifth dimension. The expectation that you have of actually leaving Earth is in alignment with our original teachings.

THE POSSIBILITY OF LIVE ASCENSION

I want to just digress for a second and explain about some of the ideas of resurrection, which is actually a galactic term. That term was downloaded into the energy of the prophets that have walked this planet in the past 3,500 years. The idea of the resurrection in the way it originally was explained to the masses was that your body in death would remain in the death state for a period of time. After a period of time, through a miraculous energetic intervention, that body would reform itself and then transmute into the higher realms. This experience was defined as being resurrected. In this concept of resurrection, one must first reach the death state, and then when experiencing the death state, one would then be able to be resurrected or re-formed in a higher fifth-dimensional body in the fifth dimension.

This idea actually fits in with the spiritual technology of the Arcturians. It is a known galactic truth that resurrection does occur on a regular basis. Yet from our perspective, we would also ask this: If resurrection can occur when the body is no longer alive, then wouldn't it be logical to conclude that resurrection could also occur while the person is alive? Why is it necessary for the person to go through the death state in order to be resurrected? In your ancient Greek and Hebrew, the translation of resurrection means "to restore the dead." Within the confines of the word "resurrection," there is then this concept that the dead are restored or brought back to life.

Our understanding of galactic spiritual energy has shown and taught us that it is not necessary to go through the death state in order to be restored. You can experience resurrection directly while alive, transitioning from a high state of consciousness in the third dimension to a state into the fifth dimension. In fact, Enoch and the prophet Elijah both ascended, or if you could use the term, they were "resurrected." Yet their state of being was in the live state when their resurrection happened; they were not in the dead state. The whole idea of the modern ascension is based on this technique of resurrecting yourself or restoring yourself to a higher plane while you are still alive.

Resurrecting while you are alive offers several advantages. The primary advantage is that you do not have to die in the physical state. When you die in the physical, there are naturally complicated events that occur, events that in some cases close the perceptual field and the knowledge field of the person. Of course, those fields can be reopened, but the experience of dying can be compared to going into a tunnel. If any of you have experienced driving through a tunnel under a mountain, then you know there is sometimes a period as you drive through the tunnel when there is total darkness. In that period in the tunnel, even though you know you are going forward and you know you will come out on the other side, there is still a moment of questioning and even sometimes fear about what is happening to you.

Another advantage to what we are calling the "live ascension" is that there is no feeling of detachment from the process. You are directing yourself. Part of the preparation for the ascension is to develop the awareness of your fifth-dimensional self. We want you to remember that you are multidimensional beings, which means that you are living in two dimensions at the same time; you have a presence in the fifth dimension as well as the third. It is the awareness of that presence and the visitation to that presence that enhances your ability to ascend. You know this, and you have a focus on where you are going to be. Focusing on projecting yourself is the biggest problem in understanding the ascension and performing the ascension. Where are you going to place yourself in the fifth dimension? Where is your other level of consciousness going to be? There are so many loopholes, so many places in the astral realm and the fourth-dimensional realm where you can become stuck.

THE FOURTH DIMENSION IS NOT A PERMANENT DESTINATION

People have asked me over the years, "Why are we skipping the fourth dimension, Juliano?" Remember that the fourth dimension has stages and levels in it, including the lower, the middle, and the higher fourth dimension. These are simple ways of describing the levels. The higher fourth-dimensional astral realm is beautiful. The lower astral realm is filled with ghosts and spirits and is more closely described as *Gehenna*—the Biblical Hebrew word for hell. You can use the word "hell." Hell is on the lower astral realm and is a dark place where you seem to be punished or get stuck in a chain of repetitious events that make it seem as if you are unable to escape. In many cases, you are repeating a continual unpleasant event. For example, you could be experiencing a violent act and repeating it over and over again. Yet eventually you can be freed from that. Nothing is eternal on the lower astral realm, even though the experience might seem like it will last forever.

In the lower astral realm, the spirit energy is still more closely attached to the third dimension. Beings in this realm suck energies from Earth beings in order to increase their energy fields. They are in a vibrational situation in which the only way of maintaining or even escaping from their experience by raising their energy field seems to be through a parasitic attachment to an Earth being. There are spirits on the third-dimensional plane that are of the lower vibrational energy as well. These lower beings have attached to people and contributed to some pretty awful things. For example, if young people are on drugs and their energy fields are on a lower vibrational field, ghosts or discarnate spirits can attach themselves to those students and actually direct them to do horrendous things.

All this is a way of explaining that the fourth dimension has lower layers, and you do not want to stay in those lower layers. The middle astral layer, on the other hand, is of a higher energy that is home to some very high beings. Finally, the higher fourth-dimensional realm is getting close to the fifth dimension and closer to the idea of the Garden of Eden, the heavenly gates, and heavenly palaces. It is beautiful there. Many of you have certainly visited the higher fourth-dimensional realms. There are many guides and teachers there. Incidentally, guides and teachers can go into any part of the astral realms, including the middle, lower, or higher levels.

The bottom line is this: When you are in the astral realm after you die, you are still in the Earth's incarnation cycle, which means that you will be reborn again in the third dimension into another Earth body. In certain situations, you can be reborn in an appropriate energy field on another planet, but by staying in the fourth-dimensional realms after you die, you will remain in a third-dimensional incarnation process. The ascension offers you the opportunity to be free of Earth's incarnation process and to go directly to a higher realm. This is a process of grace because it takes a higher energy vibration, energy awareness, and higher perceptual field awareness to graduate from Earth.

Many of you will not be able to reach that higher perceptual field in this lifetime without some assistance. At the same time, I can tell you that there is an incredible amount of assistance now available to help you raise your vibrations. Part of this assistance is coming from the energy transformation of the ascension itself. The energy of the ascension brings forth new light, new frequencies and new opportunities. For example, imagine you saw an eclipse of the Sun without knowing much about astronomy. After seeing that eclipse, you might begin to understand the nature of the relationship among heavenly bodies. You might even be able to figure out that one body is going in front of the other, blocking the light of the Sun. Without seeing that eclipse, you might not be able to understand that one heavenly body can move in front of another. This is the way it is with the ascension. That is, there are events, there are circumstances, and there are energy patterns occurring that are going to offer you new insight into the ascension process.

POWERS OF PERCEPTION AND THE ASCENSION

I want to talk about light and light perception as we are going into the concepts of the ascension. The idea of light is so complex and so beautiful: From the darkness of the night emerges the energy of the morning. When the light comes in the morning, then you are able to see what is in existence on the planet. If there is total darkness, you cannot see the shapes of the trees, the buildings, or the animals—unless, of course, you have night-vision glasses. But in total darkness, you do not see anything. Then the morning comes and lights up the forest so you can see the trees, and you can see how beautiful everything is in the third dimension. Your eyes have certain rods and cones in them that enable you to see certain light fields.

Now imagine that the light gets brighter and brighter. Say, for example, you are looking at the sunlight without any type of protective glasses, and that sunlight becomes very bright. Now all you see is light, but you can't see any objects because the light is so bright. You cannot make out anything, and you are literally blinded by the light. Too much light isn't good. In the fifth dimension and in higher perception, the light is stronger and stronger. With only your normal perceptions in which you are trained on Earth, you can become blinded by the light and not be able to see the higher realms.

Fortunately, you can shape, train, and unlock the codes of ascension that help you to open your perceptual field. When there is an increasing amount of light, the rods and cones in your eyes as well as your mental framework will adjust to be able to see the next realm and to see and experience the higher energy. Perceiving the higher realms is not just seeing; it is feeling. It is being able to see higher experience from multiperceptual levels. You have five basic patterns of perception, and you tend to think of them as individual abilities that do not interact with each other. Seeing and hearing could be one combination that is an example of two perceptual fields interacting. Feeling and seeing might be another combination. In the concept of the technology of the ascension, an increase in the light will also be experienced as an increase in your perceptual field and your perceptual powers so that you will not be blinded by the light. You will be able to see with higher light into the fifth dimension.

I want you to consider this: If we turned up the light frequency on the planet where you are, you would begin to see that people's bodies are really luminous balls of light. The physical form that you see now in the third-dimensional reality is an assumed body that represents many energy aspects of the person— including past lives, illnesses, densities, and the effects of experiences in the third-dimensional life. If you were able to experience higher light and then have a corresponding opening in your perceptual field, you would be able to see the true energetic pattern of the person you are looking at, and you would be able to experience that person as an energetic, luminous ball of light. The energy patterns that make up your third-dimensional body are at such a high frequency that your normal perceptual ranges and training don't allow you to see all levels of your luminous body.

In fact, if you did see the luminous energy balls now, you could become confused and you wouldn't know what to make of them—although after reading this chapter, perhaps you are now better prepared to see these luminous energy patterns. Increasing the light is an interesting discussion, because in the ascension, only some people are going to have the ability to participate fully in the increase in light that is coming to the planet. The light frequencies have already increased dramatically, but only certain people are going to be able to open their perceptual fields to use that light in order to see the higher realms.

When you see the higher perception, including the higher light, then you will also see the connection that you and other beings of light have to the fifth dimension. We call these connections "etheric cords" or "strands of light." These etheric cords are on everyone. However, some people's etheric cords or strands only go into the third dimension. Your etheric strands of light are connected to the fifth dimension now because you have been working with us. With the connection of these etheric strands of light, you will be able to project during the ascension and have your luminous body move to where those etheric cords are attached—namely the fifth dimension—and when you move the etheric body, the luminous body follows it.

I make a distinction between the luminous body and the etheric body. The physical body is an energy field. Visualize the image of a table. You can learn from physics that the table isn't really solid. The table is made of energetic molecules that spin around each other at the speed of light and are composed of neutrons, protons, quarks, and so on. If you put your hand on that table, your hand stops because you experience the table as solid, but if you are in a higher perceptual field, then you can see the table as an energetic field. Then as you experience that state of higher consciousness, you actually could put your hand through the table. This is what people like Sai Baba and others can do. They are able to reach through the third-dimensional reality because they are also in this other realm. With both awareness states—that is, an awareness of this realm and the higher realms—you can do what you would consider to be tricks, bringing objects into the third dimension.

The luminous body is the key to the ascension because the physical body follows the luminous body. Ultimately, all of the strands go all the way back to the Creator. There could be thousands of luminous strands of light on one luminous body. The true prophets and the great spiritual leaders have enhanced and strengthened their luminous strands back to the Creator. The luminous strands of the prophets connect back to guides and teachers. You have luminous strands of light now connected to the Arcturian temple, to the crystal temple, and to other parts of the fifth dimension. You who are Arcturian starseeds came to Earth in your luminous balls of light with many starseed luminous strands. I am going to give you some energetic tones to help you integrate everything I have said. Tones can raise your perceptual field and can put you into the place of what I am talking about on an experiential level. [Tones.]

Unlocking the codes of ascension also means that you open the doors of perception in your mind and in your body. You may think, "Well, where is the fifth dimension?" It is true that each dimension is like a huge ball or sphere and that the dimensions interact with each other. When you are in the fifth dimension, the concepts of space and time are totally indiscernible. In the fifth dimension, there is no space between things—and yet you cannot, in your third-dimensional mind, understand how objects can exist without space. How can there be no space or separation of objects between people? Yet not everyone is together on the fifth dimension, although you can be with the people you want to be with just by thinking about them. This is certainly a paradox.

As more light has come down to Earth with this higher ascension energy, opening the doors of ascension can unlock the codes of ascension, and you will be able to see and experience the fifth dimension right before your eyes. I have described this higher light and the effects of this higher light. It will be as if a bright light has been turned on. Instead of just seeing a blinding light, you will see gardens, and the intense loving light and loving space of the fifth dimension will be before you. You will use this light to see what is before you in the fifth-dimensional realm. Then when the bridge is offered to be crossed, you will choose to cross it. Think of the dream world. In a dream, a symbolic event or a symbolic action is often offered to demonstrate a transition. The bridge will be the symbol for crossing dimensions. That will be your ascension. You will simply walk across the bridge that will bring you into the fifth dimension. And then you will have ascended! That is how simple the ascension can be. [Tones.]

I want to also explain that the bridge and that experience will still be available to those who have died as well. It is not like you are penalized for dying. Yes, it would be preferable to ascend from life, but remember, the first lesson of ascension that was offered by Sananda/Jesus was the resurrection of the dead. You can create the awareness of being able to carry this ascension energy with you into your death. You might even be able to ascend immediately after your death. Even if your Earth karma is such that you are not able to sustain your physical life until the ascension, do not worry, because you will still be able to ascend. I love the teachings of Jesus and I love the teachings of resurrection. Keep on working on the codes of ascension. This assures you of your ascension. I will now turn things over to Archangel Metatron. This is Juliano.

A Meditation in *Merkavah* Light

Greetings, I am Archangel Metatron. Unlocking the codes of ascension is one of the most powerful lessons on the third dimension, powerful enough that one might consider coming back to any lifetime that offered the opportunity to unlock the codes of ascension. These codes of ascension are in your DNA and in certain parts of your brain. You have heard the figure that you only use 20 percent, maybe 22 percent of your brain in a lifetime. The rest cannot be awakened unless there is proper preparation and the proper circuitry established to hold higher vibrational frequency. This is saying that the vibrational frequency of ascension is higher than normal energy. Remember that Juliano described the light as being blinding if you are not able to open yourself up. No one wants to be blinded.

Certain higher energies were given to the mystics through exercises. One of the energies that was given was the energy of the *Merkavah* (also spelled *merkava* or *merkaba*), which means the "chariot." This chariot is the etheric encapsulated chair that serves as a protective device to bring you into a higher realm. It can bring you to a higher light so that you are protected and will not be blinded in higher energy. You can think of the *Merkavah* as the gigantic chariot covered in a dome of beautiful glass that has special connections and special filters so that you would be able to see where the merkavah vehicle is taking you. I, Archangel Metatron, am going to call on the energies and light of the *merkavah* to work with all of you at this point. Some of you had lifetimes in ancient Egypt, and you will recognize this word, "Merkavah," composed of *Mer, Ka*—you remember the *Ka*, the energy in ancient Egypt—and *Va* or *Vah*. This is an ancient energy that was transformed and transmitted—merkavah light!

Visualize your divine chariot before you. Step into your merkavah chariot. As you step into the merkavah chariot, you sense there is a glass dome and you reach behind you and close the dome so that it is totally encapsulating the chariot that is going to transport you. [Sings.] *Merkavah.* Close your eyes, and as you close your eyes, you are transported. You are being transported even though you feel no movement. This is the technology of *Merkavah.* As you open your eyes, you are in a divine garden known as *Gan Eden*, the Garden of Eden, a fifth-dimensional paradise. It has beautiful light. It is primordial light. It has the light of Adam Kadmon, the light that Adam saw. It is the first light. This light was the very first light in the Garden of Eden.

You open up the top of the merkavah chariot and you see this light. It is a combination of morning light, mist, and multicolored light—a multidimensional light that you have never seen on the Earth. You walk into this garden and you can see and feel and hear this light. This is holy light! You see divine beings in the garden that are in this light, walking with this light. Within you is awakened your ascension light and ascension energy—holy light, light of the merkavah garden. Blessings are in the light. In this garden, you feel how vast it is, yet you do not feel like there is any space. In this garden, you can be with whomever you want and you can chose who you want to be with. In this garden, you feel one with the energy of the garden. You feel one with the energy of Adam and the first light—*Aur Ha'Rishon*, the first light that was made. You can see that first light. With that light, you can see anywhere in the universe.

Now it is time to return to your merkavah chariot. You take one step forward and you are in the chariot. You pull the glass cover over it and then you are filled with the divine light. You close your eyes and return to the starting point on Earth. You open your eyes and go back into your room. You lift the glass cover and you are back in your physical body. The energy, frequencies, and healing are all with you as you step into your physical body. Because you are able to understand and conceive of the first light, you are able to use the energy of ascension and the light of ascension for your own ascension.

The energy of the first light is unlike any light that you know of on Earth. Remember that the first words from the Creator were, "Let there be light." You understand light in one confined way—a beautiful way—but light is the source of all creation, and light can be the gateway into the perceptual fields. Light can create things. Your concept of light needs to be expanded so that it is not just a visual experience of light but also a visceral experience. Light is a feeling experience. Light encompasses everything because All That Is is in light. [Sings.] *Light. Light.*

Let the codes of ascension for all of the starseeds who hear or read these words be opened so that they understand the true use and meaning of light, and they can use light for their ascensions. I am Archangel Metatron, in the light. Blessings.

CHAPTER 7

CONNECTING TO YOUR FIFTH-DIMENSIONAL SELF

Juliano, the Arcturians, and Archangel Metatron

Greetings, I am Juliano. We are the Arcturians. We are looking for ways to help you to connect with your fifth-dimensional, multidimensional self. At the same time, we are also exploring ways to help you connect your sacred planetary cities of light with the fifth-dimensional energies of Earth and of the fifth-dimensional realm in general as you practice identifying and experiencing your fifth-dimensional presence.

The planetary cities of light are sacred, holy, and play special roles in the development and acceleration of Earth into Earth's fifth-dimensional energy field. In order for you to work with the planetary cities of light, you must also be connected to your fifth-dimensional presence. The more that you are able to connect and identify with your fifth-dimensional presence, the more powers, energy, magic, control, and ability to influence third-dimensional events will come to you. This means that your higher powers as lightworkers lie in your ability to connect and to identify with your fifth-dimensional presence. We call this energy our multidimensional presence. The more that you can use your fifth-dimensional presence in your work with the planetary cities of light, the more effectively the transformations will occur in these planetary cities of light.

We will review and practice with you a method for connecting to your fifth-dimensional self. The fifth-dimensional self is the basis of your ascension, and it is the basis for your truer higher self. The third-dimensional self that you are experiencing on Earth is a temporary self; it is not your permanent self. Yet you are living in Earth, living with these polarities and dualities. The densities of these dualities create the illusion that you are experiencing your true self in the third dimension, and so it becomes even more important to practice and look for ways of experiencing your fifth-dimensional self.

As you practice experiencing your fifth-dimensional self, you also want to practice connecting and bringing that fifth-dimensional-self energy back into this third-dimensional body. This requires a special preparation and a special mindset. You already have the understanding of the mindset for the ascension. You understand that for the ascension, you must work to bring through a higher vibrational frequency down into this third-dimensional body. You understand that the third-dimensional body must be made vibrationally stronger in order to hold this fifth-dimensional energy. This vibrational strength also has to do with your emotional body, mental body, and physical bodies.

WORKING THROUGH MENTAL CONSTRUCTS

There are certain mental constructs that you have to formulate and work through in order to accept the fifth-dimensional energy. For the most part, you, as lightworkers, have already worked through the mental constructs. These mental constructs have to do with the fact that a multidimensional presence does exist and that you have a body in the fifth dimension. Now, let us just think about that. You now inhabit your third-dimensional body with your spirit, and this is the basis of this incarnation. The fifth-dimensional presence is based on the belief and thought form that you also have a fifth-dimensional body. That fifth-dimensional body is existing simultaneously with your third-dimensional incarnation.

Simultaneous is only a word to be used in the third dimension. Nonetheless, your fifth-dimensional body exists right now, and you are able to have it. You are able to go to that fifth-dimensional body with your mind and with your spirit. When you go into that body, you can experience its perceptions, powers, and abilities, and this gives you an experience of a heightened perception and heightened abilities.

For example, your healing abilities are much higher in your fifth-dimensional body than they are in your third-dimensional body. Many of you experience that when you connect with your fifth-dimensional body, and you can do healings that are seemingly impossible in the third dimension. Go into your fifth-dimensional body and call on those abilities. This will assist you in activations and healing. You can also use your fifth-dimensional body to receive light from other dimensions. In the third dimension, you can download energies from the fifth dimension. In your fifth-dimensional body, you can go up into the sixth- and seventh-dimensional energies and download that type of energy into your fifth-dimensional energy body. We need to bring that energy into this incarnation on Earth.

This process includes connecting and working with the planetary healing light and energy. You have planetary healing abilities in the fifth dimension that are far superior to the third-dimensional healing abilities for this planet. Wouldn't it be wonderful for you to be able to access and bring down those planetary healing abilities into your third-dimensional body? You would be more effective in activating the planetary cities of light. You would also be more effective in creating the sacred spaces and the sacred energy field, more powerful in doing this activation, and more able to maintain the planetary cities of light.

You will understand that the creation of a just society must first have a sacred place and a sacred city as a foundation. When there is a sacred city of light as a foundation, then the just society can follow. Part of the creation of the planetary cities of light involves allowing the energies of a just society to manifest. The planetary cities of light and the sacred energies happen first, and the just society can follow. Planetary cities of light are connecting with galactic sisters and brothers in galactic cities. I want to also announce that it is important that these planetary cities of light on Earth become well known around Earth and well known among all the lightworkers on the planet. You may be in one area that might seem remote, but now other people around Earth will know about your area. They will know that it is a sacred area, a planetary city of light area that is going to become the foundation for the just society.

YOUR INFINITE BODY

One of the roles of the groups of forty is then to find and discover ways of announcing and publicizing that these areas have become planetary cities of light. As the workers of the planetary cities of light, you will also seek ways of publicity. This publicity could involve holding events in the planetary cities of light for lightworkers or organizing certain exercises or writing stories and little paragraphs about what it is like to be in that planetary city of light area. In the exercise that we are going to do now, I want you to connect with your planetary healing abilities to receive information on how to better work with your planetary city of light.

The purpose of the exercise is to connect with your fifth-dimensional presence and to receive and activate your higher abilities in the fifth dimension, including your planetary healing abilities. We are going to use a technique that is familiar to all who have been following the Arcturian work: visiting the crystal lake. The crystal lake, which is approximately one mile in diameter, has a shoreline around it. Each one of you now has a fifth-dimensional presence, a fifth-dimensional body by that lake and on that shoreline.

What does that fifth-dimensional body look like? The fifth-dimensional body is greatly similar to your third-dimensional body, but with a sense of perfected health and energy and a light vibration that is far more advanced than your physical presence on Earth. This does not mean that your physical presence on Earth is bad, but it does imply that the fifth-dimensional body has a vibrational energy charge that is far more advanced than this third-dimensional physical body.

The fifth-dimensional body does not deteriorate with age. The fifth-dimensional body is not affected by the space-time continuum, gravity, or finiteness. It is infinite, and it is participating in an infinite energy field. You might see this fifth-dimensional body as younger than your third-dimensional body now. The most important thing for you to understand is that this fifth-dimensional body is vibrating at a higher energy than you are now in your third-dimensional body, but it is also reciprocally involved with your third-dimensional body, so even though your fifth-dimensional body is at a higher vibrational frequency, it can assimilate and receive your spirit. We are going to help you send your spirit from your third-dimensional body to your fifth-dimensional body.

MEDITATION: JOURNEY TO THE CRYSTAL LAKE

To begin the exercise, I am going to make a tone to activate you energetically for this traveling. [Tones.] Feel your spirit, your essence, and rise out of your third-dimensional physical body. Feel it rise out of your crown chakra. Know that I, Juliano, have placed a blue corridor above each of you that is reading this and wants to connect to the fifth dimension and to the Arcturian crystal lake. Know that you can travel through this corridor with me to the crystal lake. Allow your spirit body to rise and to go into this corridor now. You are in the corridor and its blue energy field, and you are already experiencing the fifth-dimensional vibration.

The highest speed in the universe is the speed of thought. Travel with me now to the crystal lake at the speed of thought. Come through the corridor and move above the crystal lake, where you can look down and see 1,600 fifth-dimensional bodies sitting cross-legged in a meditative pose around the lake. It is a beautiful lake with strikingly blue energy. Take a moment to find your fifth-dimensional body. As you find your fifth-dimensional body, move above it and align yourself with it. Enter your fifth-dimensional body now, and feel the dimensional presence you have. Feel the perceptions you have and the spiritual energy in which you are able to vibrate. Experience in all ways its heightened perceptions.

This is a body that is more of your truer self. It is a body that is experienced in eternal energy and eternal light. It can exist beyond the space-time Earth continuum. You are now in this fifth-dimensional body, which is on a special fifth-dimensional lake called the Arcturian crystal lake. Perhaps it is a new experience to try and adjust to your perceptions. Also become aware that I, Juliano, am going to raise your vibrational energy even more. In this fifth-dimensional body, you can experience a higher spiritual energy that is far beyond what you can experience on the third dimension. You have a vessel and a structure that is able to go vastly higher in spiritual light. I will raise the crystal out of the crystal lake to help you.

You have to remember that you come from the third dimension and that you therefore bring the third-dimensional presence into the fifth dimension. By the nature of that transfer, you still have some of what I call a confining energy. The crystal in the crystal lake is so beautiful and powerful that I have it in a lake underwater to attenuate the energy and prevent it from becoming overpowering. I now raise the crystal approximately ten feet above the water. You can see the top of this huge crystal radiating a spiritual frequency of light that is exactly in alignment with your third eye. This opens up your fifth-dimensional third eye very wide. You now have a perceptual range that sees far into the fifth dimension and into all realms, places, and times. You may use that perception to look down on your third-dimensional incarnation and presence. See your third-dimensional life without any judgment, without any attempt to change any aspect of it. Instead, just gaze at it. Know that looking at your third-dimensional self has a heightened effect on your spiritual vibration on Earth. It raises your spiritual energy because you are looking at your Earth self from such a high perspective.

As you return your gaze back to the crystal lake, look into the crystal with your third eye. Look for your healing powers, your psychic powers, and your planetary healing powers. Look for your fifth-dimensional abilities—whether they are in writing, medical healing, or planetary healing. It could be in music, in architecture. See that higher and gifted part of your fifth-dimensional self. Call on that to come through your third eye and into your fifth-dimensional essence. As I raise the crystal even higher, the visual and spiritual intensity goes higher and higher.

While you are here in your fifth-dimensional presence with the crystal lake, know that each of you may also have a special physical concern, a physical contraction, in your Earth body that you want to resolve. Maybe you want to bring some extra energy back with you that will help you to resolve and to expand that contraction. Now open yourself up through your third eye to receive that energy for that contraction. We will sit briefly in silence while you process all of this with your fifth-dimensional body.

You are accessing your abilities to be shamans for Earth healings along with your abilities to be planetary healers. The core of biorelativity and of Earth healing lie directly in experiencing and communicating with the whole spirit of Earth; therefore, we do not recommend a piecemeal approach in which you try to fix this section or that section. Instead, there first must be a total relationship with the whole Earth spirit. Access and connect with your ability to be that person who can connect to the spirit energy field of Earth. This is the core work.

Continue to receive this vibrational energy from the crystal. You are able to hold so much more light, so much more vibrational spiritual energy here than you can in the third dimension. Your ability to relate to the Creator is also so much higher. Your connection with your spirit guides is also much easier when you are connected to the fifth dimension. Now please gather the last bit of light and energy that you can, because we are going to prepare for your departure. Remember, access your abilities as a planetary healer. Access your abilities to help make sacred the planetary cities of light. Access your ability to receive all knowledge of the galaxy and other planetary cities of light in the galaxies that you have in your fifth-dimensional body.

On my command, your spirit will rise out of your fifth-dimensional body. It is so much easier to leave. Command your spirit to rise out. I know you want to stay in the fifth-dimensional body, but know that you are going to bring back a powerful energy infusion that is going to be energetically charging for you in the third dimension. Your spirit now rises out of your fifth-dimensional body on the crystal lake. You are now about ten feet above this body. You are familiar with the body and are in resonance with it. Rise out of this place and go up to the top of the crystal lake. Together we will leave the crystal lake, we will leave the fifth dimension, and we will travel through the crystal lake corridor back to Earth. Leave on my command at the speed of thought, the highest speed in the universe. The highest energy in the universe is thought.

Come back through the blue corridor to Earth, to a place approximately ten feet above your physical body on Earth. Become aware that you are going to reenter your physical body in perfect alignment. Because of this perfect alignment, you are going to be able to bring back a higher percentage of this energy into your physical Earth body than ever before. This interaction will slowly seep into all aspects of your physical body and all aspects of your physical Earth life, including your abilities to be planetary healers, to be medical healers, and to heal yourselves. Command your spirit to reenter in perfect alignment. Say these words, "I command that I reenter in perfect alignment." On the count of three, reenter your body. One, two, three—now! You have reentered your third-dimensional body with the highest charge of fifth-dimensional energy. Slowly it will begin to seep into you. You are a being of light.

Remember, it only takes several people to bring about change. Look at the change that one person such as Albert Einstein had on the planet. He was a great starseed. He had great connections to the universal laws. He is an example that one work, one person's thoughts and ideas, can have such a profound effect. Know now that you are able to connect to your fifth-dimensional energy and your fifth-dimensional self. You can return in your meditations to your fifth-dimensional body, and you can access the crystal lake to download information and bring it back exactly in the same pattern that we have done. I hope that you will continue to do this because this is a critical moment in Earth's development; your input and your energy are vital. Yes, there are a great many imbalances on Earth. It is so highly charged. At the same time, the receptivity of Earth to the lightworkers and to the spirits of the lightworkers is also at a high stage. I am going to turn the next part of the lecture over to Archangel Metatron. I am Juliano. Good day.

CONNECT TO THE LIGHT OF CREATION

Greetings, I am Archangel Metatron. I sit at the doorway of the stargate because I know that this is also the great portal into the fifth dimension. The stargate is different from the Arcturian crystal lake. In the crystal lake, you can enter and experience the highest vibrational energies, but you can comfortably return to your third-dimensional body. When you go through the portal of the stargate, you are actually cutting your ties to your Earth body.

Many of you want to do that, and I know that you will have the opportunity to do it soon because the moment of ascension is coming. There are many different Earth energies that are coming into a flux and reaching a point of highest division. I want you also to know that the balance and energy that Juliano was talking about in biorelativity also applies to the balance of energy of the cosmos. Earth has a relationship to the cosmos so that part of the work of the starseeds is to balance the third-dimensional Earth with the energies of the cosmos and of the Creator.

I am going to use a special phrase, a sacred name of God, that will help you connect with the Creator. What does the word "Creator" mean? The Creator is one who creates. All of this that you are now experiencing is a creation. All of this unfolding is part of the creation. Hear these special tones, these special words: [Tones.] *Oh Seh Shalom. Ohhhh Seeeehhh Shaaalommm. Oh Seh Lay O'Lam Vayed.* He who makes the world forever. He who makes your soul; your soul is forever. It is this connection to your eternalness that is also the key to your personal power on Earth. Each of you can open the doorway to your eternal light. Each of you has that connection to the eternal light. Part of the understanding of that connection has to do with your multi-self. Your self is in layers, just as there are layers that go to the highest light of the Creator, which is known as the *Ain Sof Aur*. There are layer like a coat that you take off so that you can have the vibrational energy field to experience that light. Now you understand that you can take off the coat. You can go into the fifth dimension. You have a fifth-dimensional body, you even have a seventh-dimensional body, and you have a body that is connected and eternal.

The Creator—blessed is he, *Baruch H'ashem*—has created this third dimension. You are a participant in his creation, and you have multidimensional abilities—understanding is a true gift. *Baruch H'ashem, Baaruuchhh H'Aaaashhhem.* Imagine a spiral light around you. The spiral of light comes to a point on the top of your crown chakra. That spiral of light also goes upward and opens to the cosmos. It is also on your side and also below you. You have all these spinning spirals of light around you. You are able to connect to all levels of the Creator light, all levels of the planes of existence. You have true multidimensional abilities.

In the first moment of creation, Adam had this ability of multidimensional presence and could see throughout the whole universe and other universes. In the first moments of creation, the first being had infinite abilities and perception in all realms. This infinite perception has been stepped down, allowing the formation of lower worlds. A result of the lower worlds is the third dimension that you are now in. The low world, the third dimension, also has the ability to receive the light from the highest source. Even though Earth is on a lower vibration, it is part of the *Oh Seh Shalom*, the *Oh Seh Lay O'Lam Vayed*. It is part of the making of the world. It is also called *Ma'seh B'rai Sheet*, the making of the beginning. Even in the third dimension, the core essence of this connection to all the realms is still present. The Arcturians talk continually about the evolutionary step that humankind must take in order to save this planet. This evolutionary step has to do with the expansion of consciousness and the connections to the higher realms. It has to do with the ability to bring down the energies from the higher realms so that this third dimension is able to realize its full essence, which is sacred and holy. The third dimension is a sacred place.

When you are connected to your fifth-dimensional self, as you have been in this exercise, then you have special abilities to bless and create sacred places and to hold sacred energy. And when you help to solidify sacred energy, then all the people in the area will act in their highest vibrational light. Isn't this a great thought—that you can create a sacred place and create a sacred energy field, especially through the planetary cities of light? So when people enter that energy field, they have a tendency to act in their highest ways and in their highest light. That is true healing power.

[Tones.] *Oh Seh Shalom Bin Romav, Hu Ya Ah Seh Shalom.* Let he who makes peace create this sacred energy for the whole world and the whole planet. Let there be a great understanding now that we can go to your spiritual foundation and learn to communicate directly. The key to the communication directly with Earth is to understand that Earth is also part of God's creation. He is the maker of this planet. There are laws and certain ways of relating to the creation that will allow a new harmony to manifest on Earth. Know that this creation was begun with the words, "Let there be light." I end this lecture with those words, "Let there be light shining through Earth and to all the lightbeings so that the new harmonic light can manifest on Mother Earth." I am Archangel Metatron. Good day.

CHAPTER 8

PLANETARY HEALING THROUGH THE FOUR BODIES

Juliano, the Arcturians, and Chief White Eagle

Greetings. I am Juliano, and we are the Arcturians. Your transformation as a person and as a self is a process that focuses on your energy field. You can divide your energy field into the four bodies. This includes the mental, physical, spiritual, and emotional bodies. When we look at the composition of your energy field, we note that these four bodies interact simultaneously to create a specific light frequency that encompasses it. When we recommend and guide you in certain exercises, such as the cosmic egg and pulsing exercises, we are working simultaneously on all four bodies.

There is a saying in transactional analysis that for healing purposes, you can divide the self into the parent, child, and adult in the service of the ego. I take this statement and expand on it to say we can divide the energy field to do certain higher healing work in the service of the greater self. So if you look at the cosmic egg or at the pulsing exercises, then we can divide the four bodies up specifically so that we can work with each body—the emotional, the spiritual, the physical, and the mental—using the cosmic egg and the pulsing techniques.

What is the advantage of breaking down the energy field into these four bodies and then doing this specific work? This technique offers more intense work in terms of protecting and accelerating the energy field, and dividing the bodies helps to release certain blocks that may be in the belief system, the emotional body, or even in the spiritual body. In some cases, blocks or illnesses in the four bodies are karmic and originate from other lifetimes. You can bring a weakness into the current lifetime, and that weakness can become a certain illness. Working specifically with each body fosters greater healing.

There are also circumstances in which we need to work with specific bodies because the work we do with the general energy field doesn't seem to be enough. In those cases, we have developed advanced techniques for the individual bodies that use our healing chambers and the Arcturian crystal temple. We can focus on thought-projecting your energy bodies to a higher vibrational crystal or healing place where amazing energy transformations occur that transcend the third-dimensional reality. In these healing chambers and in the Arcturian crystal temple, we are able to accomplish more powerful clearing, releasing, and cleansing of the emotional, mental, physical, and spiritual bodies than what you might accomplish by only using the techniques of energy pulsing and the cosmic egg on the third dimension.

QUANTUM HEALING THROUGH QUANTUM CELLS

In the fifth-dimensional healing chambers and in the Arcturian crystal temple, we are able to transcend the normal laws of cause and effect, becoming involved in what we call quantum healing and quantum light. In this case, the energy body sent to us in the thought-projection exercises is recoded, and the energy body is then reinstalled with a higher vibration. When the healing is completed, the higher etheric body is sent back into your physical body. The energy body then goes into a perfect alignment that allows energy from the more refined vibration to enter the energy field of your third-dimensional physical presence. At that point, spiritual osmosis occurs. Spiritual osmosis involves the transmutation of energy through a cell-by-cell process so that newer downloaded information and healing energy is transmitted into each cell of your energy field. This enables you to receive as high a percentage as possible of the healing energy experienced in the Arcturian fifth-dimensional healing chambers and in the Arcturian temple.

If you are able to download and receive a 100-percent healing in your etheric body, then what percentage of that healing would you be able to download into your third-dimensional physical body of energy? That varies from person to person and depends on the interaction of the four energy bodies. Let us look at the mental body. Does the mental body believe in fifth-dimensional energy and healing? What percentage of the fifth dimension is based on the emotional body? Some emotions are still carried into the energy field on the third dimension. For this reason, we divide the energy bodies. For example, we will transmit only the mental or the emotional body to the higher realms because the physical body is the one that is most confined to the polarizations and cause-and-effect laws of the third dimension.

With this type of healing technique, you seek to download as much higher energy as possible so that it can seep into your cells. In certain cases, we are able to plant or install a quantum cell—a higher-dimensional cell that comes from the fifth dimension and is etherically planted into the spirit body. From there it is given instructions to go into the emotional, mental, and physical bodies. That quantum cell can then generate healing light and energy that creates a new healing structure, and this energy can overcome blocks that normally could not be transcended because the old energy is so dense that the physical body will not respond as sensitively as one would prefer.

In this case, when the quantum healing cell is received, it begins to generate a higher field of energy and healing. The results can be fantastic: Not only are we dealing with quantum light, but that quantum light also becomes self-generating, like a sort of time-release capsule. Sometimes the body cannot absorb everything at once because it would become overloaded. You have time-release capsules that are created to work over six hours, twelve hours, and even twenty-four hours, allowing the body to have a chance to absorb everything. In a similar way, the time-release quantum cell can be used in the spirit, mental, and emotional bodies.

TRANSFER EARTH'S ENERGY FIELD FOR HEALING

Everything that we have spoken about up to this point is based on personal healing. It is, however, of utmost necessity to state that these principles of personal healing also work on planetary healing: Earth's energy field can also be projected to a higher energy field. The transfer of the energy field of Earth would require coordination beyond the ability of one or two people, however. It would require a large group of people—in some cases as many as a thousand people working simultaneously—to project the energy field of Earth. Just imagine and consider what a tremendous task it would be to thought-project the energy field of a planet and then to purify and download that energy back into the Earth.

What does this mean? Just as you have experienced on the personal level, sometimes you cannot overcome certain blocks on the planetary level. To overcome these blocks, you can use the technique we have described to thought-project the Earth energy field to a higher plane in which you can work in the more etheric realm and then bring that planetary energy back so that Earth can accommodate and process the healing energy. In order to thought-project the energy field of Earth, it is necessary to have anchor points. These anchor points for thought projection and accommodation are the twelve etheric crystals. Without the twelve etheric crystals, you would not be able to thought-project the energy of Earth. It would be too great a task, and further, there would be no way to get a handle on the thought-projection energy of a planet.

There will be twelve etheric crystals that can serve as anchor points for thought projection. The last two etheric crystals will be downloaded in June 2009 and in November 2009, respectively in Istanbul and the rainforest near São Paulo, Brazil. These twelve etheric crystals have the ability to reach inside and work with the energy field of Earth and to then lift the energy field of Earth. Through biorelativity exercises, starseeds have the power to thought-project the energy field of Earth to a higher dimensional place.

As you know, the Arcturian crystal lake is approximately one mile in diameter, and the Arcturian crystal temple is there at the crystal lake. Yet the crystal temple and crystal lake are too small for this thought projection of the Earth energy field. So where should you thought-project the energy field of the planet? The answer is that you can project that energy to the moon-planet Alano. The moon-planet is approximately the size of Earth and can energetically accommodate the thought fields and the etheric energy field of Earth. At the same time, Alano has the power to work with the planetary thought field of a planet such as Earth. This can only be done after the twelfth crystal is downloaded. We will be working with this idea in Brazil when we will have the opportunity to perform the first exercise of transferring the etheric energy of a whole planet to a higher place. Then, at that higher place, there can be cleansing and healing, after which the etheric energy field of the planet will be downloaded back into Earth.

Of course, as we do this, we encounter the same issue that we have spoken about on a personal basis: you must come into perfect alignment with the physical body (or as perfect alignment as possible) so that the energy can be downloaded in the most effective way. This is where the twelve etheric crystals come into play again. The twelve etheric crystals are in a situation to be in core alignment with the energy field of Earth as it is departing as well as when it is returning. Therefore, it is important to do an exact alignment of Earth with the twelve etheric crystals.

Remember that the twelve etheric crystals are not equidistant from each other. They are not, from a third-dimensional perspective, placed in what you might perceive as the most strategic locations if you were thinking from a third-dimensional perspective. From the third-dimensional perspective, you would want the crystals to be equidistant from each other and cover all the potential continents and countries as much as possible. Yet we are working in the fifth-dimensional energy with spiritual energy. We go with where the energy is most accessible at the time. Therefore, the way these etheric crystals have been downloaded is totally effective.

STARSEEDS AND EARTH'S EVOLVING PROCESS

The Earth has a great deal of lower subconscious energy. That subconscious energy is based on certain patterns of violence, upheavals, and transitions. These patterns of transitions also are based on Earth as a planet. The Earth is a living planet, and so it too is going through significant changes. On the surface level, you would understand these changes as volcanic eruptions, earthquakes, storms, and other processes that we relate to a primordial stage in the development of a planet.

Let me expound further on that. In more evolved planets, the shifts and changes you are now seeing on Earth are not part of the higher-dimensional planet's process. That is to say, there are not earthquakes or volcanic eruptions on fifth-dimensional planets. There are no physical upheavals on these higher dimensional planets such as those you are now seeing on Earth. Part of the current upheavals on Earth are related to blockages caused by overuse of certain waterways or due to air currents and so on. Nonetheless, Earth has had a history of great upheavals, including collisions with asteroids or comets. Granted, those asteroids and comets may have been bringing certain life-energy forms and cells to Earth that were needed because they are part of the beginning and earlier processes of a planet. In the later developmental stages of a planet, it is not necessary and, in fact, it is not useful for a planet to be hit by asteroids and comets for obvious reasons. Those reasons include that the asteroid can be a life-ending, species-ending event. Being hit by comets and asteroids would be part of an earlier primordial process on a planet.

Yet Earth also still evolving. An evolving planet is going through a process. Some things you are now seeing on Earth that have to do with earthquakes and upheavals are part of the instability that can be shifted when the planet itself evolves. For the planet to evolve requires a higher etheric energy process. That process usually, from our experience, can only be achieved when a group of starseeds are able to use biorelativity exercises. Starseeds can use thought-projection exercises to project the entire planetary etheric energy to a higher-dimensional purifying place. Then that purified energy field comes back to the planet.

Just as I explained in the discussion of personal healings, the quantum-cell light field can be brought down into the planet so that it can incorporate and begin to accelerate a new life force energy. Many of you have incarnated on Earth at this time to experience this planetary healing process. Many of you are excited to have the opportunity to participate in the planetary healing exercises. Earth represents a perfect opportunity for you to develop, refine, and practice planetary-healing experiences and processes.

The energy fields of the whole planet could also be broken down or separated, just as your own fields are separated during personal healings. The Earth's energy fields are comparable to the four etheric bodies of the human and thus can be separated into the mental, physical, emotional, and spiritual. You can work on each one of those Earth bodies separately. You also can work on the different bodies of the planet. Working with the Earth's energy bodies is more complicated because there are energy fields representing the biosphere, the Inner-Earth energy fields, and also the many species on the planet. There also are certain energy fields in the Earth bodies that are representative of Earth's interaction with the space brother- and sisterhood.

I want to speak in more detail about these concepts: The Earth has an energy field just like your mental body. Earth has an etheric energy field that is related to the Galactic Central Sun. Right now, there has been a great opening on the galactic interface that allows more light to be received from the Central Sun, and more light can be received from higher beings such as myself, other Arcturians, and ascended masters. It is required then that one have more knowledge of the different layers of energy. It also is fair to say that Earth has been programmed just as you have been programmed and are the result of your genetic codes that have come from other lifetimes and from your parents. Sometimes those genetic codes produce certain inevitable results. These results may exhibit themselves as illnesses, and an illness may look like it was already implanted in your cells and in your genes. Given the right opportunity, the illness manifests—often as a result of stress—but these results can be shifted through lightwork.

The process is the same with Earth. We know from our study of Earth that its programming has been manipulated at times by other beings in ways that were not for the highest good. For example, we know that sometimes beings of a lower vibration from the fourth dimension wanted to come to Earth and program the planet to either harvest certain energies or minerals, or to take certain valuables from the planet. I think that this is not that unusual in history. Even in your own history, you have sought domination over certain groups of people so that you could utilize certain farming techniques. That is just one example.

Nonetheless, even though all this energy, including the codes of Earth, is being assimilated now, you would still want to go through a cleansing of the Earth's energy. This cleansing is also related to the subconscious of Earth. We have described subconscious patterns on Earth. That means that Earth has a subconscious just like humans have a subconscious. Many people have wondered what would happen when all of the twelve etheric crystals were downloaded, and what has happened is that the energetic field of Earth as a whole can be worked with now: The twelve etheric crystals allow alignment with the Arcturian stargate and the Central Sun to be maximized. Chief White Eagle will also speak now, and then I will be return to work with you on a special pulsing exercise. I am Juliano.

WORKING WITH EARTH AS A WHOLE

Hey ya ho ya hey! Hey ya hoooh! Greetings, I am Chief White Eagle. Never before in our history have we had such a powerful opportunity to work with all of Mother Earth. I know there is much sorrow and sadness on the planet because of Earth's state. That includes the disrespect to her animals, her oceans, and her air. All of this damage has happened in a relatively short time compared with the Earth's history. At the same time, there has never been such a great opportunity for humanity to work with the whole energy of Earth. This is difficult to even grasp when you think about it or try to dissect it scientifically, but from the Native people's experience, we are always talking to Earth. We are always working with Earth, so it is not that unusual to be able to foresee or to create the necessary environment and attitude to work with the entire planet at one time. This is really the highest form of biorelativity.

We now have the ability and the global outreach to work with the energy of the whole planet at one time. This opportunity will create a very heightened perceptual field. To really grasp the whole nature of a planet, you have to understand its position and energetic interaction with the galaxy. Just as you have what you might call a luminous body, so the Earth also has a luminous body. Just like you have cords of attachment or etheric lines that go out to other places, planets, and energy fields, so also does Earth. In fact Earth, my friends, even has etheric cords to her fifth-dimensional body.

Yes, the Earth also has a fifth-dimensional body. Remember, we said that Earth is a living spirit. Being a living spirit, it has higher energy and higher etheric presence. The Earth needs to find a way to communicate with that higher etheric energy, and the connecting link that allows the Earth to communicate with its higher parts is humanity. That is the role of the planetary healer. That is why when we pray, we pray directly to the Mother Earth. We do not think that Mother Earth is God, but we understand that we are all God's creatures. The planets are God's creatures, and we know that the Earth responds to our biorelativity processes.

Never before have we had the opportunity to work with the whole energy field of the planet with the global perceptions that we now have. One of the greatest accomplishments to help the biorelativity process has been the pictures taken of Earth from the Moon when humans were there. This perspective is most useful. Now you also have pictures of the Earth seen from the outer planets of your solar system, and those images of your planet are also useful to receive, allowing a better understanding from this image of the relationship of Earth to the solar system. It is important to understand that Earth, the Sun, and the solar system are interacting with energies from inside and outside the solar system and that Earth's energies are also interacting with the Central Sun. When doing biorelativity exercises for Earth, you need to consider the energy field of Earth in her solar system. It will become necessary to work with the interactive luminous light cords that Earth has connected to the solar system and beyond.

Mother Earth, this is Chief White Eagle. We honor you today at times of the full moon, the vernal equinox, and the heightened sacred time of Easter. These are sacred energy times. Mother Earth, we recognize now as we are approaching 2012 that we are in what we Native people call sacred time—a time when many things are possible that are not possible at other times. Sacred time is when there is access to different perceptual fields and heightened energies beyond this dimension.

Mother Earth, we are willing to be conduits of that energy during this time. We are willing to work to stabilize and bring you into alignment with your higher fifth-dimensional energy. We are willing to work to purify your energy field through the Arcturian work with the moon-planet Alano. We are honored to perform this sacred task, and we will be working to help ensure that the planet Earth also evolves. We will be evolving with you. It has always been the mission of the Native peoples to share our evolvement with the evolution of the planet. For that reason we call you our Mother Earth. All my words are sacred. *Ho!* I am Chief White Eagle.

MEDITATION ON THE FOUR ENERGY BODIES

Greetings, I am Juliano, and we are the Arcturians. Become aware of your energy field and of the outer edge of your energy field. Bring that outer edge into a concentric egg-sphere shape that we have called the cosmic egg. As you are doing that, know that all holes in your aura are sealed. There are no energy leaks in your aura as you create this beautiful, smooth cosmic shape. Become aware that your aura has a pulse just as you have a pulse in your physical body. It may not be exactly on the same level as your physical pulse, but nonetheless, it is pulsing. By becoming aware of the pulse, you are able to have control of the rate of the pulse through your thinking. Become aware that the faster your aura pulses, the higher your vibrations become. Notice that your physical pulse rate remains steady, even as you control and accelerate the pulse of your aura. The higher your vibrations become, the higher the energy you possess. Lower vibrations cannot penetrate into a higher vibrational energy field. Try to pulse it using the tone *tat, tat, tat, tat, tat, tat, tat.* [Tones.] Your energy field pulsing becomes higher and higher.

We are going to divide your energy field. The mental body is now going to pop out as a total etheric energy body in the same shape as your cosmic-egg body. Now you have been able to divide out the mental body and project it right in front of you. That mental body has the perfect shape of the cosmic egg. The alignment of the mental body will be at a higher rate. Start pulsing the mental body, and it will achieve a higher vibration. This higher vibration of the mental body means that you will be protected from lower vibrational beliefs and lower mental energy. I know that there is lower mental energy around your planet, so this ability will be helpful to you.

Now project your emotional body above the mental body. You have your whole energy field in the cosmic egg as well as the projection of your mental body, and you also have the projection of your emotional body. There is a lot of energy in the emotional body. Bring the emotional body into a perfect alignment in the perfect shape of the cosmic egg. Now raise the vibration of the emotional body. Your emotional body will begin to pulse at a higher frequency, and only higher emotions and higher emotional energy will be experienced. Lower emotions will not be able to affect you, and your physical pulse will continue to remain steady, without any acceleration.

Now project your spirit body. The spirit body appears as another energy field. For the spirit body, you can first ask it to show its beautiful blue color to you. A blue color comes into the spirit body. Work with the energy field of the spirit body and raise its vibration. Now put the whole spirit body into the shape of the cosmic egg. Next, project the physical body—your best representation of your physical body just as it appears in your mind. Project the physical body above all the other bodies. Then see the cosmic-egg energy field around your physical body. Now only higher physical energy will be able to come to you. Lower physical energy and people with lower physical interests can no longer come into your energy field. They are all kept away. Your projected body is now going into a higher physical energy, while the pulse of your third-dimensional body remains steady. Now the four projected bodies are separate.

Next, we will work with the mental body again. I want you to thought-project your mental body to a corridor above you that connects to the Arcturian crystal temple at the Arcturian crystal lake. Project your mental body into that crystal now. Your mental body becomes a higher purified form and energy. You release certain lower vibrational energy, and then the mental body will be projected back to where it was, separated as one of the four bodies in front of you. Then I want you to thought-project the emotional body into the Arcturian crystal in the crystal temple in the crystal lake. Thought-project there *now*! Any emotions that seem too overwhelming can now be released and purified in this crystal. Take a moment to allow your emotions to be purified and raised to a higher vibration. Very good. Now the emotional body can to return to its place in front of you.

Next, thought-project your spirit body into the crystal in the crystal lake. Your spirit body enjoys the high spiritual light and energy of this crystal. It is also able to open itself up to higher spiritual interactions beyond even the Arcturian crystal temple and crystal lake. Experience the spirit body there. Very good. Now you can return the spirit body to its place in front of you and thought-project the physical body to the crystal in the crystal lake. The image of the physical body is there, and the physical body receives a cleansing and release of all blocks. The physical body is vibrating at a beautiful frequency. The physical body is now projected back into its proper place in front of you.

All four bodies have now experienced cleansing and higher spiritual calibration. The four separate bodies now reintegrate in perfect alignment with your physical energy field. Where there were four separate fields and a cosmic field, there is now one energy field. All the four bodies are reintegrated within your three-dimensional body. You will be vibrating at this nice frequency for a good period of time. Know that through spiritual osmosis, you will have a time-release capsule so that this energy will slowly penetrate all your bodies over the next thirty-six hours and you will experience an upliftment. Blessings to you all. I am Juliano. Good day.

CHAPTER 9

ISTANBUL: SACRED HAVEN OF THE ELEVENTH CRYSTAL

Juliano, the Arcturians, and Chief White Eagle

Greetings, I am Juliano, and we are the Arcturians. We are gathered here in Istanbul to provide the ceremony for downloading the eleventh crystal. This crystal has special meaning. Numerically, it is number 11, which is considered a lucky number in numerology. Just as 7 is a special number, 11 is also considered a powerful number. I would have to say that this crystal provides an energy that makes the other ten crystals work most effectively.

Crystals can be described in terms of electromagnetic energy and grids. Electromagnetic energy grids work best when all the crystals on the grid are connected to each other. When all of the crystal energy is connected, then the power from all of the crystals becomes more effective. We have chosen a place for the eleventh crystal that has great clarity. It is a place that has a great ability to make connections with other energetic points. The ability to make connections is a high power. If you remember, we began our lectures many years ago discussing the Arcturians through the concept called "connecting with the Arcturians." Your power and energy is multiplied and increased when you are able to connect to the fifth dimension and to fifth-dimensional beings. This crystal will help the world connect to fifth-dimensional wisdom and knowledge.

The hidden knowledge that we are talking about, which this crystal represents, is the knowledge of the fifth dimension. The knowledge that the fifth dimension exists will be revealed to this planet soon. When the knowledge of the higher dimensions becomes known more generally, then the planet can quickly make major changes. When people understand more about the fifth dimension, then they will understand that there is a need to connect to it. There is a need to accelerate everyone's energy so that all who want to can enter the fifth dimension.

Most importantly, everyone who is working to solve Earth's problems will be happy to understand that there is this connection. They can use this connection to bring newer light, newer knowledge, and newer wisdom to the problems that are facing humanity and the world. Think about what it means to you personally to know that there is another dimension. I want each of you to understand what a revolutionary concept and what revolutionary information it is to know in your heart, with complete faith and with complete wisdom, that another dimension of a higher vibration exists that is going to connect to the third dimension.

We can describe this connection symbolically. We have described it by using the concept of two large spheres. Each sphere represents a dimension. The fifth dimension as a sphere will touch the third dimension as a sphere. We call this touching an intersection of the dimensions, and it will create a powerful experience because the light and energy of the fifth dimension will immediately be downloaded into the third dimension. When two dimensions intersect, the energy from the higher dimension will flow into the lower dimension. This is the universal law known as "spiritual osmosis." Higher light will go into lower light and will slowly fill that sphere.

There has never been an intersection of the dimensions on Earth. In the past, individual spiritual leaders and spiritual people have sought to create a connection to the fifth dimension, and they tried to explain and provide examples of the way to connect to the dimension. Now there is going to be a sustained energetic connection and intersection. This intersection is like plugging a wire into a wall; then, you can turn on a light and the light will stay on. At this point in the history of the fifth dimension intersecting the third dimension, we, the Arcturians, are creating a special corridor that allows the sphere of the fifth dimension to be permanently connected to the third dimension here at this crystal area, at this point in Istanbul. You who are here right now will feel the tremendous linkage this corridor provides between the fifth and the third dimensions.

You are here at a time that can be described as a moment in eternity, a moment in eternal light. The linkage of the corridors from the fifth dimension and the third dimension are becoming more solid. Now you who have come here today are assisting us in bringing down the eleventh crystal. We have some work to do with you. I thank you for coming here to provide the human power to download this crystal. I want to emphasize the word "power." Spiritual power is required to help perform this energy work. You who have come here today are showing great spiritual power to be here at this moment with this light, with this beauty, and in this great energy crossroad. You are here to help connect the fifth dimension with the third dimension. What could be a greater service to humanity at this time then to provide the means of connecting the fifth dimension to the third dimension?

MEDITATION TO BRING IN THE ELEVENTH ETHERIC CRYSTAL

You are now sitting in a circle. Feel the circle and the energy of the circle. Now the circle begins to move: It goes around and around, and you are moving in the circle. As you are moving around in the circle, your spirit feels light and it is able to leave your body. I, Juliano, have provided a beautiful corridor right above your group. As your spirit leaves your body, join me in this corridor. I will wait until everyone has been able to leave their body. If you have difficulty leaving your body, then please just visualize what we are doing to the best of your ability.

We begin to follow the corridor. Going up the corridor, we travel at the speed of thought. As we travel with the speed of thought, we go through this corridor and we travel to the Arcturian crystal lake on the fifth dimension. We arrive to the outer area of the crystal lake in Arcturus in the fifth dimension. As we arrive, we look down around the lake and we see that for each person from the group, there is a fifth-dimensional body waiting. Please enter your fifth-dimensional body now. We are now in the crystal lake, and each of you is in your fifth-dimensional body. I, Juliano, call on the crystal in the crystal lake to begin to rise. Slowly it rises. As it rises, you feel the intense light of the fifth-dimensional crystal. It now rises totally out of the water.

The crystal is now out of the water. Now, with the powers that I have, I am going to create a perfect etheric duplicate of the crystal. On the count of three, you will see and experience two crystals instead of one. One, two, three! There is now a duplicate crystal. I, Juliano, am using the light and energy of the original crystal to charge the new duplicate crystal with all the light and energy that is necessary for it to have. The second, duplicate crystal is being filled up with great spiritual light and energy. It is now ready to be teleported back to Istanbul. Each of you can now use your power of thought projection to help me transport this crystal back to Istanbul. I want you, with my assistance, to visualize the raising of the crystal from the crystal lake. We are going to transport the duplicate crystal back to Istanbul. The original crystal will stay above the water at the crystal temple during the transportation.

You will now also practice multipresence. You have a presence in the third dimension, and you now have a presence in the fifth dimension, and your presence is now needed in both dimensions. You have the power to do this with my instructions and help. Together, our thoughts now transport this duplicate crystal. We transport it out of the crystal lake. In the fifth dimension, we do not need to pick things up; we move things with our minds. We can now transport this crystal with our minds out of the crystal lake through the corridor. We now travel through the corridor with this crystal and, using our minds, we transport it at the speed of thought. Now we arrive in Istanbul with the duplicate crystal. A huge light comes over the whole city now as the crystal is coming into alignment with the Bosporus Strait. It is coming into the area at this special historical place you have chosen called *Anadolu Hisari*—the Anatolian castle. The crystal is in alignment in the fifth dimension and the third dimension. Huge light connections are already beginning to form.

As these light connections are made, you now return to the crystal lake. We will leave this crystal over the Bosporus Strait that we brought down from the fifth dimension, and we will return to Istanbul to do the actual downloading back on the third dimension—so return to your fifth-dimensional body on the crystal lake. This beautiful eleventh crystal is now in alignment from the fifth dimension with the third-dimensional Bosporus. Follow me and return to your fifth-dimensional body on the crystal lake in the crystal temple.

The crystal lake is filled with light, and you have now returned to your fifth-dimensional body. The original crystal is still above the water. It will stay above the water until the crystal over Istanbul is downloaded. Feel the energy of being in the fifth dimension. Feel the energy of being on the crystal lake with the crystal above the water. You are going to shimmer your body back into the third dimension so that when you come back into your physical body, you will have the fullest possible fifth-dimensional light that you can bring in. Shimmer your fifth-dimensional body now.

Reappear into your third-dimensional body in Istanbul. Beautiful! Hold that light in your third-dimensional body. You will need all that energy to do the exercise. Now, repeat: Return to the fifth-dimensional body on the crystal lake. Now prepare yourself to return to the third dimension. Your spirit leaves your fifth-dimensional body, but you know that you can return to it at any time. As your spirit leaves your fifth-dimensional body and the crystal lake, you follow the corridor and travel at the speed of thought back into your third-dimensional body back in Istanbul. You see a huge light over your body because this new etheric crystal is exactly over where you are sitting. Look for your physical body; find a perfect alignment and reenter your physical body now. You have reentered your third-dimensional body. The circle has stopped going around, and we are ready to download the crystal into the third dimension.

Project and send your thoughts up to where this crystal is, directly over the Bosporus and Anadolu Hisari, and command the crystal to come down and enter the third dimension. You are the anchors. The beautiful eleventh crystal is now coming into the third dimension over the Bosporus Strait. Huge light, love, and connections to the fifth dimension all are in this crystal. Now we bring the crystal itself down into the third dimension with your help. We bring the crystal right to this location into Bosporus. The crystal is now entering Bosporus and is going right to the bottom. Huge energy comes down with the crystal, connecting to the other ten crystals that have already been downloaded around the world. We are connecting with all of the other members of the groups of forty around the world now who are with us in thoughts. Hold this connection, and we will meditate together in silence for five minutes to anchor this light. Begin the meditation. [Pause.]

The crystal has been successfully downloaded! The hidden knowledge of the existence of the fifth dimension will now be more widely known to humanity. It will become known to everyone that the fifth-dimensional energy can be brought down into the third dimension. It is time for this hidden knowledge to be revealed to all seekers of the truth. It is time for spiritual light to connect to all aspects of the third-dimensional reality. This crystal here in Istanbul will provide great light to Turkey. Turkey has great pride in its ability to be a leader, as Turkey has already been a leader of spiritual light in the world. Turkey will now again show itself to be a leader of spiritual light to this part of the world. This spiritual light will spread throughout the Middle East and the Far East, to many different countries. More spiritual people will be attracted to studying and experiencing this spiritual light that is coming out of this etheric crystal that you have helped today to download into the Bosporus. I am Juliano, and we are the Arcturians.

A BLESSING OVER THE BOSPORUS STRAIT

Greetings, I am Chief White Eagle. [Tones.] *Hey ya ho ya hey!* The Native spirit masters are so happy when a new sacred place is identified on Earth. Earth has many corridors and many sacred places. Now, this place in Istanbul is an area through which much spiritual light can enter. It is also a place where spiritual light can work with third-dimensional light and also with thirddimensional spirits who are stuck and need to be released. We feel the energy of this crystal. Our fifth-dimensional workers are drumming in joy! Feel this energy now. This is an energy that you have been helping to bring down. You have become a sacred person because you are participating in the downloading of sacred energy and of higher energy.

O Great White Father and Great Mother, I, Chief White Eagle, am here today with gratitude so that you can bring and protect this great area of Istanbul and Bosporus. Let this place represent peace and love, light, and brotherhood.

Let this place represent and help people to connect to the fifth dimension. This area has many lightworkers, Great Mother/Father, Protector of All. These lightworkers are being shown the way to teach and to connect their country along with other countries and other lightworkers to the fifth dimension.

Today we ask for a blessing for this area. We ask for a blessing over the Bosporus Strait and a blessing to all here who have participated in this wonderful ceremony. Let each one who has participated in this ceremony today experience the light for his or her own personal life. Let their personal lives be blessed, O Father/Mother, for they are working to promote light for the planet. Today we ask for your gratitude, your blessing in the name of your love and your light, O Father/Mother, Creator of All. Thank you.

The Native American fifth-dimensional masters, including myself, Chief White Eagle, will be here now in the Bosporus. You have helped to place a corridor that will allow the Native American masters to be here. I know that we are accepted by the Turkish people, for they love us and our spirits. We are all brothers and sisters! I am Chief White Eagle. *Ho!*

CHAPTER 10

PLANETARY SPIRITUAL ALCHEMY

Juliano and the Arcturians

Greetings, I am Juliano. We are the Arcturians. Now is an opportunity to raise the spiritual light quotient of planet Earth. Never in the history of this planet has there been this opportunity. I ask you to consider the enormity of this process and the magnitude of the work involved. The spirituality of the planet and you, the Adam species, have not kept up with scientific technology. We know from our travels throughout the galaxy that this is a dangerous position for a planet to be in; when the scientific technology of its inhabitants exceeds the spiritual light quotient of its inhabitants and of the planet, it creates an imbalance that often has the outcome of the destruction of life forms and possibly of the entire biosphere of the planet.

Throughout the history of Earth, there have been great spiritual masters who have been able to influence millions of people on the planet. Consider the great spiritual masters and the huge numbers of people who were influenced by them. One would still have to say that the years 2009 to 2012 represent the strongest possibility and opportunity in Earth's history to raise the spiritual light quotient of planet Earth. Why is that? First, the current scientific technology has led to fantastic communication links that were not possible earlier in your history.

Second, because of scientific space exploration, the beautiful image of the "Blue Jewel," as we call her, or planet Earth is embedded now in the consciousness of many. In order to raise the spiritual light quotient of any planet, one must be able to visualize the planet from an outer perspective. This outer perspective was made by satellite imagery and from angles and perspectives photographed from the Moon. Even though this is not a distant perspective, it still provides the necessary image to work with consciously and unconsciously. It gives us, the

Arcturians, an opportunity to more easily direct you in your accelerated imagery and your accelerated, guided visualizations.

PLANETARY HEALERS ON THE CUSP OF EVOLUTIONARY CHANGE

The Earth responds to your telepathic communications, and visualizations are the height of telepathic communications. Therefore, the visual imagery that you use in your planetary meditations can have a dramatic effect on shaping the Earth changes and the evolutionary process of the planet. It is important to realize that not only is the Earth a living spirit but also that, as a living spirit, the Earth is going through an evolution. You and the Earth are both on the cusp of an evolutionary change. As you know, each evolutionary change that has occurred for the inhabitants of planet Earth always transpires as a crisis situation; a crisis situation goes hand in hand with evolution.

The process of nature is that change basically occurs out of necessity. You may even know that from your own personal history. If you review your own changes and your development, you may agree that the major changes that you have successfully made—especially the most dramatic and far-reaching of them—probably occurred concurrently with a crisis. I think you have a saying: "Necessity is the mother of invention." Well, from our perspective as planetary archeologists and planetary anthropologists, we can say that crisis is the mother of evolutionary change. That means that evolutionary change dramatically occurs in the midst of danger.

Everyone who is listening and reading these words knows firsthand the tremendous danger that exists at this time on Earth. The idea of planetary stability and the idea that everything will continue in a normal, stable unfolding is but an illusion. The planetary evolution now has to be guided by planetary healers. The crisis and the danger inherent in this moment are amenable to dramatic changes and dramatic shifts through planetary healers and planetary spirituality. The planetary healers that are present now can raise the spiritual light quotient of Earth in order to provide the foundation for the dramatic change that must occur for Earth to evolve.

Earth is a living spirit, so when we talk about the Earth surviving, we are talking about Earth surviving as a living spirit—a living spirit in the third dimension. Yes, you can look at other planets such as Mars. You can see that there are no life forms on that planet. You could say, quite conclusively, that there is a dramatic decrease in the spirit of Mars. I say dramatic decrease because it is not like Pluto or other planets that have absolutely no life. Mars did have life on it at one time. Mars was inhabited, and the remnants of the spiritual life forms and of the spirit of Mars are still in the ethers around the planet. Those spiritual energies exist in the outerdimensional realms of Mars in the fourth dimension.

I know there has been some discussion about how to revitalize and reengineer Mars to hold life again and to rekindle the spiritual energy of the planet. It is true that the spiritual energy and the spiritual life force of Mars can possibly be rekindled through some dramatic reengineering. This is far beyond the capabilities of your scientists on Earth now. From a practical standpoint, we can say that the spiritual energy of Mars is dormant and may possibly be reawakened. Yet the spiritual life of Earth is very awake. The evolutionary process of the spirit of this planet needs to be studied because humankind now has limited knowledge of how a planet evolves and lives and what it means for a planet to have a spiritual light quotient. You, my friends, are on the forefront of this evolutionary shift.

We, the Arcturians, consider you planetary healers. Planetary healers understand that a planet evolves and that a planet has a spiritual light quotient. Planetary healers understand that this is the first opportunity in the history of Earth to systematically work as a unit around the entire globe, the entire planet, with the expressed purpose of raising the spiritual light quotient of the planet. Raising the spiritual light quotient of a planet is totally linked to raising the spiritual light quotient of humankind. Remember, I said that there has never been a moment in the history of this planet at which the evolution and survival of the spirit Earth were linked to one species. It is also true that only humankind can institute the changes in the planet, and that can only be done through the process of raising the spiritual light quotient of humankind and raising the spiritual light quotient of Earth.

The 1,600 Arcturian starseeds are committed to planetary healing. Do not be concerned by how small that number might seem, because one spiritually focused person—especially in this environment on the Earth now—can gather much light and can influence many people. This has happened repeatedly in the history of this planet, even without modern communication or modern technology. Many times, one person has dramatically influenced people. But it has taken hundreds—and in some cases, thousands—of years for the full effects of that one person's spiritual intervention to change the masses. You do not have time on Earth now to wait for one spiritually powerful person to effect a change, because you cannot wait 300 years for the full effects to occur.

Using Reverse Time Acceleration for Planetary Healing

This means that we need acceleration. The only way that you can accelerate planetary healing, evolution, and the distribution of spiritual energy in a timely manner is through connecting to fifth-dimensional energy. In the fifth dimension, time is not linear, which means that you can activate and accomplish many things that would take years, even centuries, on Earth. We seek the opportunity to connect you to the fifth dimension. By connecting you to the fifth dimension, many of the meditations and much of the work that we do with you is accelerated in time. You may have the experience in other instances when you connect to the fifth dimension that time seems as if it is occurring quickly. Yet when you return to your third-dimensional body and the third-dimensional Earth, a long time has elapsed. You might feel like, from your perspective in fifth-dimensional meditations, only five or ten minutes are passing. Actually, it could be an hour—and that is a modest time acceleration.

We want to use this concept of time acceleration. In a focused meditation in fifth-dimensional light, we can accomplish and shift energy on the Earth in an even shorter Earth time. What you would experience as a long time in the fifth dimension may actually only be a short time in the third dimension. We call this "reverse time acceleration," or RTA. This is possible—and it is necessary now. It may not be helpful to focus your work and meditations on the fifth dimension, accomplishing many wonderful things, only to find out that what you thought was a short period of time from the fifth dimension was actually a year in Earth time. Quite frankly, Earth may not have a year to let things just unravel the way they are right now without a more powerful and immediate spiritual evolution. And so we want to use RTA, reverse time acceleration. In this way, using fifth-dimensional energy, we can effect change in a shorter period of Earth time—that is, quickly institute a change that may have required months or years in other ways.

Let me give you an example. When Jesus/Sananda was on the planet, in many ways, the full effect of his energy and light did not dramatically influence the planet for perhaps 200 to 300 years. I realize that there were many people around him the years immediately after his death that were dramatically changed. But his effect did not influence countries or lands until much later. We could say that this was a normal time effect. If Jesus/Sananda were to appear on the planet now, it would not take so long for him to affect everything. This is one of the main messages and metaphors that I could use to explain to you the effect of reverse time acceleration.

The work that Jesus/Sananda has been doing has been going on for centuries. When he returns, it would take him less than five seconds of Earth time to make the evolutionary changes necessary on the planet and in the human species so that everything would be moving in the highest light and the highest good. This example shows you the power of reverse time acceleration, and it shows you the power that a spiritual presence can have on Earth now. Your work as planetary healers is accelerating.

MEDITATION TO CONNECT THROUGH THE ETHERIC GRID

We have worked consistently and dramatically with the groups of forty to download the eleventh etheric crystal in Istanbul, Turkey. This crystal has been referred to as the one opening up hidden knowledge to the world. Its main function to connect the fifth dimension to the third dimension so that more third-dimensional people become aware of the fifth dimension. This crystal dramatically accelerates the process as the veil between the third and the fifth dimension is gradually being lifted.

Even so, one might ask, "How will I be able to most effectively use the fifth-dimensional connection, the fifth-dimensional energy, to institute the changes necessary to accelerate and activate planetary healing and my personal healing?" This is a continual question that most of the starseeds have been asking for many years. All starseeds are interested in their personal development as well as planetary development. Every starseed wants to be able to use this fifth-dimensional connective link for his or her evolution and ability to be more effective as a personal healer and a planetary healer.

The etheric crystals, including the eleventh etheric crystal, form a grid of spiritual and electromagnetic energy. With this crystal, and with the downloading of the twelfth crystal on the horizon, each of the planetary healers, each of the Arcturian starseeds, will more effectively be able to plug into what we call the Arcturian Tree of Life etheric crystal grid. The Istanbul crystal is also sometimes described as the Asian crystal in Istanbul because it was downloaded on the Asian side of the Bosporus. The downloading of this Anadolu-Bosporus crystal makes a connection available to the electromagnetic grid energy of the crystal links. In many ways, it is a doorway for starseeds to connect themselves to this etheric grid. This etheric grid is a fifth-dimensional force on the Earth and a way for you to connect to fifth-dimensional energy.

All energy, including both third-dimensional and fifth-dimensional energy, is electromagnetic. If you want to be able to connect to the frequency of the fifth-dimensional energy, then these etheric crystals are often an avenue to plug into a fifth-dimensional etheric grid. When you connect to a fifth-dimensional etheric grid, then your frequency is immediately raised. This is similar to connecting into a higher voltage—you raise your ability to assimilate the electromagnetic volts.

In our meditation now, we will seek a better connection for all of you to the electromagnetic grid of these etheric crystals. We will use the Istanbul crystal to provide the avenue and the opening for you to connect to the fifth dimensional energy. Remember, once you raise your vibration to the fifth dimension, you as a third-dimensional being have the option of focusing and using it as you see fit.

So in some ways, it would be as if someone gave you $10,000. They can say to you, "Spend it wisely," but you have the responsibility and the power to use it as you will. What I am suggesting is that you will be able to receive this higher energy by connecting into the grid today, and then you can use it for personal and planetary healing.

You can use this fifth-dimensional connection to increase vibrations for a planetary benefit. First, our goal at this time is to connect into the grid of the etheric crystal linkage by visualizing the Anadolu-Bosporus crystal in Istanbul. You may have difficulty visualizing it, as many people are not aware of it geographically. I would like you to visualize a waterway that separates Europe and Asia, and because there are two bridges, I would like you to visualize a second bridge that goes across. At the far end of one bridge is an old castle. Across from the castle on the waterway, almost in front of that second bridge, is where the etheric crystal is downloaded. Visualize a strait or a waterway that may be a half-mile or more wide with a beautiful etheric crystal in the water. As you hear these words, begin to connect with that energy. [Sings.] Anadolu, Istanbul, etheric crystal in the Bosporus. Anadolu, etheric crystal in Istanbul in the Bosporus.

We will go into a meditation now. Feel this crystal energy connection activating all of the chakras in your body. This crystal has the power to activate both you and the planet. It has the power to remove the veil for you so that you experience more fifth-dimensional energy and light and receive the vibrational energies of the fifth dimension now. This Anadolu crystal is opening up an area between your heart and your throat chakras. This is, from your perspective, a new chakra and a new energy center. We have modified the Tree of Life to twelve spheres instead of ten spheres.

Realize that there are more chakras and more ways of activating yourself energetically than the traditional level of chakras. Now, there is a new level, a new sphere, a new chakra between the heart and your throat. This new level can be called the chakra of hidden knowledge. In *Kaballah*, it is known as *Da'at*—knowledge—unifying the ten Sephirot of the Tree of Life. In the crystal world or etheric world, it is called the eleventh crystal—the Anadolu-Bosporus crystal.

Planetary Spiritual Alchemy

The ancient mystics knew there were ways of transforming the Earth reality. This was practiced in the study of spiritual alchemy. Spiritual alchemy was metaphorically described as the desire to transform lead into gold. This transformation, of course, would break the laws of physics because there is no way that lead can be turned into gold in normal, third-dimensional logical physics. But in spiritual alchemy, there is a special state of higher consciousness, and when that state of consciousness is achieved through various accelerated, energetic exercises, one has the power to change physical reality—lead into gold—by saying a certain word such as "abracadabra"—*avra kehdabra*—Aramaic for "I will create as I speak." This is one formula of words that, said with the right intention, will work effectively with spiritual energy and exercises. One can thus transform lead into gold. This is an example of using fifth-dimensional energy to transform a third-dimensional energy. It is a very small and modest work; transforming lead into gold would not save a planet. But transforming lead into gold would be a step in the integration of fifth-dimensional energy to effect a change in the third-dimensional reality and in the third-dimensional physical world.

In terms of planetary healing, we can say that there is planetary spiritual alchemy—PSA. In the concept of PSA, one can induce a planetary change through the right sort of spiritual exercises and practices and then through saying certain sounds and words to effect that change. In order to do that, you have to raise the vibrational field of the planet. This can be accomplished through the twelve etheric crystals. The interaction of the planetary healers with the etheric crystals can create the environment for Earth changes when certain powerful words are spoken. In order to effect the change, one has to have an idea of what change is possible and what change would be most effective for planetary health.

Earth is a complicated spiritual energy. What change would you make to Earth? There are so many complex interactions within Earth; thus, it would be difficult to know what change you would want to make when you were finally setting everything up and saying "abracadabra." What would you change? Would you reverse the polar ice caps so that they were frozen again? Would you clear all the air? Would you stop volcanic eruptions? Realize that taking one such event is isolating that event from other interactions. It would be difficult to say which change would be the most effective and the most needed.

We want to emphasize that the concept of biorelativity is focused on telepathic communication with Earth. In that telepathic communication with Earth in biorelativity, we have two processes. The first process is the transmission of energy to Earth. The second process is receiving communications from Earth. Only when there are these two energetic linkages can you receive the information that would allow you to receive the correct energy through which change needs to occur for the highest good of the planet—both for the human species and for the evolution of planet Earth.

We remind you that we continually have meditators on Arcturus who assist in communicating and receiving energy and light from our planet so that we can perform exactly the shift and change that is necessary. We institute the needed change and work with a biorelativity system similar to what we have been teaching you—a system that centers on working with etheric grids. We also work with the etheric crystals, establishing and raising the light-frequency energy of the planet as well as of the people. Then people can interact with and receive messages from the planet about what change needs to be done, as planetary healers then use planetary spiritual alchemy to do it. On Arcturus, we would get our meditators and other group members together on our planet to also participate in a PSA experience.

In individual spiritual alchemy, there is a lot of preparation and a lot of study necessary. In planetary spiritual alchemy, there is an equal amount of study and preparation that needs to be done: The downloading of these etheric crystals on Earth has lasted several years at least and has been a process of preparation for the PSA experience. Now that the eleventh etheric crystal is connected, the opportunities for each person to connect to the energy of planetary spiritual alchemy are raised.

A New Planetary Harmony

The first level of planetary spiritual alchemy has to do with providing harmony on Earth. The changes have been rapid, and Earth does not have enough time to integrate and balance everything so quickly. You have a hard time integrating and balancing yourself when the changes are too rapid. So does the Earth as a planetary spirit. You have to consider the age of Earth, and then you have to consider the rapid amount of changes that have occurred in the past hundred years and even the past fifteen to thirty years. The Earth needs to come into a balance with all of this, because the changes are happening so quickly. Therefore, one of the first lessons and issues in performing planetary spiritual alchemy would be in harmonizing Earth. This harmony has to be tied in with fifth-dimensional energy, because there is no way Mother Earth can assimilate everything with only third-dimensional energy and light. It is too much to integrate—even you are probably struggling because you have witnessed so many changes on the planet.

Obviously, if you look at everything that is happening now, Earth is going to become more polarized in terms of the effects of certain Earth changes. Changes in the human species—politically, sociologically, economically, and environmentally—are also becoming more polarized. To process these changes for the planet and to help Mother Earth to bring herself into harmony, it is necessary to connect the light from the fifth dimension and to work with Earth, helping her to receive fifth-dimensional energy from the Central Sun. That Central Sun light, which comes into alignment approximately on December 22, 2012, needs to be focused through planetary spiritual alchemy. This will ensure Earth's survival by allowing her to come into a new harmony.

Fifth-dimensional light from the Central Sun can come to the core of the Earth. It can be directed to her with the PSA energy, helping her to accelerate her ability to come into a new balance, which will ensure that humanity can survive on her. This means that all of the predictions of bad events that are going to happen, such as temperature increases, will have to be recalibrated. Earth and humankind will have to recalibrate so that Earth can assimilate all these changes and shifts while still holding a planetary balance that will ensure the survival of humanity and Earth in a new, fifth-dimensional harmony. I am Juliano. Blessings.

CHAPTER 11

HOLDING AND SUSTAINING FIFTH-DIMENSIONAL LIGHT

Juliano and the Arcturians, Adama, and Lord Arcturus

Greetings, I am Juliano, and we are the Arcturians. We will be talking about the connections between the fifth dimension and the third dimension in order to learn how one can enhance these connections. It is true that when one is working in a large group, one is able to go to very high energy levels. These high energy levels can often surpass what one would normally experience individually. Of course, this is in part due to the group energy, for a group energy that is focused on the fifth dimension can raise many people's vibrational levels. Yet when one is going to be alone, the connections that were made in the group are often not as strong as one would hope. That is another way of saying that the fifth-dimensional energy connections do not seem to transfer when one is away from the group.

We note that many people are struggling with their own connections to the fifth dimension. For those reasons, they seek out group contact to create a better acceleration energy. It is also true that being in powerful energy places, such as the energy fields of the planetary cities of light, will also raise one's vibrational field. We continually work with the groups of forty to raise the energy levels of the planet through a process we call "planetary osmosis," which is seeping through the whole planetary system. Planetary osmosis is a way of describing how fifth-dimensional energy is going to many different places on the planet. Our activations of the cities of light are a major step forward in enhancing the process of planetary osmosis.

We have been able, with the help of the members of the groups of forty, to activate twelve planetary cities of light. The last planetary city of light activated was Mount Shasta, the host city of the Arcturian conferences, because of the powerful energy emitted from this beautiful mountain area. Mount Shasta is connected interdimensionally to Inner Earth. This is particularly important because Inner Earth is bringing forth powerful fifth-dimensional light energy to the starseeds and to the planetary cities of light.

EARTH-FRIENDLY, FIFTH-DIMENSIONAL CONNECTIONS

The interdimensional Inner Earth has a definitive role to play in holding fifth-dimensional energy and light on the planet. There are several reasons for speaking about the power of interdimensional Earth that emanates specifically from Mount Shasta. The idea is that you can connect to the fifth dimension through the Arcturian stargate and the Arcturian crystal temple. These are very powerful connections. The fact remains that these places—the stargate and the crystal temple—are fifth dimensional. Of course, we have made special corridors in order to more easily facilitate your connections to these fifth-dimensional energy fields. In particular, we have set up the crystal lake as a special energy place for our third-dimensional Earth friends. You can say that it is Earth-friendly for you to travel through the fifth-dimensional corridors to the stargate, the crystal temple, and the crystal lake.

Let us look specifically at the interdimensional Earth of which we are speaking. In particular, let us speak about the interdimensional portal of light that is so strong in Mount Shasta. This portal of light and interdimensional corridor at Mount Shasta allows a particularly strong access to fifth-dimensional energy that is being radiated from the interdimensional Earth. This offers specific advantages to the starseeds. Why and how? The main advantage is that this is already fifth-dimensional Earth energy, albeit interdimensional Earth energy and Inner Earth energy.

Earth energy is ingrained in your DNA, which means it is a familiar, home-based energy field. As you seek more contact with the interdimensional Earth, you can integrate and accelerate your own fifth-dimensional energy field to a new level. You can bring your energy to a level that perhaps did not seem possible. More importantly, you can use the interdimensional Earth energy from the Inner Earth to sustain your fifth-dimensional energy as you travel around the planet and as you leave the Mount Shasta area.

This portal of interdimensional light at Mount Shasta was increasingly activated on 9–9–9. After 9–9–9, the interdimensional Earth, or the Inner Earth as some call it, has created a greater flow of light to all starseeds. I would like my friend Adama to now speak to you about the interdimensional Earth and the Inner Earth, and then I will return to speak more about the relationship of holding the fifth-dimensional light and the four bodies. Now I turn this part of the lecture over to Adama.

CORE COMMUNICATION FOR PLANETARY ASCENSION

Greetings, my Earth friends. I am Adama. I am from Inner Earth, from the great portal that is emanating so strongly from the Mount Shasta area. My name, Adama, comes from the name Adam, which is Earth, for we are of our Inner Earth. Our relatives and beings are connected and committed to holding the fifth-dimensional light in the Inner Earth.

Many eons ago, the Earth was integrated into fifth-dimensional light, and there were starbeings like myself who came to Earth to work and open the portal to the fifth dimension from Inner Earth. Think about the inner core of a planet. You will immediately realize how logical it is that the core—the inner structure, the inner etheric energy of a planet—shall first be formatively connected to the fifth dimension. It makes perfect sense that the inner core of a planet is etherically connected not only to fifth-dimensional energies in the solar system but also to fifth-dimensional energies of the Central Sun and in other galaxies.

Through the Inner Earth core connections we have the ability to communicate intergalactically, especially to Andromeda. We consider Andromeda our sister galaxy. We understand that this core of Inner Earth that we inhabit is already in the fifth dimension and already has fifth-dimensional powers and energies that can be transmitted to all the starseeds. We want ways to broaden the transmission abilities of Inner Earth to more parts of outer Earth.

It is strange to talk about inner and outer, but you know from working on yourself that you have an inner self and an outer self. You know that it is the inner self that contains all of the codes for your ascension. It is the inner self that you look to to unlock your inner codes of ascension and your inner codes that open up to the fifth dimension. Think how natural it is to work interdimensionally with Inner Earth. Maybe now you can feel the gratitude and the success of having an Inner Earth already activated. Perhaps you can appreciate now that this portal from the Inner Earth is serving as a vital link to the planetary ascension and to the planetary cities of light.

We have, through Juliano and the groups of forty, activated twelve planetary cities of light, and we will activate even more of them soon. This is just the first phase of this activity. I want all of you to understand that Inner Earth energy fields are opening up to all the twelve activated cities of light from this powerful 9–9–9 energy in which we have been participating. As I speak, portals of interdimensional fifth-dimensional light are now being opened to each of the twelve cities. This means that each city now has connections to Inner Earth. They now have connections to me, Adama, and to the many people in Inner Earth and to Inner Earth's energy field. The Inner Earth energy field is a self-generating etheric energy ball of light that is now radiating through the Inner Earth to all twelve cities.

The tremendously powerful fifth-dimensional, interdimensional, Inner Earth light is going to each of these cities of light and being transmitted to all of you who are listening to and reading these words. The Inner Earth contains a basic foundational energy that is working for the activations of the planetary ascensions and for your personal ascension. I, Adama, am so pleased that we have reached a point of greater knowledge and greater awareness of Inner Earth and of its relationship to the planetary ascension. I am so pleased that you have activated these cities and that you are willing to open up this corridor from Inner Earth in Mount Shasta so that it radiates through the whole planet.

SUSTAINING YOUR FIFTH-DIMENSIONAL ENERGY

It takes a certain level of consciousness and spirituality to be able to focus and work with Inner Earth. I want to tell you that Inner Earth is able to communicate with the inner Central Sun as well as with inner planetary systems throughout this galaxy and throughout other galaxies. The Inner Earth has specific interactional portals that connect to other corridors that can lead to interdimensional travel. There are many interdimensional beings in Inner Earth who work for planetary ascension.

The twelfth etheric crystal, as you know, is going to be downloaded into São Paulo, Brazil. This place was chosen for many reasons. Juliano has explained some of these reasons, including the Brazilian rain forests, from the Arcturian perspective. From our perspective, this area in Brazil has deep connections to Inner Earth. This area near São Paulo has the capacity to receive powerful light from Inner Earth. So realize that you can connect Inner Earth's energy with fifth-dimensional etheric energy from Arcturus and from crystal lake. This connection can create a powerful magnetic energy field of light that is sustainable on the fifth dimension and sustainable on the third dimension.

We are working with the Arcturians to help develop methods of sustaining the fifth-dimensional light throughout Earth. I emphasize the word "sustaining." When you work with fifth-dimensional energy and light, you may find that it is hard to sustain this higher energy in the third dimension. I promise you that as you work with Inner Earth, we will open up more portals and energy fields. Because of the activations on 9–9–9, each of you is able to sustain your fifth-dimensional energy, perspectives, and connections to the corridors. These portals will also be a great enhancement to the Arcturian etheric crystals that are already downloaded.

Remember that these etheric crystals are downloaded into Earth. We are speaking of the Arcturian etheric crystals, of course. They are not downloaded on top of Earth; they are *in* Earth. Does this not point out again the knowledge and the power of Inner Earth? Think about biorelativity and Inner Earth, because we are reaching a point where the biorelativity exercises are becoming crucial for maintaining certain stabilities. There are several levels of biorelativity. One level is to sustain and stabilize, and another level is to shift proactively. To shift proactively, one can go into Inner Earth and work with Earth-balance energies.

YOUR CORE RELATIONSHIP WITH INNER EARTH

One of the most powerful interventions in biorelativity is to access and work with Inner Earth energies. The Arcturians know that the key to proactive biorelativity is working with the feedback-loop systems in Earth. This can allow greater control of air systems, ocean currents, and solar-flux energies. All these Earth energies can be modulated through Inner Earth. Obviously, this biorelativity activity has to be done through specialized instruction and permission, and it only can be done by higher beings who understand the ramifications of working with Inner Earth energies. In this way, dramatic effects can be realized.

These Inner Earth energies also serve a great higher purpose for your personal ascension and personal healing. Your DNA is totally linked to the inner core of Earth. You have incarnated and manifested on Earth; therefore, your human physical body obviously has a special core relationship with Inner Earth. This core relationship with Inner Earth is absolutely necessary and part of your incarnation energy. That is to say that you have special linked energy to inner core Earth and to interdimensional Earth. The inner core of Earth has certain corridors linking to the fifth-dimensional Earth and to the fifth dimension in general.

Remember that thinking is the fastest light energy on Earth and in the universe. The speed of thought is faster than the speed of light. To work most effectively with the speed of thought, you can go to special sacred places where your energy is enhanced. Mount Shasta is a special sacred place. The twelve planetary cities of light are special sacred places, as is the Inner Earth. One way of enhancing the speed of thought is through interdimensional travel. In this way, you can also receive interdimensional messages from other beings, planets, galaxies, and inner-core planetary systems. It is, however, difficult to travel to different areas of the universe without knowing specifically what the names of those areas are. If you don't know the names or at least the location, then it is difficult to thought-project yourself there, even if you are traveling at the speed of thought. This is why the Arcturians created the crystal temple and crystal lake. These powerful areas give you a place to focus your energy. This has been extremely helpful.

Inner Earth is a place in interdimensional space where you can receive higher energies and thought waves from other fifth-dimensional planetary systems throughout the universe and the galaxy. By receiving those thought waves, you can travel interdimensionally at the speed of thought to those places. Feel your abilities now to thought-project and to bilocate yourself into Inner Earth and the interdimensional space where I, Adama, am waiting in the garden, directly under Mount Shasta, California. This is approximately, in Earth measurement, two to three kilometers below the Earth of Mount Shasta. I invite each of you now to thought-project your energy into this beautiful interdimensional garden, where there is beautiful sunlight from Inner Earth.

You all appear here in your lightbodies. As you enter this interdimensional space, you immediately transform yourselves and enter into your fifth-dimensional lightbodies, which is also present in Inner Earth. As you come into your fifth-dimensional lightbodies here in the garden with me, you can feel a huge acceleration of fifth-dimensional activation in your DNA codes. [Tones.] *Kadosh, Kadosh, Kadosh, Adonai Tzevaoth.* Let those sounds activate the DNA within your lightbodies to help you be more connected to Inner Earth and the interdimensional Earth. Now I send you a special healing light that you may direct to any part of your third-dimensional bodies when you return. Hold this healing light in your Inner Earth body, and we will go into silence for one to two minutes. [Pause.] Rays of interdimensional light are now connecting to the inner Arcturian planets. We help you connect to interdimensional Arcturus. I turn you over now to Lord Arcturus. I am Adama. Blessings.

CONNECTING TO THE SISTER CITIES OF LIGHT

Greetings, fellow starseeds, bearers of light and builders of the adytum. I am Lord Arcturus. I am one of the commanders of the inner Arcturian light mission. I welcome you now to the inner core of Arcturus. We have many interdimensional links to planetary systems around this galaxy and sister galaxies. I am very grateful for the lightwork that the Arcturian starseeds do here on Earth.

We have many responsibilities and commitments. Our primary commitment is to assist fellow starseeds through their ascensions, and our primary responsibility is to provide interlinking connections to the stargate so that after you have completed your Earth lessons and incarnations, you will easily travel through the stargate and be able to continue your journey to higher planetary systems.

We look at our work as providing an entranceway for you to go to higher levels and higher planets. At the same time, we work on a deeper core level to help activate the ascension energies of Earth. Activating the ascension energies of Earth requires great spiritual efforts. I can assure you that we are ready, and we hold great spiritual technologies that offer assistance.

Anytime a new fifth-dimensional energy is activated, all other planets in the fifth dimension benefit. We are all linked. Here we are speaking of the holographic light and holographic connections. Maybe now you understand. From this place in the inner core of Earth, you can connect holographically to inner core energies in many fifth-dimensional planets. Other planets, like Arcturus and Earth, have interdimensional cores. There are interdimensional Arcturuses, interdimensional Pleiades, and interdimensional Alanos. Through interdimensional work, you can accelerate your travels throughout the fifth-dimensional galaxy. That is right; there is a fifth-dimensional galaxy.

The entry level of Earth as a fifth-dimensional planet will positively affect all fifth-dimensional planets. We, the Arcturians, are connected to these fifth-dimensional planets in the deepest way, and we are prepared to welcome a fifth-dimensional Earth to the family of fifth-dimensional planets. We are not, however, prepared to welcome the third-dimensional Earth with its planetary polarizations and dualities into the family of planets on the fifth dimension. But we already accept the Inner Earth, and we will accept and facilitate the fifth-dimensional Earth through Inner Earth's work to create a transformation and ascension of planet Earth.

I, Lord Arcturus, now connect the inner core of Alano, a moon-planet close to the center of the galaxy, the Central Sun, and Inner Earth. There are planetary cities of light, which we call sister cities, that are on Alano and that connecting with the twelve etheric planetary cities of light on Earth. In particular, we will connect with Mount Shasta. The twelve sister cities on Alano are now connected through Inner Earth to Arcturus and Inner Earth to the planetary cities of light. These planetary cities of light will become planetary star cities of light. Please note this shift of planetary star cities—that they will now be places of starbeings, star energy, and star activation. There will be many visitations in these cities.

The work of planetary ascension is a task all of us on the fifth dimension are participating in through the Arcturians. We on Arcturus are not only connected through the stargate to other systems but also through our inner core, Inner Arcturus. We are connected to the inner cores of many different planets. My friend Juliano will now guide you back to your Earth bodies and will speak to you about sustaining and holding this fifth-dimensional light. I am Lord Arcturus, and I am working from the inner cores of many planetary fifth-dimensional systems. We help to solidify the connections of Inner Earth to the other inner planets in the fifth dimension.

Open Your Bodies to Receive Quantum Healing

Greetings, I am Juliano. Project yourselves back to your Earth bodies through the speed of thought and reenter your physical bodies in perfect alignment now. As you come back into your physical body, be aware of the many messages of sustaining fifth-dimensional energy. You have made some core connections, and we have activated many of these connections through your DNA.

Holding fifth-dimensional light and sustaining it involves sustaining the energy in the mental body, which includes ideas and beliefs. It also involves the emotional body, which includes emotions of love and higher feelings. And it involves the physical body as well, which includes the ability to hold etheric energies from other dimensions. Finally, holding fifth-dimensional light also involves the spiritual body, which is able to gather, collect, and sustain spiritual energy. Spiritual energy is the core energy of your soul.

When we talk about dimensions, this includes interdimensional travel and travel at the speed of thought. We are getting close to the core soul light when we talk about dimensional travel. Soul energy is activated when discussing dimensional energy. Dimensional energy can create an activation of spiritual energy. Each one of these levels is called a body. For example, the spiritual body is eternal and infinite and knows no boundaries of space or time; it knows no life or death because it is infinite and eternal. The physical body, of course, is finite. But the physical body can benefit from the fifth-dimensional spiritual energies.

The physical body can benefit from fifth-dimensional emotional and mental energies because these energies nourish the physical body. It makes your physical body open to quantum energy, thought, and healing. As we speak these words, say to your physical body, "Cells, be open to any quantum healing that is necessary for me now. I am ready to receive." You see, we have now established a groundwork for receiving the spiritual light, the spiritual energy, and the quantum energy for healing. Say again in an affirmation, "I am open to receiving quantum healing energy. I am open to receiving this in my physical body. I am open to receiving this in my emotional body. I am open to receiving fifth-dimensional quantum light in my mental body, my belief systems, and my concepts. I am open to holding this energy in all my four bodies. I stay connected. This connection now is strongly unified with Inner Earth. Being in an Earth-based incarnation, I now have an easier connection to Inner Earth and fifth-dimensional energy. This link will help me to sustain my connection to the fifth dimension and to other fifth-dimensional planets."

All of you want to activate your connections to the family of planets in this galaxy and to the family of fifth-dimensional planets. The Earth is now being welcomed into the fifth-dimensional galactic family of planetary light. These activations of the planetary cities of light have been an important step toward connecting with your galactic families and your star families. It is so precious that you are able to understand and hold this star family connection. The star brothers and sisters are fifth-dimensional, and they are communicating with you now and sending you love and light. I am Juliano, and we are the Arcturians. Good day.

CHAPTER 12

ALIGNMENT WITH THE ARCTURIAN STARGATE

Juliano, the Arcturians, and Chief White Eagle

Greetings, I am Juliano, and we are the Arcturians. The starseeds in the groups of forty are working to complete the alignment with the stargate. The stargate is the point of ascension that allows those who have completed the lessons on Earth incarnation to transit into the fifth dimension. This is a major soul occurrence, and it certainly calls for celebration. Many have asked what their soul purposes are—and indeed, one of the main lessons and purposes of your incarnation now on Earth is to transit through the stargate.

In order to travel through the stargate, it is clear that you must complete the Earth lessons or the Earth schooling here. Many of you are very close to completion and being able to graduate from the Earth school. The Earth school is filled with many lessons, and the lessons are increasing in variability—and sometimes in difficulty—during this time of polarization and duality. I would like to compare this to going to a university. Some of you would like to study, but you would like to have the broadest curriculum possible. Therefore, you might choose a university that offered many different courses and many different subjects and a variety of different languages and different cultural opportunities. This variety is what Earth represents in terms of soul lessons. Earth represents variability, and Earth school allows you the experience of duality and polarization. Earth school offers different spiritual and religious experiences that represents, at this point, an opportunity to be on a planet that is going directly into alignment with the Arcturian stargate. This alignment is going to allow an acceleration of your soul force and will be the perfect opportunity to ascend and transit through the stargate.

As a planet, Earth inhabits this portion of the galaxy that is referred to as the Sun solar system. Each solar system in the galaxy is named after its sun, because the constellation or the star represents the central force of that solar system. The name of your star is the Sun, and the name of your solar system, therefore, is called the Sun solar system. If there is a solar system in the star Spica, then that solar system is called the Spica solar system. If there is a system in the constellation of the Pleiades, then one of the stars in that constellation, such as Algol, could have a planetary system, and that system would be called the Algol solar system.

The Sun solar system has a unique position in the galaxy, and part of the awakening energy that is necessary for the Sun solar system is now occurring. In other words, the Sun solar system is gaining and is in a position to be activated and to come into this alignment with the Arcturian stargate. The Arcturian stargate, the Sun solar system, and the Central Sun form a powerful triangular-activation light force field. Earth must do its share of energy transformation and energy awakening, because it represents the most powerful life force in the Sun solar system. Actually, in this section of the galaxy, Earth is one of the major planets that is awakening.

You Need to Learn This Life Lesson

We teach galactic spirituality as one of the sides of the sacred triangle. Galactic spirituality centers on the awareness of the soul's relationship to the galaxy and beyond. An understanding of galactic spirituality states that each soul that incarnates on a planet can expand its consciousness. Each soul has awareness and seeks to align with all highly evolved spiritual beings in the galaxy. To say this in a simple way: Galactic spirituality is the force that seeks awareness and knowledge of all higher life forms in the galaxy. Its basic premise is that there are many highly evolved spiritual beings in the galaxy and that many of those highly evolved spiritual beings are masters—and humanity's relationship to the Creator is enhanced through the communications, meaning, and knowledge gained from these galactic masters.

Why would becoming aware of the galactic civilizations and galactic masters be of assistance in your soul development? Each evolved life form in our galaxy inhabits a specific section of the galaxy that we call sectors. You are in the Sun sector, in which Earth is the main planetary guardian of consciousness. Each galactic civilization has a unique perspective and a unique view on life as well as its own evolutionary process that its members are experiencing. Each galactic civilization has its own ascension, if you will, and each galactic civilization has its own specific lessons that are often—not always, but often—available within those planetary systems. This means that there are certain life lessons and certain soul lessons that are only available on Earth, certain life soul lessons that are only and perhaps best experienced on Arcturus, and certain life lessons that are only experienced and best enhanced through Spica or through the Sirians.

Therefore, we seek to say that each galactic civilization offers a viewpoint that is a different and detailed view of the Creator life-force energy. Each galactic civilization has a unique view, because it is true that the Creator life-force energy only shows a limited part of itself on each planet. This means that you on Earth experience a unique, life-force Creator energy. This God force is called *Adonai*. It is focused on Earth, and it is your perception of the Creator life-force energy that is offered from your unique perspective of the Earth. If and when you go to another planetary civilization in the galaxy, then you will be able to see another perspective and another view of the Adonai light and the creative life-force energy. This will enhance your soul development.

Not every planet has duality like Earth. Not every planet has numerous religions or numerous races like Earth. Indeed, not every planet has the many millions of species that now exist on Earth. Some of you have already remembered your experiences on other planets. You have come to Earth at this time and have difficulty accepting and in dealing with dualities. Part of that is because you remember what it was like on other planetary systems where duality was not present. And yes, while those other planetary systems may not have had duality, I guarantee you that they also had life lessons and soul lessons. So you need to understand that you are here on Earth because you needed this life lesson. You needed this experience here to complete your soul evolution, and now this particular energy on Earth is coming into alignment with the stargate.

This will create an opportunity for what we call the manifestation of the "ladder of ascension." The ladder of ascension is an etheric energy force field. It is an etheric elevator or an etheric escalator that allows you to ascend to the Arcturian stargate and be raised up. I want you to just meditate for a moment on this concept of being taken up to the stargate, where you can experience the feeling of completion of your soul lessons on Earth. Meditate on what it means to complete your soul lessons on Earth and to actually reach the point after so many incarnations when you are in a position to say, "I am completing my soul lessons on Earth. I will be able to graduate." Affirm the following: "I am now ready to graduate from Earth, because I am completing my soul lessons here. I am ready to graduate from Earth school, and I am completing my soul lessons here."

ALIGNING EARTH WITH THE STARGATE

There is no doubt that this is an accelerated time on Earth. There is no doubt that Earth changes, as they have been called, are accelerating and will continue to accelerate. It is also true that as you get closer to completing your soul lessons on a planet, your spiritual energy will become stronger and your personal power will become more activated. This activation includes your abilities to be both a personal and a planetary healer.

The planetary healing work now focuses strongly on aligning Earth with the stargate. We have worked with the group and through the channel to download eleven etheric crystals into Earth. Each one of these etheric crystals is an etheric duplicate of the crystal in the Arcturian crystal lake, and each of these crystals that have been downloaded has a specific energy field. The energy field of each crystal works on two levels. On the first level, it works on bringing down energy into Earth from the Arcturian corridors and from the Arcturian crystal lake. On the second level, each crystal has a unique dialectic energy field that has activated itself through interaction with the other crystals.

We have unified these eleven existing etheric crystals by activating the diagram known in the *Kaballah* as the Tree of Life, the *Etz Chaim* in Hebrew. We have added two additional places on the Tree of Life, because this new Arcturian tree-of-life force field that we are working with interacts directly with the fifth dimension and with the Arcturian stargate. The interaction of these etheric crystals will become more enhanced when the twelfth crystal—the crystal in Serra da Bocaína in Brazil—is downloaded.

The twelfth crystal has a unique power of its own, and that unique power is to enhance the communications and the self-regulation of the biosphere of Earth. The etheric crystal in Serra da Bocaína, Brazil will provide a self-regulating energy force field that previously was not available to people. This will be downloaded in the center of a rainforest area because we see that the rainforests are becoming the key energy force fields for maintaining the biosphere for the whole planet.

This means that Brazil and all those areas in South America holding particularly strong rainforests are going to be playing a more major role in the world and in the world's ability to hold the biosphere force field intact. Brazil then, in particular, moves into a prominent role in the spiritual and biospheric light field. That is one of the powers of this twelfth etheric crystal. The second level is that there is a magical power in the number twelve. The twelve levels of activation create a dynamic power grid. This dynamic power grid, which is formed from the twelve etheric crystals, can and will be aligning with the Arcturian stargate.

Remember that the twelfth crystal completes the grid. The completion of the grid will be at the site of that downloading at Serra da Bocaína. The intentions and energy fields of those workers that will be there with that twelfth crystal will be very strong. The workers' intentions and their thoughts will help bring Earth into the alignment with the stargate. This is the first time in the history of planet Earth that twelve etheric crystals will be downloaded into the planet by the Arcturians and that the alignment with the stargate will be activated.

COMPLETING YOUR PREREQUISITES

What will this mean for Earth? What will it mean for the groups-of-forty project? What will it mean for you personally when Earth becomes aligned with the stargate? On a personal level, each of you will feel a boost in your soul power that can be manifested on Earth. One of the most important experiences for you on Earth now is to bring down as much of your soul energy and power as possible onto Earth. Your soul power and your soul energy can help to manifest many things. The more you are in alignment with them, the more that you can manifest and the more personal power that you can allow to come through. This alignment will help you to accelerate your Earth lessons, and Earth changes will also continue to accelerate with more intensity.

These Earth-change accelerations also bring the acceleration of lessons, and learning these lessons requires a certain receptivity. Let us go back to the example of the university. When you were looking for a planet to incarnate on, you wanted to come to a planet that would provide you with a diverse curriculum. This diverse curriculum included many different subjects that were only available in certain planets, so you chose the planet that had the widest possible choices that were available. But just because there are many courses available doesn't mean that you are immediately open to each course. Some of the courses require prerequisites. You know about prerequisites: For example, you have to have a background in mathematics in order to take calculus. If you take the calculus course without an earlier background, then you might not be able to understand and integrate all of the mathematical theorems that were present.

So in Earth energy, we can say that there are prerequisites, and some of them have to do with learning about dualities and polarizations. Others have to do with learning to detach and also learning to use unity thinking. Unity thinking is one of the major life lessons on this planet; unity consciousness or unity thinking is the ability to see that there is a higher unity above the duality. That is one of the major soul lessons for most everyone who has come to this planet—for what better way to understand unity than to see duality and to understand that the duality is an illusion? The illusion is so strong here that the unity is hard to perceive. This is one of the great soul lessons that one can learn here.

With the alignment of the stargate, each of you who is doing ascension work will receive a boost in your energy so that you will be able to see the unity with a greater clarity. Each of you will be able to see the great divine plan and how you are part of that plan. This is on a personal level. Coming into alignment with the stargate enhances your clarity. The prerequisite coursework that you need to have and the knowledge and the wisdom that you can gain from the prerequisite coursework is now going to be downloaded into your consciousness. Let me repeat that the prerequisite knowledge and wisdom will be downloaded into your consciousness when the stargate is in alignment with Earth.

COMPLETION OF THE STAR CORRIDOR

On a planetary level, there is also a great activation coming. The twelfth crystal will enable the etheric energy field of the planet to come into the alignment with the stargate. That means that Earth's higher astral energy is going to fit into the corridor that directly leads to the stargate. It is like completing a new freeway that has a bypass. You are completing a new road, and you are now able to very easily cross through a city by traveling on this completed road. The alignment with Earth's etheric energy field is now going to be opened up. This is a completion of a pathway, a roadway—a star corridor of light to the stargate.

Some have asked, "Does that mean that the stargate and the star corridor are now only going to be connected from Brazil?" The answer is that each etheric crystal is holographically tied into the others. Whatever the one etheric crystal is able to experience, all of the etheric crystals will be able to equally experience. This is a dialectic energy field. In our terminology, dialectic means that there is a holographic energy connection in which what one part experiences, the other part also experiences, and that each portion of the grid is able to enhance and elevate other portions. When the grid energy field is completed, then the highest energy can be experienced at any entry point into that etheric grid. In the energy field of the Tree of Life, there are twelve etheric crystal energy grids connected dialectically.

It would be helpful for each of you to be at the nearest etheric crystal that you can locate. We realize that not everyone can come to Brazil for the downloading of the twelfth etheric crystal, but we also realize that you may be able to be at one of the other etheric crystals, such as Lago Puelo, the Bodensee, Mount Fuji, or Mount Shasta. Being at those areas when the downloading of the crystal occurs will enable you to holographically experience the same openings to alignment with the stargate. This will also help the planet, because it is a great honor and it is a great spiritual achievement for Gaia, the spirit of the Earth, to have its starseeds bring its energy field into alignment with the stargate.

Perhaps you view the stargate as a place where you go to. This is correct, but perhaps you didn't know that energy from the stargate also comes down to the

Earth. Not every planet in your galaxy ascends. Not every planet in the galaxy achieves the higher etheric energy field that would allow twelve etheric crystals to be downloaded and would also allow the alignment to occur with the stargate. Therefore, there is a reciprocal downloading of etheric energy from the stargate back into Earth. This etheric downloading becomes activated at the downloading and completion of the twelfth etheric crystal.

Many of you have been working on subcrystals. Subcrystals are derivations and etheric reproductions of the downloaded crystal. There is a crystal at Montserrat where the Spanish starseeds created subcrystals in different areas on their peninsula. These subcrystals are serving wonderful functions, because they are able to serve as spiritual regulators and spiritual transformers. We will use the example of the electrical current to explain this concept. Imagine that there is a 5,000-volt energy current coming from a power plant that then has to be transformed into a lower voltage so that the people can activate and use that voltage. In the same way, the subcrystals are taking higher energy from main etheric crystals and bringing it to other areas.

These subcrystals will now also receive a higher uplifting when the twelfth crystal is downloaded. I emphasize again that the number twelve and the activation of the number twelve will create a powerful energy force that transcends each individual one. It is the power of twelve that holographically creates a new energy field of light in alliance with the Arcturian stargate. I now turn things over to Chief White Eagle. I am Juliano.

Moderating through Biorelativity

Greetings, all my brothers and sisters, all my relations. [Tones.] *Hey yah hey! Hey yah hoh yay hey!* All my words are sacred. I am Chief White Eagle. Wow! What a time to be on Earth. What a time to experience the energy of this planet. Earth is alive, and she is responding to the blocks and looking for ways of releasing the energy, trying to find a new balance. We are always in touch with Earth. We communicate with her on all levels, at all times possible. The spirits of our grandmothers and our grandfathers are deep in the mountains, oceans and canyons.

Many different possibilities of energy shifts are now possible on the planet. These energy shifts are bubbling. It is as if Earth wants to find a balance that will work to hold the biosphere. You need to understand that Earth, as a spirit, wants to keep the biosphere. Earth, my friends, is a spiritual force. She is a spiritual planet. She is a planet of great honor, of great respect. She is known as the Blue Jewel. Earth wants to keep the life-force energy field on her, but it is required that Earth have assistance, because this new balance is in uncharted territories for her and is not readily attainable for her spirit. Therefore, Earth needs guidance. A new spiritual technology for Earth called biorelativity has come now. This spiritual technology can be developed to maintain the biosphere.

I know that there have been increases in earthquakes and storms. I know that some are predicting that this is just the beginning and that there will be a series of more earthquakes and storms to come. Yet look at the situation from this perspective: one, Earth has to release this energy; two, it is inevitable that this energy has to be released; three, how could the energy be lessened? How could the energy be pacified so that it is released with the least possible harm to the biosphere? How can that energy be released for the least possible harm to human inhabitants and also the least harm to the animal and plant worlds that are in the path of energy release?

I, Chief White Eagle, say to Mother Earth and Father Sky: We are gathered here to ask for a path of peace and a path of release that does minimal harm to any living being. We ask that these storms and these quakes be released at a moderate level so that there will be the least destruction. I ask that each one who is reading and listening to my words send the words to Mother Earth through our thoughts: "Moderate and in balance; moderate and in balance."

This may mean that there could be storms, but they won't be as strong. You might have to have three storms that would be moderate but as not damaging to equal the combined strength of one storm. In this way, the energy of that storm would be released but would be released moderately. This may mean that instead of having one earthquake at a scale of 9—which is very possible in the near future somewhere on this planet—then you might have three earthquakes that measure at the scale of 5, or four earthquakes that are above 6 on the Richter scale. This is how we see biorelativity working more effectively—the necessary energy releases can be moderated. We know that Earth is coming to a much more active period, and these biorelativity exercises can help Earth to moderate.

We see the twelve etheric crystals and the activation of these crystals as a time when Earth is aligning with the star families. When we say the words "all our relations," we are talking about all our relations—not only on Earth but with the star families as well. I ask that each of you become aware that you are gaining two things with this twelfth crystal. First, you are gaining alignment with the stargate. Juliano has beautifully explained how that will affect you and the planet. The second thing you are gaining is an alliance with your star family. This includes a powerful alignment with the Arcturians and the Pleiadians as well as the many other starbeings that are throughout the galaxy.

Now each of you who are in tune with this energy will gain the possibility of receiving more information directly from other planetary systems of higher light. Each of you will gain knowledge and information about how these planetary systems have come to offer solutions to some of the problems facing Earth. What a great gift, to be able to connect with your star family members throughout the galaxy and to bring through their knowledge and their wisdom back into the third dimension and the Earth. I am Chief White Eagle, including my star family relations. *Ho!*

CHAPTER 13

MANIFESTING FIFTH-DIMENSIONAL ENERGY

Juliano and the Arcturians

Greetings, I am Juliano, and we are the Arcturians. Of course this is a very exciting time with many energetic openings. To summarize the gathering in Brazil and the Group of Forty, I would say that the most powerful energy that emerged out of that gathering was the ability to connect with the starseeds to create a powerful energy field that culminated in the downloading of the crystal and the activation of the tepee that was built specifically for this exercise and for the caring and holding of the energy of the Arcturian temple on Earth. To categorize newer techniques that would come out of this would be difficult, because the most important aspect of the work is the ability to connect and hold a powerful fifth-dimensional energy. I want to repeat that the energy of the downloading of the twelfth crystal represents a connection to the fifth dimension that has not been previously available on Earth.

What this means is that there are further opportunities that had not existed before for the fifth-dimensional energy to manifest directly into the third dimension. If one looks at the techniques and the increase in biorelativity power, then one has to say that the key factor in any technique of energy work now lies in the ability to connect, to download, and to manifest fifth-dimensional energy into the third dimension. That is the most powerful energy technique possible at this time on the planet.

Let me explain some aspects of fifth-dimensional energy. Downloading the last crystal essentially created a new energetic force field on the planet. That force field of dialectic energy is the interactive force of twelve etheric crystals simultaneously. They create an energetic force which, when focused and concentrated, is able to accelerate thoughts, biorelativity projects, the activation of corridors, and the downloading of new information and new ideas. Each specific problem now facing Earth—energies, extinction, and planetary survival—has a fifth-dimensional energy solution.

That solution is a transcendent energy that goes beyond normal logic. Normal logic will tell you that if human beings continued their current consumption of oil products with the accompanying discharge of greenhouse gasses into the environment, it would take a hundred years to bring it back into a pattern of normal. And it would take a century *only* if people stopped polluting at this point, which they will not do. However, if there is a fifth-dimensional solution, then disaster can be transcended.

I want to repeat that the key factor in the Brazilian work was the connection that enabled all twelve etheric crystals to interact on a continual basis to enable the downloading energy for the Arcturian temple to manifest on Earth. That energy force field is very strong, and it is continuing to emit an unbelievable source of light. To help you to connect to the energy, I want you to visualize a beautiful tepee in the Atlantic rainforest approximately 350 kilometers from São Paulo that was built specifically for this purpose. This tepee is in the center of the etheric crystal, and it has become a radiating force of light that is generating very positive attractive energy. This has given an unbelievable spiritual boost to the country of Brazil and to the area there. This is very welcome for that country and the entire area.

PREDICTIONS FOR FIFTH-DIMENSIONAL ENERGIES

Predictions about the future of Earth have been made on two levels: There have been predictions on third-dimensional levels that are based on logic and linear processes, and there are predictions that stem from the fifth-dimensional energy and the connections being made on this planet. I believe that most of you will want to focus more on the fifth-dimensional energies and the fifth-dimensional contacts. I will look for you at both levels of predictions. I will review the predictions for 2010 because some of these predictions extend into 2011 and beyond.

As I spoke in a previous lecture several months ago, the polarizations that you are becoming aware of are becoming stronger, but then there is going to be a reconciliation. The unfortunate part of this process is that things have to become more polarized before people at each polarizing camp become conditioned and willing to reconcile. You will see, for example, some further polarizations in the economy that could mean greater differences between the rich and poor. And in terms of the wars that are going on, people will become more entrenched.

Other polarizations on the planet and in the biosphere will culminate in several catastrophic weather events. It is not overly helpful to list too many catastrophes, because people become so worried about them, but it is like this: Because there continues to be polarization about what to do about global warming, there is a lot of inertia. These catastrophic events will make it clearer that the destruction of the biosphere is a real problem and that people will have to reconcile their differences to do something constructive.

If you look specifically at what I could predict for the fifth dimension, I believe that increasing links to the fifth dimension are now going to manifest. Let me give you an example: Where the twelfth etheric crystal was downloaded has become a sacred spot in Brazil. More importantly, more people are going to be drawn spiritually and magnetically to Brazil. Brazil is going to become known for generating fifth-dimensional magnetic light around the planet, and it is going to specifically be a receiver of Central Sun light from the fifth dimension to the planet.

The planetary cities of light will become more active and will be able to activate additional planetary cities of light. The starseeds on this planet and those who are working in the fifth-dimensional way are also going to become more unified and effective in holding the fifth-dimensional light. There will be a greater ability to become politically involved for the greater good, and there will be greater success in that area. The Arcturian work is going to become more popular and more energizing for people.

Harnessing Accelerated Thought Energies

I am very pleased that these twelve etheric crystals are becoming known worldwide and the magnetic energy will be the basis for the biorelativity work. Now we will help you to project your thoughts. There are exercises for working with biorelativity through the crystal grid. This etheric crystal grid is connecting with fifth-dimensional energy and light and bringing down a charge that was not available prior to the downloading of the twelfth etheric crystal.

There is a question about how to harness the energies that were downloaded for healers. The process for this is based on thought energy waves. Thoughts can be amplified. In the concepts of quantum healing, light has been discussed several times with the channel in several healings. The idea behind this technique is that if you have a thought like an affirmation and you want to increase the effectiveness of that affirmation, you can emblazon the affirmation with a fifth-dimensional light we call quantum light—we have also used the term omega light.

This is an example of what I call thought amplification. In normal, third-dimensional thinking, let's say you had to hold that thought in your mind for a hundred hours—because in the fourth dimension, thinking can change reality, but sometimes the thinking requires a longer process. That longer process could be defined in terms of hours that the affirmation needs to be repeated. Even then, when it becomes effective, the actual manifestation of the energy may still take a long time, even several years. Therefore, in order to be affective as healers, you need to work with your thoughts and amplify your thinking. Say, for example, you want to heal somebody and you actually think the words, "I am able to heal this person. I am able to send healing energy to this person's organs" (or whatever). With that thought, you are connected to fifthdimensional healing light, and the light can come through your hands and can heal that person.

Imagine that you can take your thought and put it in the grid of the twelve etheric crystals called the Arcturian Tree of Life. [Unless you already have it in your mind, see the diagram in the appendix of this book. You can also use the map found there.] Let's say that you are close to Mount Fuji. So you send your thought: "I am going to heal this person." Your thought then goes to Mount Fuji, and then all of a sudden the thought passes through all the twelve etheric crystals, including Mount Fuji. Then that thought comes back to you amplified. Before this enhanced process was available, your work might have taken ten hours. Now you are suddenly able to project an energy thought and manifest it in a matter of a few minutes. You have been able to accelerate your thoughts because, like with a particle accelerator, you have the twelve etheric-crystal grid to help you.

The other thing you can do to accelerate your healing is to ask the Arcturians to also download healing energy into that grid for the person you want to heal, allowing your thoughts to mix with our thoughts. We have downloaded this etheric grid at great effort over a period of years. The channel himself and his wife personally traveled thousands of miles over the years to establish this grid so that you can interact with our thoughts. When you send your thoughts through the etheric-crystal energy field, they are accelerated and returned to you. Then you just do your healing the way you normally do, but with much more powerful thoughts and healing energy manifesting through your hands and also your mind. The power will seem unbelievable.

When we talk about biorelativity, we are in a similar situation. Your telepathic communications with Earth will be accelerated through the twelve etheric crystals. Then when you want to manifest healing, let your thoughts go through the twelve etheric crystals, and healing will manifest through the crystal in Serra da Bocaína, because that's the crystal that shows the third and fifth dimensions interacting. If you want to manifest, say, the energy of compassion, look at the energy of compassion and go to the crystal that shows compassion. If you want the energy of harmony to manifest, then you go to that crystal, the Montserrat crystal. Do this after you have accelerated your thoughts through the twelve etheric grids. This may be very complicated, but we are only just beginning to formulate these processes. I am Juliano.

CHAPTER 14

THE ROLE OF THE TWELFTH CRYSTAL IN BALANCING POLARITIES ON EARTH

Juliano, the Arcturians, and Archangel Metatron

Greetings, starseeds. I am Juliano, and we are the Arcturians. The downloading of the twelfth etheric crystal has completed a special energetic grid that is representative of the Tree of Life. The Tree of Life is a symbolic glyph or blueprint that was given to Moses on Mount Sinai. It was passed through many generations of mystics and many prophets. The goal of this blueprint is to provide a path for ascension. In actuality, the diagram of the Tree of Life is developing and has been presented to humans to provide an explanation for how the universe works, how soul evolution works, and how each soul follows a particular path in order to evolve.

All souls are in a process of evolution. Evolution is to the soul what breath is to the human body. This means that your soul thrives on evolution and expansion. Your soul *needs* expansion. We, the Arcturians, have made a galactic addendum to the Tree of Life. This addendum is actually an acknowledgement of the galactic process you as a starseed are experiencing, and for the first time, this galactic process is being superimposed on a planet: Mother Earth. The superimposition of the Tree of Life within the planetary meridian grid of Earth has provided a new energetic and holographic connection to galactic evolution. I think we will all agree that nothing could be better or more appropriate now for Earth than to participate in the planetary process of galactic evolution and galactic participation.

I want to elaborate on this, because downloading the twelfth etheric crystal has created a holographic link for Earth. A holographic link allows Earth to receive and transmit energy to higher galactic sources. These galactic sources include the Central Sun and the Arcturian stargate. They also include other high-energy sources, high-energy planets, high-energy suns, and even high-energy galaxies. You know there are other evolving galaxies. There are other planetary systems in other galaxies. What is truly amazing is that the completion of the twelve etheric crystals has enabled Earth to intercommunicate and interlink with the higher evolutionary systems in our galaxy, especially in the Andromeda galaxy.

Let us talk about the holographic nature of the original Tree of Life and the holographic nature of the Arcturian Tree of Life. We have designated additions to the Tree of Life, placing them in such a way as to support the coming forth of hidden knowledge, which will now be spread more easily throughout the planet, and to support the manifestation of the fifth dimension onto the third dimension. If you look at the twelve spheres that represent the twelve etheric crystals, each of which represents one of twelve powerful energy points on the planet, then you can understand that they are all interacting and holographic. By holographic I mean that they are representing parts that are transmitted, transposed, and projected onto an interstellar, intergalactic energy screen.

DOWNLOADING CHANGES INTO EARTH'S SUBCONSCIOUS PROGRAMMING

Each of you has a subconscious. Each planet has a subconscious. Each galaxy has a subconscious. There are ways of communicating with the subconscious. Ways exist for Earth's subconscious to receive higher messages and higher energy from sources beyond Earth. The Arcturian Tree of Life has become an antenna to receive some of these transmissions. That is to say, Earth responds to subconscious messages in the same way you as a human being respond to subconscious messages. In fact, there is a process by which you can communicate with the subconscious. This process has to do with repetition, with the creation of affirmations and with the expansion of emotions. It also has to do with an interesting phenomenon that has best been described by your computer developers that is called the downloading of programs. Your subconscious is able to receive affirmations and emotions, and it is also able to receive downloaded programs about how you are to be and how you are to act. Some of these programs come from your parents; some come from your cultural upbringing. Some of these programs come from other significant people in your lives, and some of these programs come from other lifetimes. These are called psychic impressions, and they are transmitted genetically and holographically from one lifetime to the next.

On Earth, you are given the freedom to change your subconscious and to begin the process of reprogramming your subconscious so that you can evolve.

Many people have inquired about why there are so many people wanting to come to Earth. We have said before that one reason has to do with the fact that this is a freewill zone. The freewill zone means that you can choose—even about things that appear to be predetermined. The fact is that what you call "predetermined" from our perspective simply means that it has been programmed, or more specifically, programmed into the subconscious. Remember that any program in the subconscious can be changed.

I agree that such changes take intensity, focus, and concentration. Most importantly, they require knowledge. For the most part, you have all been learning how to work with your personal subconscious. If you still think you need updates and instructions on that, I am glad to offer them. I would like to point out one great insight now, however, and that is that the planetary subconscious also exists, and the planetary subconscious can be changed, just like your subconscious can be changed. Earth's subconscious is filled with a plethora of programs. Many of these programs are very primitive, just as some of your own programs are primitive. It is in fact true that you are not that far away from your primordial self, the self who existed in a more primitive environment—even just a couple of lifetimes ago, for example. So you can understand very easily that Earth as a planet still has many primordial programs.

I also need to add to this discussion the fact that some of the Earth's subconscious programming has been downloaded and tampered with by otherdimensional beings. These otherdimensional beings have not been of the highest nature. Sometimes the conflicts you are seeing on Earth are really the result of galactic conflicts—conflicts on Earth that don't even make sense, conflicts so catastrophic that you would never be able to assign logic to them. This would include terrible events such as the Holocaust and some of the catastrophic destruction of civilizations that has occurred on this planet. What I am suggesting is that some of these types of events actually came from outside of the Earth's subconscious and were downloaded from other areas.

You might ask, "Why is this happening?" Remember, because this is a freewill zone, these things can happen. At this point, it is necessary to be on guard and to have a ring of protection around Earth's subconscious so that these types of intrusions from lower-energy sources can't occur. The good news is that the planetary subconscious is changeable and programmable; the planetary subconscious is actually able to receive higher messages from higher sources. To explain that in more depth, I want to come back to the comparison between this information to your personal subconscious.

Using Quantum Light to Accelerate Subconscious Change

I have worked with many of you on your personal subconscious as a path, as a way of changing. I have reviewed with you the process of personal change via the subconscious and have expressed some ideas, including affirmations, repetition, focus, and concentration. Now I want to add the idea of imagery, focusing on images as a way of communicating with the subconscious. A good example would be the concept of gaining material wealth. Many of you might focus on money or wealth as an image. We personally do not recommend focusing on that; rather, we would recommend an image of satisfaction, of having all your needs met, of having a sense of harmony in your life. We recommend this rather than an image focusing on material items. When you focus just on the material, it is not comprehensive enough. This is one method of working with your personal subconscious that has been taught and will continue to be taught on Earth.

Another aspect about the personal subconscious is that it is very amenable to inputs from higher sources. These higher energetic sources in particular can have a very dramatic and powerful effect on your personal subconscious. In a normal working of the subconscious, you might have to, for example, repeat an affirmation a thousand times, or maybe you would have to work on an image daily for two years. These are simply examples. Yet if you were able to concentrate on a higher energetic source, a source that would have an ability to transmute the normal laws of cause and effect and would be able in a very short time to have the same effect on your subconscious, then you would obviously want to use this source.

We have referred to this many times as the omega-energy light and also as the quantum light. The omega-energy light is a light source that comes from the soul level. In terms of the Tree of Life, it would be at the top, at the crown of the Tree of Life. If you were to receive or use radiated vibrational light from that highest source—in this case, it might be radiating from Mount Fuji—to illuminate an affirmation or an image, then that image or affirmation would have an immediate and powerful effect on you. This is because it would be able to directly communicate to your subconscious, because it is a higher energy—a higher vibration.

This is another way of saying that the subconscious does differentiate between lower vibrational sources and higher vibrational sources. I want to tell you that you do have a safeguard in your subconscious. If you are coming from a lower source—for example, say that you are depressed or are focusing on negative thoughts—those lower thoughts generally will not manifest at the same rate as thoughts from higher sources. It could take a longer time for them to manifest because of the lower energy with which you would be working. These thoughts can have the same outcome if you focus on them, but a higher energy source can transmute and work wonders; it can accelerate the laws of the subconscious so that events can unfold more rapidly.

If you were focusing on your subconscious and sending an affirmation—"I am an electromagnetic, loving starseed," for example—if you use the omega light to illuminate that message and then downloaded that message into your subconscious, then the affirmation could manifest much more rapidly in your life. This is the idea behind the Tree of Life and the downloading of the twelfth etheric crystal in Serra da Bocaína. This downloading means that fifth-dimensional energies and fifth-dimensional thoughts can now be made manifest in the third dimension. We look for the highest source of light to illuminate our powerful thoughts so that we can shift our subconscious.

The corollary to this is that the planet Earth has the same process. Up until this point in the evolution of planetary awareness and global awareness, no one that we know of has spoken of the existence of a planetary subconscious. When I am speaking about your personal subconscious, every one of you understands it and every one of you would be able to follow my instructions quite easily to work with this process. You might need guidance or assistance in connecting with omega light, but with assistance or by yourself, each of you would be able to do this work. Yet how can this be done to Earth's subconscious? Earth has been manifesting what has been downloaded into her subconscious. As you already know, this downloading contains some pretty powerful programs. Some programs have to do with the end times, some with world wars, some with world domination. But there are other programs that have to do with Shangri-la, fifth-dimensional energies, and planetary cities of light.

There is a definite process through which you can begin to download higher-energy programs into Earth's subconscious. I told you that the personal subconscious can be accelerated by using higher quantum light. In the same way, change in Earth's subconscious can also be accelerated through the use of quantum light and also through the use of higher extraplanetary sources. There are other higher planetary messages coming in—from Arcturus, for example—that Earth can receive and that can be downloaded into her subconscious. There are messages coming from the Pleiades, from the fifth-dimensional Central Sun, and from the moon-planet Alano that can be received and downloaded into Earth's subconscious.

If these messages are received and downloaded with the highest integrity and from the highest sources, they can supersede some of the drama-filled lower energies that are seemingly dominating Earth at this time. In order to receive these messages, the Arcturian Tree of Life can be activated on Earth to be a fifth-dimensional antenna. This fifth-dimensional antenna can be used to receive these messages and then these messages can be downloaded into Earth, following the path of the Tree of Life. A message will come in at the top of the tree and then go through all of the twelve etheric crystals before being downloaded and manifested into Earth. You already have the twelve etheric crystals downloaded into Earth, and you therefore have the process, the means, and the technique of bringing this energy into the subconscious of Earth and then manifesting it.

A Visualization of the Twelve Crystals and Tree of Life

I would like you to visualize the twelve etheric crystals around the planet. I want you to try and visualize them as all standing up vertically in the Earth so that they form a holographic image that participates in interdimensional space on Earth. If you cannot remember all the places, that is okay; just visualize the linkage and visualize the name "Arcturian Tree of Life," and it will help you. Visualize the Tree of Life standing on the Earth, and at the same time, hold the tree in your etheric cosmic-egg energy field. You are now also participating in the Tree of Life in your own personal energy field. You can visualize the Arcturian Tree of Life on Earth. You can use these energies, and I want each of you to know that we want you to use this energy; we want you to use this system for your own personal development as well as for planetary development.

At the top of the Arcturian Tree of Life on the Earth, the top sphere known as Mount Fuji, I, Juliano, am connecting to the energy of that top crystal. Don't think of these crystals as being in a hierarchy of importance; just look at this crystal as being in the number-one position on the chart. I am connecting with that crystal now, connecting that sphere with the moon-planet Alano, which is a fifth-dimensional moon planet close to the Central Sun, in the Central Sun belt. I am providing a corridor link between Alano and Mount Fuji, and I am putting into words a message that Alano is giving to Earth.

Perhaps you and I will meditate together as we receive this message for Earth from the moon-planet Alano. The first message is that planet Earth can balance these dualities for higher evolution. The moon-planet Alano says to Earth, "Earth, you can balance these polarities. You can balance these dualities for higher evolution." Now I ask you to look at the top of your Tree of Life and to receive that message for yourself. Tell yourself, "I can balance these dualities for higher evolution. I can balance these polarities for higher evolution." This is so beautiful—Earth receiving this message from another planetary system. The language by which one planet communicates to another is not verbal like the words I am speaking. I, Juliano, am able to transcribe the energy into words.

ALANO'S MESSAGES FOR EARTH

- Earth can balance dualities for higher evolution.
- Because there are now so many starseeds on the planet, Earth can hold more fifth-dimensional energy and light.
- The rapid acceleration of change will lead to a higher evolutionary shift for humankind.
- The energy of biorelativity grows stronger and stronger between humanity and Earth, and so Earth needs to know that she is now ready to receive and work with the energy of biorelativity.

There is a second message coming through from moon-planet Alano: "Earth, you can hold more fifth-dimensional energy and light, because you have so many starseeds on you now." This energy message is coming through the top of the Arcturian Tree of Life, and now it is moving down into all of the spheres. As it travels down into all of the spheres, it goes down into the planet. In particular, because we just returned from Serra da Bocaína, the tepee at the center of the etheric crystal is radiating a powerful, etheric red light, illuminating that whole valley of Serra da Bocaína. As this message moves about the planet, you can tell yourself—in terms of your own personal tree of life—"I am able to receive and hold fifth-dimensional light because I am a starseed." Everyone who is listening to and is reading these words is starseed, because if you were not, then you would not be attracted to these messages.

The next message coming from the moon-planet Alano is that this rapid acceleration of change will lead to a higher evolutionary shift for humankind. One piece of explanation is needed here: Earth is very aware of and very involved with humankind. Earth as a spirit, as a planetary being, is very aware of the human species and with what the human species is doing. Earth knows that the outcome of her evolution as a planet is inextricably linked to human evolution. Earth in essence needs human beings to assist her in evolution. At the same time, human beings need to work with and communicate with Earth for their evolution.

For your own personal tree of life, I would like you to affirm, "I am connected to and participating in the evolution of higher consciousness for humanity." Now, hold that thought for your own personal tree of life, just as the planetary tree of life is also receiving that thought. You might ask: "How is it that we work with so many affirmations?" We are all using group energy; we are all connected. The Arcturian Tree of Life is helping us all to participate and connect.

One more message is coming through from the moon-planet Alano. "The energy of biorelativity grows stronger and stronger between humanity and Earth." This means that humanity's telepathic abilities to communicate with Earth—for a higher good, for the resolution of dualities—is improving and getting stronger. Earth needs to know this; Earth needs to receive that message just as you need to receive that message for yourself. You can use the energy of biorelativity that has been downloaded into your subconscious, saying: "I can use the energy of biorelativity to communicate effectively with Earth." Earth needs to know that she is now ready to receive and work with the energy of biorelativity. Some have asked how to send a message to the Earth's subconscious. All you need to do is to put your thought—as I am doing now—into the top of the Arcturian Tree of Life (which is now symbolized by Mount Fuji), and then that message will be transmitted through all appropriate spheres and sources to the subconscious of Earth.

Now I am receiving a message from another source. I am now connecting with the Arcturian stargate. Remember, we said that the downloading of the etheric crystal in Serra da Bocaína would not only complete the grid for all twelve etheric crystals but would also bring a special alignment with the stargate. In particular, it is going to help to radiate and align Brazil—and Serra da Bocaína in particular—with the Arcturian stargate. A brief explanation is in order: The Arcturian stargate is the portal that allows you to leave an incarnational cycle. You can only leave the incarnational cycle after you have graduated and learned your Earth lessons, or through grace, such as from ascension, when you have a rapid acceleration and can complete the process of going through the stargate. The stargate, then, is a portal for human evolution that provides transportation to other higher places in the galaxy.

The Arcturian stargate is also a spirit being—just as Gaia, the planet Earth, is a spirit. The Arcturian stargate is a spiritual place, a spiritual energy. Now the stargate is sending energy to Earth. I am going to work with that energy. The Arcturian stargate is opening a special portal to Earth to receive starseeds. In particular, that portal is now in alignment with Brazil and the twelfth etheric crystal. This alignment will facilitate the ascension for all starseeds who have permission to pass through the stargate, if they so wish. For your own personal tree of life, you can now say: "I am in alignment with the energy of the Arcturian stargate." Alignment with the stargate means higher light; it means that higher energy is coming to these places. Those people who are receiving and working with this energy can have a more rapid evolution, a more rapid acceleration, because that is what each of you really wants. You want to accelerate and evolve as quickly as possible. The next affirmation is: "The energy from the Arcturian stargate will accelerate my evolution."

For Earth, the same message applies. The energy from the Arcturian stargate will accelerate Earth's evolution. These twelve etheric crystals and the formation they make in the Tree of Life are holographic transmission antennas. It is so beautiful that we can help you download these messages, for yourself and for the planet. In closing, I would like to have Archangel Metatron speak with you, as he is guardian of the Arcturian stargate and the Tree of Life. I am Juliano.

REPAIRING AND RESTORING THE WORLD

I am Archangel Metatron. Blessings to *B'nai Elohim*, children of the Elohim light. You are the guardians of the light of our Creator in this dimension. You are the children of this light who are about to evolve and mature into the light of *Elohim*. Each one of you is now preparing for a beautiful evolution, the beautiful glory of being the children of the *Elohim*. To be in that energy is also to have the power of the *B'nai Elohim*. This power includes the ability to transcend duality—the ability to ascend, to unify the third dimension with the fifth dimension in a process we call the unification light: *Yichuda Ha'aur*, the light of unification. It is a special power that you are all developing now, and that power is manifested in the twelfth etheric crystal at Serra da Bocaína, which is the manifestation of the fifth dimension into the third dimension.

The manifestation of the fifth dimension into the third also means that you can unite the third dimension with the fifth, because in holographic light and holographic energy, the dimensions go back and forth. Yes, the fifth-dimensional light and energy, the Arcturian stargate energy, is going to manifest on Earth. At the same time, you as the starseeds, through the power of unification, *Yichuda*, you are going to connect this energy, this third-dimensional energy, with the higher fifth-dimensional energy. That is your soul mission, one of the soul missions many of you have, because there needs to be a link to hold this energy. That is what the *B'nai Elohim* can do—the children of *Elohim*, the children of Creator.

Some people also use the term "co-creator." As you are evolving and begin to leave the planetary Earth, each of you might be called on to go to other planetary systems as ascended masters. You may even be called on to return to this planet as an ascended master. You will need this skill to always be able to connect the third dimension to the fifth dimension and the fifth dimension to the third dimension, to be able to go both ways. That is the power of the unification—the power of unity.

This is the true *Tikun Olam*, the true repairing of Earth. That is, the *Tikun Olam* is the restoration of the *Gan Eden*, the Garden of Eden, the paradise that is really the fifth dimension on Earth. It requires the alignment of the fifth with the third, the manifestation of the third from the fifth and the unity of the third to the fifth. It is also your *Tikun Hanefesh*, your restoration of your third-dimensional body. You are repairing and restoring your third-dimensional body with fifth-dimensional light and becoming a fifth-dimensional being. It is *Tikun Olam, Tikun Hanefesh*: restoring the world, repairing the world and repairing your own human body.

This is why, when resurrection appears in some of the earlier Biblical phrases, it is really referencing the ascension in which you will unify your third-dimensional body—not the physical third-dimensional body but the spirit body. You can even focus on that body as the repaired body. Hold that light—the light of restoring, the light of repairing your perfected third-dimensional body in the fifth dimension. You will ascend into that body so easily. *Kadosh, Kadosh, Kadosh, Adonai Tzevaoth.* I am Archangel Metatron. *Baruch Hashem.* Blessings.

CHAPTER 15

CHARGING PERSONAL AND PLANETARY SPIRITUAL BATTERIES

Juliano, the Arcturians, and Archangel Metatron

Greetings, I am Juliano, and we are the Arcturians. We wish to explore the concept of downloading energy—in particular, the downloading of higher energy from other dimensions. This is an important concept for many reasons. Many starseeds may be struggling to hold their spiritual light and their spiritual energy. Planet Earth is struggling in a way that is different from the past, even as Earth has gone through some dramatic changes over the history of her existence. Earth is being called on to make adjustments and to make energy transformations in a very short period of time. Earth changes will soon require a great deal of energy and input from higher dimensions to balance the biosphere.

The concept of a battery serves as a helpful metaphor for this discussion. As you know, the battery is a device that stores electrical current, and it is measured in certain electromagnetic energy descriptions such as volts or amperages. The car battery, for example, is a device in your automobile that must be charged by an alternator that sends energy from the operating engine to the battery. The stored electrical power in the battery can then later continue to provide energy to start and run your vehicle.

Sometimes the alternator, as the source of the electrical charge of the battery, breaks, and then there is no way to charge the battery unless there is a new alternator. In this case, the battery runs on reserve power—stored capacity. The stored electrical current from the battery can provide the necessary charge for the operation of the vehicle until a new source—in this case a new alternator—can be placed so that the charging can continue. In some batteries, the storage reserve can be as long as an hour or more. This means that your automobile would be able to run for a given period of time without a charging source.

YOUR LIFE-FORCE CHARGE

Let us follow this metaphor and consider you as a battery. Instead of electrical current, you are holding spiritual light with a very fine charge. Your capacity to hold this spiritual energy is dependent on you as a vessel, on how you train yourself. Yet even before this storage capacity is developed, there is another function of this that I need to describe. Many of your spiritual and mystical religions already suggest the concept that I am going to introduce. This concept is that every person is given an initial charge at birth, an initial life-force energy that determines how long that person is going to live on the planet and how much energy he or she can expend.

Some people like to measure this energy capacity by the number of years that you are able to survive on Earth. You might say that one person has a capacity, or a life-force charge, to live eighty-five years. Another person only has the capacity to live seventy years. Some people only have capacities to live ten or twelve years. It is beyond the scope of this discussion to elaborate on why some people are given more of a life charge than others. Let me just say that a lot of it is predetermined by your soul family and by your soul mission. But let me also say that we, the Arcturians, believe that this energy capacity is not only based on years. I would not say to you that you only have enough charge for a given amount of time; rather, your time on Earth can be based on how you are able to sustain and receive energy.

There are certain activities, for example, that shorten your battery's capacity—your own self-capacity. A very simple example would be engaging in war, drugs, or alcohol. These substances produce what we can call lower vibrations. Lower vibrations negatively affect your ability to hold a life charge. This also means that the opposite is true. Higher energy and higher activities can sustain and lengthen your ability to hold a charge, to maintain the spirit in this body for a longer time.

Many of you who are starseeds are older and have already transcended the charge that you were given when you came into this Earth. Many of you were programmed with a charge for a given length of time, and it might have been for seventy-two to seventy-four years. Through your spiritual and energy work, you have accumulated an additional capacity and an additional charge to sustain yourself longer than the time that was originally given to you at entry point into the Earth. This then reiterates the point that you are given a certain life charge for this incarnation, but you can lengthen the life charge, especially if you are involved in spiritual activities.

The charge and the length of time that you spend here is not the sole measurement for your life success. An example of someone who was only on Earth for a short time was Jesus/Sananda. He carried a tremendous energetic charge. The charge that he carried far transcended thousands of lifetimes that normal people would be able to sustain. The energetic charge that he distributed throughout the planet cannot be measured at all by the length of years that he walked the Earth.

PREPARING FOR NULL ZONES BY STRENGTHENING YOUR RESERVE CAPACITY

I want to now explain this concept of the reserve capacity because many of you are struggling with holding the spiritual energy that you have sustained or achieved. For example, you might have received a high spiritual vibration after attending a spiritual workshop, but after a week or two, the spiritual energy you obtained is dissipated, and you no longer feel the charge. For whatever reason, the work that you did at the workshop did not affect—or you did not allow it to affect—your storage capacity for spiritual light. One of the most important concepts for you to develop is strengthening your spiritual storage capacity. It is necessary to be able to hold the spiritual light even when a charge is not being delivered for whatever reason.

If your alternator in your car is failing, then hopefully you have the best battery, one with a big reserve capacity. Such a battery will have the reserve charge to take you to the nearest repair center. There you can either install a new battery or a new alternator so that your charging can be continued. You may not necessarily need a new battery, but you may need to get yourself to a new charging source.

There is a reason why I am giving you this metaphor. I know it is obvious to many of you that the energetic spiritual charge that is working and sustaining many of you is sometimes being cut off or blocked. For a variety of reasons, the charge is not getting through, and you may lose your spiritual focus—your centeredness. If you ever feel that the charge of spiritual light that has been sustaining you may be weakening, I want you to remember this discussion: You must, at that point, tap into your spiritual reserve capacity. Many of you like using acronyms, so spiritual reserve capacity can be called "SRC." We have talked about the SLQ—the spiritual light quotient—and today we talk about the spiritual reserve capacity. I, Juliano, want to ask you: How is your spiritual reserve capacity? How long could you sustain yourself if you were suddenly spiritually cut off?

You might ask, "What are you talking about, Juliano? What do you mean, cut off? Why would spiritual light and spiritual energy be cut off?" The answer to that is somewhat complex. The first answer is that sometimes the densities on Earth are so strong that the spiritual light can be temporarily blocked. Sometimes the environment that you are in and the people that you are around can create a denser field that is hard to lift yourself out of. This could even be in family situations or in work situations. Sometimes there are environmental catastrophes such as earthquakes, tsunamis, storms, or blizzards that make spiritual connections. Sometimes there are illnesses in the body that focus your energy away from your spiritual work and spiritual light.

Many of you have already heard about the concept of the null zone. I know this concept was popular several years ago. Some people had thought Earth was supposed to enter a null zone in which the energy would be blocked out and there would be no electromagnetic current able to flow—all the computers would fail and other such things. This never happened, and so people felt that the idea of the null zone was not a correct notion.

In reality, the concept of the null zone is a very accurate description of certain occurrences with spiritual and electromagnetic energy: One example of a null zone would be if someone using electromagnetic energy or current and went into the Bermuda Triangle; then normal current wouldn't work anymore. There are also null zones in Earth's path around the Sun. More importantly, the Earth and the solar system's paths around the center of the galaxy contain null zones. Because Earth revolves around the galaxy over such a long period, no accurate historical descriptions of the path of the whole solar system or of the Sun around the galaxy exist.

The closest approximation or attempt to describe any energy that would come to Earth during this long galactic path is the Mayan understanding of what will occur in the year 2012. In this concept, a description is offered of an energy shift that is coming from the galactic source, or the galactic center. Even that description is not very detailed, because all you are getting is this one description at the center point known as the winter solstice of 2012, but there is no other information about other energies that could be forthcoming on that path. I would say that the Maya were probably more aware of that long-term energetic charge, but this information was lost.

It is unusual or a sign of weakness for you to experience being temporarily cut off from spiritual light or your energetic charge of spiritual energy, but I would expect and hope from the knowledge that we are getting now that if you were temporarily cut off from spiritual energy, then you would be able to operate on your spiritual reserve. I also hope that we can explore certain lessons on how to hold and to improve your capacity to hold this light so that you have the longest reserve capacity possible. This will be important during the coming times of Earth change.

Downloading Spiritual Light from the Fifth Dimension

Now I will make a slight digression. Some of you in earlier lifetimes had your spiritual batteries and capacities totally drained through some traumatic events.

Examples of a traumatic event might be a holocaust, a violent elimination of a culture—such as when the Native Americans were overridden through wars and terror—or someone experiencing some type of nuclear trauma. You have heard me talk before about nuclear traumas. There is something within the nuclear energy field that totally depletes the spiritual capacity of the person and the battery power so that when they come back into another lifetime, these people might be operating on a deficit for a while.

I know this may sound strange to you, but after such traumas, there could be a deficit in spiritual power and energy in the next lifetime. Sometimes you might even have negative energy to come back into another lifetime. You might find in the next life that you have a lack of capacity to hold spiritual light and that you also have difficulty in gathering that light or finding it. At this time, there is a tremendous grace that comes from an opportunity to expand your spiritual capacity, to store spiritual light and energy, and to learn the ways of downloading the higher spiritual light.

This brings forth the topic of downloading spiritual light, particularly downloading spiritual light from the fifth dimension for the planet. Earth also operates on the same principles that we are discussing for you personally. Earth has a spiritual capacity and an ability to store spiritual energy and spiritual light. Your energy field can expand when you bring down higher energies and spiritual light, expanding the time that your body can stay on the planet. Focus the time on Earth as measured in terms of experiences and light.

The changes that you go through have put a strain on the physical body, in part because the physical body wasn't programmed initially to follow this path. Because of this, you need a greater spiritual light and spiritual energy to solidify these changes and to hold this energy. The Earth charge—its alternator—is not producing and cannot keep up with the spiritual current that you need. That is like saying to you that your car now suddenly requires more electrical power but the alternator in your car can't keep up with it and you need a bigger alternator to produce more electrical current. In the same way, in order to sustain yourselves at the spiritual level that you want to hold, you need more spiritual charge. The older methods, Earth methods for charging spiritually, cannot keep up with what your needs are. You must look to another source, and that other source is the fifth-dimensional energy field that we originate from.

Earth also needs a higher source of electrical or spiritual charge because as a spirit body, as a planetary spirit, it is having difficulty holding the spiritual charge that is necessary to sustain the biosphere. The current Earth energy sources are struggling to keep it in balance. It is true that Earth will continue even if the bio-

sphere is thrown out of balance from humanity's perspective. Earth is a living being that has a life expectancy of billions of years. We are not talking about Earth
losing its physical body, but we are talking about it losing its spiritual energy.

You cannot have life without spirit, and you cannot have spirit without spiritual energy. If the Earth loses its spiritual charge, then the biosphere will collapse.
What can be done to sustain the spiritual charge to keep the energy of Earth going, and at the same time, what can be done to improve and increase the spiritual
light for you as lightworkers? How can we create a spiritual reserve capacity or
lengthen or expand the spiritual reserve storage capacity of Earth? How can we
expand and lengthen your spiritual capacity in your physical incarnation?

THE IMPORTANCE OF SACRED ENERGY FIELDS

I will first speak about the charge of spiritual light for Earth and how we perceive
the improvement of the receiving storage capacities of Earth. Earth is able to
hold energy—especially spiritual energy and life-force energy—through its sacred power spots. There are many special power spots on the planet, and Earth
is able to hold and transfer its spiritual energy through the ley lines, which we
have compared to the meridians in Chinese acupuncture. From our perspective,
the activation of the twelve etheric crystals is especially important as additional
sources of powerful charge. This means that Earth can hold fifth-dimensional
energy with the assistance of etheric crystals.

It is also true that fifth-dimensional energy is a highly refined current, a spiritual force and an electrical charge that can withstand certain Earth abuses and
drains. Because of the nature of this type of etheric energy, it has a greater ability
to be stored. Fifth-dimensional spiritual light has such powerful characteristics,
and one of the most useful characteristics in particular has to do with the ability
to be stored. We know that defining and creating these twelve etheric crystal areas has added huge spiritual energy reserves throughout the planet. It has helped
to make those spiritual areas have greater capacity to store energy and a greater
capacity to transfer energy.

The unfortunate fact is that many of the other sacred power spots on Earth
have been damaged because they have not been properly protected and many of
the ancient peoples' sacred energies have not been sustained. These ancient peoples were guardians of sacred spots. Many of the grandfather and grandmother
spirits that were living in the mountains, forests, and lakes while holding this spiritual energy for the planet have left. Why? To hold their sacred energy, they need a
protective energy connection to the third dimension. If there is not a protective,
sacred energy field that is interacting with them, then it becomes harder for them

to stay. It then follows that it also becomes harder for the power spots to hold the energy and to keep the spiritual reserve capacity.

However, a newer energy source from the fifth dimension has the ability to transcend and to be able to reestablish the sacred power spot's storage capacity of spiritual light and energy. That is one of the functions of the twelve etheric crystals that we have been working on so hard with you. This is why it is important to continue to work on connecting with the etheric crystals and why we designated meditation times for you.

One suggested meditation is that you visualize each of these crystals and each of these areas as sacred power spots. Visualize etheric crystals being downloaded into Earth as special fifth-dimensional power spots. They have now been given the function and the purpose to store spiritual energy, just like a battery stores electrical current. These etheric places now have the function of storing higher spiritual light and higher spiritual energy, and their storage capacity is far stronger than that of normal power places on Earth. These designated etheric areas now have extraordinary ability to store powerful spiritual light and spiritual energy, and that capacity is needed now more than ever.

The spiritual storage capacity can become lengthened even more through focused group meditations. For example, focus and meditation performed hourly on the twelve etheric crystals all around the planet will be very effective. It just so happens that a charge from one crystal then goes to another crystal. This is similar to the idea of parallel batteries; placing batteries in parallel is another metaphor for using the twelve etheric crystals as energy fields. One battery standing by itself has a certain amount of voltage that it can give, but when you connect the battery parallel to another, suddenly the charge of that battery and the capacity of the two batteries together are doubled. In a similar way, the twelve etheric crystals are accelerating and charging each other because they are all interconnected.

WORKING WITH THE PLANETARY CITIES OF LIGHT

In many of our previous discussions, we have talked about the dialectic energy capacity of the Tree of Life, which is represented on the planet by the twelve etheric crystals. When connected, the charge of all of the twelve etheric crystals far transcends the doubling effect that we have described in placing two batteries in parallel. To give you another example, imagine that you have two six-volt batteries. Together, they could produce twelve volts and have a far greater capacity. This is just doubling the power, and each of them is sustaining a certain charge.

In the etheric world of energy and etheric crystals, I cannot describe how much spiritual light and energy you are creating—because it is more than double, triple, or quadruple the energy. You describe things in the mathematical world as ten to the fifth power, ten to the tenth power and so on. This is approximating the kind of dialectic energy that I describe when we talk about increasing energy from the etheric crystals. What you also accomplish when you do this type of etheric crystal meditation is that you create new types of energy patterns, which also creates a greater reception to fifth-dimensional light.

Some have asked about how we should work with this energy in relation to the planetary cities of light. The planetary cities of light are also sub-batteries, if you will, and they correlate to these etheric crystals. The planetary cities of light already have some capacity to function in the same way as the etheric crystals. One new planetary city of light is Aufkirchen, near Munich. This location already has gathered a large spiritual capacity, and higher spiritual light is going to come to this beautiful city. You may wonder how the planetary cities of light are similar to the etheric crystals. They are similar in that they are battery-storage devices for spiritual energy. They can download higher spiritual charge, store it for longer periods of time and can now begin to transmit that energy outside of their boundaries. The crystals' main function and goal to the planetary cities of light is to both hold that spiritual charge for a given city and to transmit that light to other areas.

It is important to emphasize that the planetary cities of light are given the task of holding the spiritual energy. Why is that important? Some cities of light are already in high spiritual energy areas. But even in higher areas, there still are drains on the cities. After all, these cities are still in the third dimension, and therefore negative energy can sometimes come in: These cities still have the same problems that all cities have, including unemployment, pollution, environmental hazards, and whatever other dense Earth energies exist, and these energies can even affect a planetary city of light. So it is a tremendous task and a great accomplishment to hold and to ensure that the higher spiritual energy is to be held in that city. The exercise of shimmering a barrier around the city helps to hold the spiritual energies within the area. A good meditation to help this situation is to visualize a shimmering light as a spiritual battery that can hold and attract more spiritual energy and more spiritual light.

We also created the image of the energetic basket—which was first discussed in Argentina in Buenos Aires, where a spiritual basket was raised around the city. The image was that the city of light would be in a basket of light. This basket was then partially raised and the fifth-dimensional energy was brought down. The energy field of the city held that light, and from there that light was spread throughout the planet. The idea of shimmering the basket focuses on the fact that this shimmering raises the capacity of the planetary cities of light so that they can hold a higher fifth-dimensional energy. It is the shimmering that accelerates the planetary city of light so that the spiritual battery, namely the basket, can hold spiritual light.

These principles for the planetary cities are exactly the same for you as individual lightworkers. There is a certain refinement when it comes to talking about lightworkers. That refinement has to do with the fact that you all have a mental, spiritual, physical, and emotional body. Each of these bodies has a charge. Each of these bodies has a capacity to hold certain energy. The concept of working with yourself to improve your spiritual capacity and your spiritual reserve actually focuses on working with each of these individual bodies. The emotional body, for example, needs to be transformed into more universal concepts. Compassion, forgiveness, love, and acceptance are all emotions that create a greater spiritual capacity for your emotional body to hold emotional spiritual light.

In a similar way, the mental body can hold more spiritual light when you work with higher concepts of the cosmos. Higher mental concepts include universal love, universal light, eternity, concepts of time expansion, unity consciousness, multidimensional energy, and the fact that other dimensions exist. These are some of the concepts that can make your mental body have greater spiritual light and capacity. The spiritual body also can be expanded through the shimmering exercises and by connecting with the fifth dimension.

It is clear that there needs to be a new spiritual power source on Earth; at this point, there is not enough spiritual current. There needs to be an upgraded current, and that upgraded spiritual current needs to come from other sources. I can tell you that no planet has ever been able to survive the crisis that Earth is currently facing without connecting to higher spiritual sources from the fifth dimension. We could debate this, and we could argue that maybe it could be done without this connection. But our experiences and travels throughout the galaxy have been pretty extensive, and we haven't seen any planet being able to survive without connecting to the fifth-dimensional energy. This means the guides and teachers who are coming from the fifth dimension are needed for this connection.

The physical body responds to certain types of diet, to certain types of exercises, and also to stress. It can also be programmed to receive spiritual light and spiritual energy. You call this the white healing light. The physical body can be programmed so that your correct visualizations will be most effective. One of the particularly effective ways you can visualize yourself is to realize that you are an energy field instead of just a solid body. The energy that you have that may be creating illnesses is really a congestion or a blockage. If you can, focus on the energy flowing within your body. This is a great step forward for the physical body. I do want Archangel Metatron to speak with you because he has a great message for you, even though it will be short. I love you all. This is Juliano. Good day.

THE GIFT OF *IBBUR* CAN HELP YOU HOLD CHARGE

Greetings, I am Archangel Metatron. The love from my Father Adonai is so strong. Know that the greatest source of spiritual charge is God's love for you. Your love for God, your love for the Creator—your love for creation—is placing you in the same vibrational field, the same energy that the Creator is emitting for creation. Your loving God, which is a central concept in the *Kaballah*, also helps you to be on the same vibration. Many people have asked: "Why does God need our love?" You are not asking the right question. The question is: "Why does humankind need to love God?" The answer is because it puts human beings on the same spiritual vibrational field as God.

Juliano has given a presentation on the downloading of the fifth-dimensional light, and he has asked me to talk to you today about the concept of *Ibbur*. Ibbur is the Kaballistic description of cohabitation with a positive spirit. In the energy of *Ibbur*, spiritual seekers, the lightworkers, open their energy fields to cohabitation with a higher angelic presence or a higher angelic guide. The *Ibbur* can also come from a higher ascended master, from a higher-dimensional master.

This experience of *Ibbur* provides a tremendous spiritual charge to your physical body, your emotional body, you spiritual body, and your mental body. It does not at all diminish your own abilities but actually raises your abilities. To do the higher spiritual work that you need to accomplish, you need more spiritual charge. Sometimes, for obvious reasons, your life circumstances do not help you to hold your charge. A great gift from the spiritual masters and from the ascended masters is to offer you the ability and experience of the energy of *Ibbur*. *Ibbur* includes the cohabitation of higher spirits, such as Archangel Michael. I, Archangel Metatron, am also willing to work with you and provide you the spiritual charge. Remember, I am not saying I will take over your karma. I will help you do what is already in you.

I am going to say to you that you have within you the ability to do great things. You can do great Earth healings, connect the energy fields of this planet with the twelve etheric crystals, and you can work as starseeds and spiritually connect with each other. Each of you can connect with the higher dimensions and amplify your light. Maybe you need a boost, or a "pick me up," as they say. We, of the ascended master world, we of the higher dimensions, are ready to cohabit if you are. We can do this for short periods of time, such as at night during your dream state. We can help you during crisis. We can help you do certain work that you want to do but maybe don't feel you have the energy to do.

You can call on Chief White Eagle, on Juliano, and on me, Archangel Michael. Juliano has a corps of students that he works with. P'taah also has a corps of students he works with. There are many higher spiritual guides. They are needed—they need to work with you and you need to work with them. Make a space in your energy field, and you will feel the joy and love from the higher guides and teachers.

Shalom Aleichem. Amen. May your guide and teacher work with you. May you connect with Him in full light and love. May your consciousness be enhanced, and may you improve your abilities to do your life mission and your spiritual mission far beyond what you can even imagine. I am Archangel Metatron. *Shalom.*

CHAPTER 16

A NEW MODALITY
OF HEALING

Juliano, the Arcturians, Sanat Kumara, and Archangel Metatron

Greetings. I am Juliano, and we are the Arcturians. You, as the Arcturian starseeds, have come to the Earth as planetary healers. Planetary healing is a new modality of healing that you are destined to practice. You are destined to teach others about the process, expectations, and methods of planetary healing. Perhaps we can first look at the idea of healing. What is it? In one aspect, healing means to make whole, to bring into harmony, to bring into unity. Healing implies that the object, person, or planet being healed can manifest its full destiny and unfold in its highest potential. This means that in any approach to healing, one wants to connect with the highest potential and the highest energies that are within that which is to be healed. In this case, we are of course speaking of the highest potential of planet Earth. When we look at the planet, we are able to visualize what that potential looks like.

What does the potential of Earth look like in the fifth dimension? The planet, its highest energy, and its highest expressions are also linked to higher dimensions. The Earth is on an evolutionary path that will bring her to a fifth-dimensional presence. To be more specific, Earth's evolution will bring her to fifth-dimensional potential as a planet. This idea that the planet is evolving has other implications, because it also implies that the planet has a form of unity, that the planet is one system. It implies that there is a governing system that works within this planetary process. There are a few people now on the Earth who will acknowledge and speak about this planetary process, this planetary evolution. This is controversial because when we are speaking of Earth evolving, we imply that the Earth is a living organism and a living spirit.

This idea of a planet as a living organism is certainly not out of the realm of popular human imagination: It was even portrayed in the popular movie *Avatar*, in which the unified spirit of the planet Pandora was acknowledged and protected. Even so, when we are speaking of a planet, there are many limitations in the perceptual view humans tend to have. A planet does not obviously seem to be a living organism. A planet does not obviously meet the rules of life forms as you know them. There are contradictions in scientific theories that would say that a planet does not meet the criteria of a life form.

I want you to consider some of these ideas and some of these perceptions from the Arcturian perspective. From the Arcturian perspective, everything is part of the Creator. The Creator is omnipresent—meaning that the Creator's awareness is in every aspect of creation. That includes everything that is in the universe, including the galaxy, the solar system, and the planets. The second thing I want you to consider is that everything is connected. We will first begin by speaking about the connections that you have as a third-dimensional being and the connections that you have as a fifth-dimensional being. Your third-dimensional presence is connected to your fifth-dimensional presence.

THE LUMINOUS AURA OF EARTH

The etheric cords (we have also called them luminous strands) are everywhere around your etheric energy field in this third-dimensional body. You cannot see these energy fields. You cannot see the thin, luminous strands of light; they are too microscopic—"nano" thin. They are not viewable with any existing technologies on Earth. Yet if the doors of perception were opened, you would be able to see each human as an etheric luminous egg with infinite luminous strands of light connecting that person to all aspects of the universe. You would be so overwhelmed that you might not be able to make much sense of it unless you had a mental map that could hold your perception.

The point of all this is that you are connected to the galaxy. You are connected to the Central Sun. You are connected to your fifth-dimensional presence and to the Creator life-force spirit. When I say that you are connected, I mean that literally. I mean that these luminous strands around your energy field are actually linked to the fields of other planetary systems, other galaxies, and other dimensions.

If we look at Earth in the same manner, we would see that Earth also has a luminous energetic magnetic field. It is not the same as a human field, but there are interesting similarities. For example, there are luminous strands of light that come from the Inner Earth to the outer Earth and the Central Sun. There is also an energetic auric energy field around the Earth, and there are links to its fifth-dimensional body. Let me remind you that you have these luminous strands, these links of light that connect you to your fifth-dimensional body. And just like you, the Earth has luminous strands of light that connect it to its fifth-dimensional body.

In its etheric energy field—what you might call its "aura"—the Earth also has a self-regulating program we call the feedback loop. This feedback loop is part of an overriding, overseeing regulating system, similar to the one that is in your own etheric energy field as a human being. You cannot find this regulating system in the brain, because when the brain is dissected, it appears to be just cells—many neurons and many pathways. Instead, that regulatory system can be found in a higher, more refined energy field—just like your mind can. Your mind does not exist in the third dimension; it manifests and connects to you through your third-dimensional presence.

The Earth as a planetary system has linkages to other dimensions and to other parts of the whole interactive system. This is a concept that a planetary healer will be able to grasp and accept quite easily. As it stands, the existing program on the planet Earth is capable of crashing. By "crashing" I mean that the harmony and the balance that Earth holds can be disrupted, and (from your perspective) a chaotic situation can emerge. This type of program of chaos also exists within this planetary system. There have been numerous predictions about how chaos will unfold. Some of this programming includes ideas you have heard numerous times, such as ideas of purification, Earth changes, and also the 2012 shift. Even beyond that, there have been many famous prognosticators, or prophets such as Edgar Cayce, who predicted dramatic shifts in the Earth's crust causing massive earthquakes. We conceptualize these types of events as breaking or crashing the Earth's program because they would disrupt the Earth's relationship with humankind. It would make human existence on Earth extremely difficult.

Yet there is a higher order, and this means that there is a higher possibility of altering this program of dramatic and massive shifts. There is a higher regulatory energy that, through intervention by planetary healers like yourselves, can be implemented. As planetary healers, you have been effective in many ways in preventing a total breakdown from happening on Earth. Total disruption of all civilization has not occurred, nor has there been a total breakdown of the environment at this point. A planetary healer looks for the mechanism and the feedback intervention that will allow the planet to evolve and integrate at a higher level.

FINDING A HIGHER MODEL FOR HEALING

The original Earth program balance was causal-based. In this model, one puts so much energy into the atmosphere—so much greenhouse gas, for example—that the end result will be greenhouse warming. If you put so much pollution into the oceans and the waterways, then things will die. If you block certain pathways and ley lines in the Earth, there will be disruptions, including volcanoes and earthquakes. There is also a transcending view model, though. In this model, you can see things from a higher perspective. You can go to a higher energy that will allow the Earth to regulate itself so that issues such as greenhouse gases and blockages will not produce a chaotic result.

I want to add that this higher model is the same one that is used in many of the personal healings occurring now. For example, your systems were not programmed to handle as much radiation as many of you have been exposed to. Your immune systems have been exposed to unbelievable levels of radiation during your lifetime. That level of radiation could and would usually produce a great deal of illnesses. This has happened already to some degree, for example, due to the breakdown of the controls at Chernobyl or through aboveground nuclear testing. Breakdowns in systems have also occurred through the addition of many types of chemicals in your food. Add up all of the pollution, external radiation, and chemicals you are exposed to, and one might conclude that the majority of the population should be dying.

This has not happened. Why? The immune system of the human body has an adaptation that is quite phenomenal. This adaptation is so evolved that it is beyond the total effect of these causal additives. This is another way of saying that you can transcend many of the blocks and much of these chemical and radioactive energies, all of which could be lethal under other circumstances. It means you are able to live your whole life in its potential even though you are carrying energies that seemingly could be lethal. How is this done? It is possible because you are connected to a higher transcendent regulatory system, and this regulatory system is coming from the fifth dimension.

Naturally, even with this knowledge, it still makes sense to try to purify and release any of the additives or toxins in your system to the best of your ability. You do not stop trying to heal yourself; you are continually healing yourself. Healing is a process that you are going to need to continually experience. You will experience a renewed healing energy between now and the rest of the time you are on Earth. Do not look at a healing on your physical body as a one-time intervention; rather, you will need to be continually involved in your healing in order to purify and detoxify and, more importantly, to connect with your higher self and higher energy.

This energy—to heal, to make yourself whole, to detoxify—is coming from a cosmic energy source that is downloaded through your crown chakra. This powerful cosmic energy that is coming into you and that you need to call on now is called the universal light source. In the Arcturian Tree of Life, it is called the undifferentiated cosmic life source. An undifferentiated light can be differentiated or broken down into the areas it is needed. You can call on this light for specific energy healing you need. Energy healing could be needed in an organ, for example. There might not be any logical third-dimensional medicine or intervention that seems able to heal your illness, but if you call on the undifferentiated cosmic light to come into your system, it will brighten the whole system. The whole system will have an energy that can create fantastic and necessary healing for you.

MEDITATIONS FOR PERSONAL AND EARTH HEALING

I am going to use this same healing model for your planet. An energetic healing for Earth begins at the cosmic level. We will go into some of the specific aspects of the planetary healing, but first I want to lead you in a brief meditation for your self-healing because I know that you are in a continual healing process. For this, it would be helpful to be familiar with the Arcturian Tree of Life and have worked with the spheres. [For more on the Arcturian Tree of Life, please see the Notes on the Tree of Life at the end of this book.]

Visualize the light and energy at the top of the Tree of Life. The highest sphere is connected to the famous Mount Fuji in Japan. Visualize that sphere above your crown chakra. I, Juliano, am calling on the cosmic light, the undifferentiated light, to come into your crown chakra. This great sphere of light is over each of you now. Ask your crown chakra to open to this great cosmic light. Let it fill your whole energy system now. Your whole system receives this undifferentiated cosmic light. This beautiful light goes to places within each cell, within each etheric part of yourself, within each part of your cosmic egg. The light enters and charges each area.

Remember, we called your energetic egg shape the cosmic egg because you are also cosmic in your origin. Feel this connection. I send you this cosmic light. It is a light of the *pung* energy, a light of the protective energy field that shields you, keeping out other lower vibrations that might be attaching to you for some reason. Feel your energy field breathe. Feel any bodily deficiencies heal and your body strengthen. Feel as your immune system receives this wonderful upgrade of light. Most importantly, your updated program within is saying: "I am able to adapt to the changes that are occurring on this Earth. I am able to adapt in a most healthy, expanded way to the changes that are occurring in my body and on Earth." Microorganisms and any bacteria are easily pushed out of your system because you have a vibrancy with this cosmic light energy.

Now, with the same intention and with the same visualization, let us go to the Earth. The Earth is ready and able to receive cosmic downloading because Earth also has this ability and is continually receiving cosmic energy. Even those people who deny Earth's self-regulation process will readily agree that Earth continually receives cosmic energy. It is well known that even the light from the big bang, which occurred over thirteen billion years ago in Earth time, is still being received around Earth. The energy of the initial big bang, the initial expression of all there is and all there will be, is around Earth now. In this moment, the energy from the Central Sun is coming to Earth in an undifferentiated way. This means that new codes and a new regulatory process in Earth's system are also possible and available. The key link is that humans—and in particular the planetary healers—need to participate in downloading this new code for Earth.

The Earth can also expand and regulate itself with a newer energy. This will allow Earth to maintain the existing homeostasis that allows humans to live on it, even with the many disharmonies and blocks now present. We still must try to clear these blocks and to bring a greater sense of purification to this planet. The Earth does not have to experience change at a catastrophic, chaotic level—even if such change, from a causal connection, seems likely. The Earth is capable of transcending the causal energy field.

Planetary healers can assist in this process. Connect with your mind and your visualization to the energy that you know of as Mount Fuji—which is also connected deeply to Mount Shasta—at the top of the Arcturian Tree of Life. Visualize Mount Fuji directly receiving this planetary light upgrade from the Central Sun. Doing this takes advantage of the powerful alignment of this sacred time. I will be speaking some more about sacred light and sacred spaces. Connect with this newer planetary light from the Central Sun and feel it downloading into the Earth. I will now ask Sanat Kumara to speak briefly to you, and then I will return. Continue to hold this connection to the Central Sun, Mount Fuji, and Mount Shasta in your mind.

STABILIZING THE COSMIC LIGHT

Greetings. I am Sanat Kumara, the planetary logos. I am the planetary overseer of Earth who is working with the Earth's codes of ascension and overseeing the ascended masters' work with Earth's ascension. You are absolutely correct in understanding and believing that Earth has a presence in the spiritual world and that Earth has links to other dimensions. As Juliano has said, these links to other dimensions are luminous strands of light. Know that the higher beings in the galaxy and in other galaxies know how to find the luminous light emitted from a higher planet such as Earth. Maybe you ask yourself this question, "How can it be that extraterrestrials can find Earth? The universe is so vast; it would take centuries to locate a planet that has advanced life." The way the higher beings find Earth is by connecting to this cosmic energy, what Juliano called the luminous strands. Now you can also connect to other planetary systems using the same method.

We are here to speak about the power and importance of your planetary work. Juliano spoke to you about being a planetary healer. In the first stages, a planetary healing brings forth stabilization so that the undifferentiated cosmic light overrides some of the causal links. You can send this energy through all the Earth meridians—through the Ring of Fire, for example. You can also send this energy through the ocean currents, through ley lines, and through the atmosphere. You can even send this higher energy through people on the planet, who hopefully will realize that the destruction of the planet is being aggravated by war. There is nothing more destructive to Earth than the wars going on. You know that people from other centuries will look back in shock at the number of wars and killings that have occurred in this century and the past one.

Remember, the cosmic light is a light of harmony and I, Sanat Kumara, call on you to reignite your interest in the ring of ascension around this planet. Remember that the ascended masters and guides, through our work with Juliano, have asked you to work with the ring of ascension. We have called this ring of ascension a halo. It is a halo in which the guides and teachers place their energies, allowing you to mix your energies with the ascended masters' energies. You can then send a halo of harmonious light to Earth.

Allow the energies from Mount Fuji and Mount Shasta to go into the Inner Earth core through all the meridian forms on the meridian lines. Help the Earth receive this new upgraded light, this upgraded vibrational energy. I will be giving you more directions about the planet. This is the time for planetary healers to step forward and manifest, to let their healing skills and their intentions be known. May all twelve of the etheric crystals in the Arcturian Tree of Life be activated with great harmonic balls of light. May all of the planetary cities of light be activated, including the city of Taos and the other beautiful planetary cities of light. May the energies of the sacred sites on this planet be activated. May new sacred energy fields be created.

It is our intention to create more sacred planetary cities of light and more sacred areas. That which is not sacred, such as the disgraceful abuses to Earth, will be counterbalanced as quickly as possible. A new balance will be created by the designation of planetary healers and by their energies, healers who will create and hold more sacred sites on the Earth. These sacred sites, some of which we call the planetary cities of light, will be able to hold higher cosmic light. I, Sanat Kumara, tell you that the power of the sacred sites will become phenomenal in counterbalancing other, negative energies. I will return you to Juliano, and I will be speaking more to you about how to work with the planetary healing that you are all capable of participating in, the planetary healing for which you are already activated. I am Sanat Kumara.

COUNTERBALANCING THE DESECRATIONS ON EARTH

Greetings. I am Juliano. The way of communication with the Earth's regulatory system can be enhanced through the Arcturian Tree of Life and the twelve etheric crystals. Let us say that each of those crystals represents an energy field, an energy code that the Earth can respond to. The two examples we give are the energies of undifferentiated light that represent Mount Shasta and also Mount Fuji. We have designated Mount Shasta as a particular energy that we call chameleon energy because it can work in any sphere. The energy of sacredness on the Earth needs to be activated more, as a counterbalance. Sanat Kumara has told you that we need to help make more sacred sites on Earth. More than anything, this will counterbalance the desecrations on Earth. Each of you can create sacred areas, an energy of harmony and balance in the heart. The etheric crystal at Montserrat, which is in the center of the Arcturian Tree of Life, can emanate this balance and the harmony.

Clearly there also need to be more consequences for not respecting Earth. Isn't it clear that a planet can only allow so much imbalance? How can this imbalance be judged or regulated without creating chaos? We ask that the energy of compassion and kindness emerge to counteract judgment. That energy is still in Montserrat, and it still holds the messianic light that is coming to this planet. Let us always remember that this planet Earth holds the energies of messianic light. This is one of the greatest gifts that the Earth has, which is the gift of holding, receiving, and understanding the messianic light. That messianic light is a fifth-dimensional light that transcends all causal links.

Let it be clear that the energy of hidden knowledge of Earth is now coming forward. The crystal at Istanbul, the Bosporus crystal, is more activated. Let that activation also make everyone aware of hidden knowledge about Earth. This hidden knowledge will be revealed by you, the planetary healers. Part of this hidden knowledge includes the understanding that Earth is part of a galactic system and that Earth has a fifth-dimensional presence. Part of this hidden knowledge is that Earth has meridians and that those meridians can be activated and treated. The release of this knowledge means that the knowledge of the Inner Earth is going to be coming forward to humanity.

Let us remember the energy at Barranca del Cobre (or Copper Canyon), which is the shimmering light. The crystal at Copper Canyon is an effective and powerful tool for activating the shimmering energy field. The vibration of the fifth dimension is strong in that place, and the crystal there is able to hold so much fifth-dimensional energy. Feel yourself shimmering, bursting with light. The shimmering light is connected to the planetary system called Alano as well as to the ring of ascension, and now the Earth and the halo around Earth are shimmering. At the same time, the halo around your body and head is also shimmering.

Let us not forget the beautiful energy of Lago Puelo, Argentina, which is also a foundational energy. It is able to hold in place all of this light. It is able to keep the whole structure intact so that all of this light, all of this energy, all of this new coding, can come to the Earth and be held within this beautiful lake in Argentina. The mission of Lago Puelo is to provide the foundation for holding this light.

I am aware of a great teepee that was built at Serra da Bocaína. That structure could not sustain the force field there because of various factors. I am also aware of another area that can stand in its place. Do not worry, because the crystal in Serra da Bocaína is vibrating at a magnificent speed, and the teepee that stood there for several weeks, perhaps two months, served a very powerful energy. We thank all of the starseeds in Brazil who were able to hold that light. It was an intense and magnificent display of courage and dedication. There will be others who will step forward and seek methods of manifesting and holding sacred spots in each of these twelve etheric crystal areas. I love each of you. I am going to turn the next part of the lecture over briefly to Metatron. I am Juliano. Blessings.

Making Sites Holy

I am Metatron. Make the spot where you are standing holy. The most direct way of bringing any area into the fifth dimension is by making it holy and sacred. We work not only in sacred place but in sacred time. When you have a sacred place and a sacred time, it multiplies the power of your abilities to hold sacredness. Holding sacredness is a way of bringing something into a higher light—mainly fifth-dimensional light. Sacred time and sacred place can be combined with your sacred intention. As Juliano has said, you are the alchemy of this process.

The Creator, *Adonai Eloh'keynu Adonai Echad Hashem Baruch Hu, Ha'kadosh Baruch Hu*, has commanded us to raise sparks on all areas of the third dimension. This means that Earth has many sparks that must be raised to fifth-dimensional status. You have the ability to raise these sparks, because you have spiritual presence, spiritual awareness, spiritual energy, and spiritual thoughts. You are able to hold and transmit spiritual energy into specific places, making those places sacred. Only humans—only members of the Adam species on Earth—have the ability to transmit spiritual light and spiritual energy into a place and make that place sacred and holy.

We bless the planetary cities of light. Do not hesitate to bless a river, a site, or a city. Do not hesitate to bless your family and to bless your friends. You can bestow blessings onto other people because you are transmitters of the spiritual light. Blessings are a way of elevating the sparks on Earth as well as elevating people. I, Metatron, bless each of you so that you too will be elevated. Blessings, planetary healers and spiritual healers. I am Metatron. Good day.

CHAPTER 17

UNDIFFERENTIATED COSMIC LIGHT AND THE CROWN CHAKRA

Archangel Metatron

Greetings, I am Archangel Metatron. I am happy to be with you. I will be speaking about the top sphere on the Tree of Life. In Hebrew, this sphere is known as the *Kether* (KEH-ter)—the crown. It is the part of the tree that is closest to the eternal light. That eternal being is also called *Ain Soph Aur*—the light without end or infinite, undifferentiated light. What can we say about the infinite light? It is undifferentiated, but it is also stepped down.

To understand this concept, it is helpful to speak about electricity. You know that electricity can have very high voltages—often more than are needed by those using it. Say, for example, that a house needs 220 volts. If 5,000 volts came into a house, it would blow all the wires by making them too hot. Fuses will blow out and a fire might start. Therefore the electrical current coming into the house must be stepped down to 220 volts. In reality, you are luminous, electromagnetic beings. You have a spiritual electromagnetic charge that is extremely high, and you might experience the charge. We are helping you to awaken to that energy that is within you. When I'm talking about the undifferentiated light, I'm talking about a light that is stepped down from a source so magnificent that even when it is stepped down, it still could blow all your circuits, so to speak.

What is this undifferentiated light, and what good is it if it is so strong? How can human beings safely experience this light? Now we get to the truth of the Tree of Life. The tree of life is a way of stepping down energy into usable spheres. The Tree of Life offers a study in different levels of energy and which type of light you can really handle. It doesn't really help you to go to an energy field that is too high to handle, but in studying the Tree of Life, you can learn to make yourself a greater vessel so you can hold more light.

In studying the *Kaballah* and the Tree of Life, you practice holding light. One way to teach people to hold light is to explain the process so that both the mental and emotional bodies understand it. When Gudrun—this channel's wife—is speaking about the emotional body, she is helping you to release old emotions that are no longer useful so they don't stay in your system and stop other energy from coming in. The Arcturians have helped to develop a way to use the Tree of Life and its principles to heal the planet. They have been able to work with this channel to develop the basic principles of the Tree of Life and to adapt them so they could be used for healing the Earth. The first step is in bringing down undifferentiated light or cosmic energy from the universe.

In the *Kaballah*, the phrase "if God had a face" is used. Remember, we said "if." It is also said in the *Kaballah* that the Infinite Light, the Infinite Being, is *Adonai Eloheynu, Adonai Echad*—God, Creator of all, who is One, has no form. Anything you can say about God would not even be close describing the Creator. Therefore we can only try for a description that will expand your minds. God is not in time or space. God has no form. God is everywhere but also beyond everything. By talking about God as a paradox, you only begin to understand. We developed analogies and we developed symbols to speak of God so you could try and understand. In a beautiful paradox, God has a face—he has eyes and is looking on the world. If God closed his eyes, the world would end because the energy coming from God's eyes keeps everything going.

Bringing Down Usable White Light to Earth

Consider this analogy from the Tree of Life in the *Kaballah*. The Tree of Life appears as nine spheres in a special order and one additional sphere exactly on the top. I want you to understand that the energy for all the spheres comes from God. You can begin to think about God by visualizing the godhead energy at the top above the nine spheres on the Tree of Life. Understand that God and also his light and energy are coming to the Earth. There is cosmic energy involved in existence, and the Earth needs this light, but the energy is coming from many different directions.

I will also speak about both personal and planetary trees of life because in the personal tree, you have cosmic light, and you have me, Metatron, representing this higher light. In the process of personal healing, you connect to the white light—the great light. I know that many of you sometimes do personal healings in which you direct healing energy with certain rays of light to specific organs, and sometimes you also do a general healing, using descending white light. God sends undifferentiated light and tells you to let that light go where it needs to go. Then you have total faith and confidence that the healing white light will go through different channels; it will be stepped down until it can be manifested and used on Earth. That is what Mount Fuji represents.

This brings me to the discussion of the other new spiritual technology of the etheric crystals. We have talked previously about twelve etheric crystals that were brought down from the fifth dimension. These crystals were placed in a special pattern representing what we call the Planetary Tree of Life. Each sphere is placed on acupuncture points on the meridians of Earth. One etheric crystal has been placed on Mount Fuji, which is a mountain high in Japan that is connected to a very ancient energy source. The highest of all of the twelve etheric crystals is the Mount Fuji energy sphere. This crystal's role is to bring down undifferentiated cosmic light. In the planetary Tree of Life paradigm, if the highest light isn't coming down, then the other crystals will not work—the others spheres or *Sephiroth* will not work.

Sephiroth is a Hebrew word that means sphere. In the *Kaballah*, the Tree of Life is discussed in terms of spheres. The spheres are able to hold different energy. Even though we talk in the *Kaballah* about each sphere being individual, you really must look at the whole tree interacting with itself as all of the spheres work together in a unity. You cannot work with one sphere or etheric crystal alone without taking into consideration the other spheres or crystals.

MEDITATION FOR CONNECTING TO UNDIFFERENTIATED LIGHT

Let us focus briefly on undifferentiated light and how to make sure that Earth is connected to it. In the language that you know as planetary healers, we can say that the undifferentiated cosmic light is coming from the Central Sun. The Central Sun has both physical and etheric energy points. The fact is that people on the Earth are coming into alignment with this point. You now get the cosmic undifferentiated light more strongly. In planetary healing, this alignment comes about approximately every 25,782 years. The alignment in December of 2012 relates to the Central Sun alignment.

We will be saying special Hebrew letters to recognize and acknowledge the undifferentiated light for the planet. In Hebrew, the four letters of God's name are *Yod Hey Vav Hey*. [Chants the letters thirty-three times.] *Let the light of Yod Hey Vav Hey* come down to the Earth. Let this light come through Mount Fuji. Open to the cosmic light. Let the light of *Yod Hey Vav Hey*—an energy that cannot be described—make you feel beautiful. Feel the power of *Yod Hey Vav Hey*. You feel totally united with the cosmos. You feel total unity with all that is. You feel totally at peace with your life, your death, and your transformation because you know you are a part of all that is and all that will be.

In this lifetime you have advanced so much that you've been able to grasp and experience the energy of *Yod Hey Vav Hey*. Now as planetary healers you are working to make sure that this cosmic energy is also directed so that Earth can be renewed and it can come into alignment with the cosmic family. Together, chant the following: *Yod Hey Vav Hey*. [Repeats the chant four times.] Even though you cannot describe this energy and even though you cannot use words, you still can experience it and feel it.

As planetary healers, you can be sure that this energy is received by Earth. For your personal healing, you understand that you can bring this energy down into your crown chakra, which represents the first sphere in the Tree of Life. Symbolically open your crown chakra. Just move your hands open. You are connected with the undifferentiated cosmic Light through your crown chakra. Blessings to you all. Shabat Shalom. I am Metatron.

CHAPTER 18

PROJECTING TO THE ARCTURIAN STARGATE

Juliano, the Arcturians, and Archangel Metatron

Greetings, I am Juliano, and we are the Arcturians. As the ascension gets closer, we focus our energies and our teachings on the Arcturian stargate. The stargate is coming into alignment with the Earth, just as the Earth is coming into alignment with the Central Sun. There is a beautiful triangle of fifth-dimensional etheric light that aligns or creates a beautiful alignment with the Central Sun, the Arcturian stargate, and the Mother Earth.

Many starseeds have returned to Earth at this time for the specific purpose of experiencing the alignments that are before you with the Arcturian stargate. We have compared alignments before with the eclipses of the Sun and the Moon. Our example has been this: If you were a student of astronomy and you knew that there was an eclipse of the Sun of great magnitude and great power, then you would easily travel to South Africa, to the North Pole, to the South Pole—or wherever it was on Earth that would enable you to receive the highest perspective and the highest energy from that eclipse. In the same way, you as starseeds would want and, in fact, have decided to reincarnate onto Earth at this time in part to experience the alignment with the Central Sun and the alignment with the Arcturian stargate.

In cosmic alignments, there are powerful energies that would not normally be available. In a cosmic alignment, you receive and can accelerate your powers of fifth-dimensional activation, of fifth-dimensional streaming, and of fifth-dimensional shimmering. You can activate your energy with thought projections, pulsing, and dynamic interactions with the fifth dimension, which will allow you to ascend. The power of this ascension energy on Earth is twofold. The first power comes from the Earth's alignment with the Central Sun. The second power—an equally dynamic one—comes from the alignment with the Arcturian stargate.

The Arcturian stargate is a portal that allows the starseed-activated beings to participate in their planetary choice for their next incarnation process. This means that at the stargate, you can review and participate in choosing where you want to incarnate next, including which planet. It always means and also includes the possibility of returning to Earth for another incarnation. This is a great power and a great gift—to be able to participate in the planetary reincarnation process. In the hierarchy of soul evolution, consciousness and choice in incarnation are considered to be of high value. When you are able to participate in choosing the life and the planet you are going to, then you can be assured that you have reached a higher level of soul evolution.

Life between Life

Now, in a normal reincarnation process on Earth, your next lifetime is directed in part by your guides and teachers. Your next lifetime is in fact set in parameters in accordance with your Earth karma and is in many ways preset based on the needs that you have for your own learning and for your own evolution. In fact, when you are born through the Earth's incarnation process, part of the whole process depends on your forgetting everything about the reincarnation process. You are made to forget about the inter-life or life-between-life processes so that, in essence, you come to Earth in an incarnation with a relatively clean slate. I say "relatively" because you know that there are certain soul imprints that carry on from lifetime to lifetime. We have used the example of Mozart, who has a great soul imprint for music that carries on in any lifetime that he manifests. In any lifetime that he wishes to access that talent, he can use music to his greatest and highest good. Yet even with such a powerful imprint, you must still consider the fact that someone like Mozart did not have conscious memory of other lifetimes in which he was a musician. He did not even have memories of his musical experiences between his life-between-life processes.

The life-between-life process is often as important in the whole evolutionary process as the experiences that you have on Earth in a lifetime. I know that a lifetime on Earth can often be of a limited consciousness. However, each lifetime on Earth has the potential to be lived in 100 percent awareness. In fact, if lifetimes were experienced in 100 percent awareness, then people would be making different decisions about what they are doing with themselves. It is true that the third dimension is a dimension of duality and restriction. This third-dimensional restriction is such that there is not an easy opportunity readily available to experience the inner life and life-between-life memories. However, through special meditation and studies, you can reawaken your memories from past-life and life-between-life experiences. With those memories, you can also further awaken your starseed consciousness.

In the stargate, there is an entirely different operational principle. That stargate operational principle focuses on awareness. When you go from the stargate to another planet, then you go in full consciousness and in full awareness. You go in full memory of all of your life-between-life experiences and of your past lives. To be able to go through the stargate, you have to have a greater consciousness and a more evolved soul. That is what you are developing now. That is what you are evolving toward. This lifetime on Earth is bringing you closer to higher soul evolution. In fact, we have noted that in any one lifetime—but particularly in this lifetime—you can gain full consciousness of all of your past lives and of the lessons of the life-between-life experiences. We want you to develop this ability. We want you to understand that the normal consciousness that you have of yourself is a limited consciousness, limited necessarily by the restrictions of the third dimension. You expand and move up to a higher level of consciousness, and with that higher level, you quickly develop the ability to enter the Arcturian stargate.

In the transition for the ascension, we recommend remaining in full consciousness. When you approach and access the stargate and leave Earth's incarnation process, we work to help and teach you to make this transition with full consciousness. This means that as you travel through the corridor for ascension, you focus on the Arcturian stargate. You visualize and direct yourself in these soul energy spaces called "corridors." The fuel that propels you to the place you want to be is your thoughts. Your ability to project yourself through a corridor is a vital tool and a vital skill that you want to access and use when you are in the ascension corridor. This means that you should visualize and consciously think: "I am projecting myself to the Arcturian stargate." I, Juliano, am downloading a corridor of light around each of you now. This corridor of light is a stargate corridor that we call a "practice corridor" that enables and offers each of you an opportunity to experience and to practice projecting yourselves to the Arcturian stargate.

THE GRAND CENTRAL SUN STATION

There are only two stargates in the entire Milky Way Galaxy. The Arcturian stargate is the official stargate for this half of this sector of the Milky Way Galaxy. This means that anyone or any being who wishes to reenter and process themselves into another planetary incarnation has to come through this stargate—or at least it is desirable for them to come through it. Naturally, when you come through the stargate, you are doing this with consciousness, and so you will correctly choose a fifth-dimensional planet, a more evolved planet, to continue in your incarnations.

Rest assured that in the fifth dimension, you will go through an incarnation process, but it is totally different from the third-dimensional incarnation process. What is different? As I have said, in the fifth-dimensional planetary system, you enter an incarnation in full consciousness of life between lives and past lives. This means that you will even have a memory of this information I am giving. You will have memory of what you have done on Earth in this lifetime. You will have memories of other lifetimes that you have been on Earth. My starseed friends—whom I love very much and to whom I send you my blessings—you must understand what a great event it is in the soul evolution to go and approach the stargate. You have to understand what a great leap of spiritual energy it is to complete a planetary incarnation such as what you are doing now on the Earth and to graduate and go through the Arcturian stargate.

Many people have asked, "What is it like in the stargate?" The stargate is in the fifth dimension. It is a fifth-dimensional heavenly gate that has an unlimited amount of contacts with different planetary systems that are much evolved. The best way that I can describe the stargate is for you to imagine that you are in a huge train station. Perhaps you might call it "Grand Central Station," Another term would be a "Grand Central Sun Station." In that station you might see signs like: "Going to the Pleiades," "Going to Sirius," "Going to Aldeberan," "Going to Scorpio," "Going to the Andromeda Systems," "Going to Xerxes," or "Going to the Central Sun Moon-Planet Alano." You would also see many corridors in the stargate. Each one is a beautiful transitional corridor in which you are accelerated and projected into a much higher consciousness in preparation for downloading yourself into an incarnation. It is a beautiful process to go from a spirit form into incarnation form, and this process is enhanced when you are in higher consciousness.

In the Arcturian stargate, we have special teachers or guides who will work with you. Imagine coming into the Great Central Sun Station and beginning to contemplate which corridor you should take in order to go to the appropriate planetary experience for your soul. You need to decide which higher dimensional planet would be best for you. I understand that when you have so many positive and interesting choices, you sometimes become frozen and are unable to make any decision. We, the Arcturians, are going to be there helping. Also, Archangel Metatron is there at the stargate. We even have classes with group discussions. At the stargate, you do not have to immediately decide which place to go to. There is not even a time constraint. You can stay at the stargate for as long as you want to. There are many spirit guides at this Grand Central Sun train station, and you will be meeting many higher dimensional spirits. How fascinating to see all these spirits coming from different countries and going to different places!

In the same way, the Arcturian stargate will give you the opportunity to interact with beings from other levels. I know that you are all excited at the opportunity to see other beings, and you will be seeing only those beings that are fifth dimensional and higher. Some of these beings could be somewhat different in terms of their manifested forms. You are still defined in Earth body. When you go into the fifth-dimensional corridor, I know that it will be easier and most comfortable for you to manifest a fifth-dimensional body. Perhaps you can manifest a body to appear like when you were twenty-five or thirty years old. You can create a body in that certain light of the youthful figure that perhaps you feel most comfortable in.

Consider this: Species from other planets have humanlike life forms that are slightly different from the Earth human form. One different example is those human-like life forms that are hermaphrodites. Hermaphrodites carry male and female characteristics in one body. Therefore, a hermaphrodite would be able to have a relationship with another hermaphrodite, so the whole issue of whether it is male-to-female relationship or male-to-male or female-to-female relationship would not be an issue. The hermaphrodite would become involved in a relationship based on whatever sexual orientation was appropriate. This type of flexibility in sexuality might be foreign to you. However, when you experience meeting hermaphrodites, you might find yourself interestingly attracted to a planet that has that experience. You may meet a guide or teacher from that system, and you might begin to realize that this is an interesting, challenging, and expanding way of experiencing an incarnation. You may then decide to go to the corridor of the planet that offers that experience and learn what it is like to incarnate on that planet.

CHOOSING A THIRD-DIMENSIONAL PLANET

What you need to know is that incarnating from a fifth-dimensional perspective is not like incarnating into a third-dimensional perspective. When you incarnate into the third dimension, you are also bound by the laws of karma on that planet, and this may mean that you will go through some discomfort and densities in that experience. In some cases, we know that the beings on the third dimension who have incarnated from higher planes have even felt trapped on Earth, and they have had to extricate themselves from Earth incarnations with some assistance from their guides.

Some of you may have incarnated on Earth from the Arcturian stargate. The Arcturian stargate can also be a Central Sun transitional point to another third-dimensional planet, and so there will always be the possibility of returning to Earth from the stargate. Remember, returning to a third-dimensional planet or coming to a third-dimensional planet does have limitations in consciousness. You can put yourself into the position that you might have to go through another incarnation on that third-dimensional planet. What is interesting to us is that those people who have come from the stargate to Earth—we call them Arcturian starseeds—knew that an alignment with the Central Sun and the Arcturian stargate was coming to Earth during this incarnation. They knew that they were going to be activated by the Arcturian process, the Arcturian groups, and they knew that they would have an opportunity to come back through the Arcturian stargate during this incarnation.

You might think of coming to the Earth during this alignment with the stargate like an insurance policy. You might think this way: "Previously, I wanted to come to the third dimension, but I was a little bit concerned that I would be having limited consciousness. From that limited consciousness, I might find myself trapped in the third dimension for another couple of incarnations. However, I am now going to incarnate on Earth at a time where there is going to be a powerful alignment with the Arcturian stargate and when the Arcturian energy is going to be strong on Earth. Therefore I will be activated, and I can be sure that I will have the correct consciousness and activation to return to the fifth dimension."

The Arcturian stargate is a place of higher energy and excitement. Remember, if you pass through the gate of the Arcturian stargate from your present Earth life, then you cannot return to your third-dimensional Earth incarnation that is this current incarnation. We are not allowing it, and we would not encourage anyone in our meditations and exercises to go on through the Arcturian stargate to the other side. However, we will help you come to our stargate's vestibule—our foreroom, where there is plenty of opportunity to experience the closeness of the Arcturian stargate and where you can also practice the idea of thought-projecting yourself through the Arcturian stargate corridor from Earth. We can also open the gate a certain distance for your experience. Remember, the Arcturian stargate is a gate where you can briefly experience the power and light and attractive force of that light and prepare yourself for your eventual transition to there. We will be working with you on an exercise for that experience.

ALIGNMENT WITH THE ARCTURIAN STARGATE

I want to speak about the relationship between the etheric crystals we have downloaded and the Arcturian stargate. The etheric crystals are multidimensional and multifunctional. Generally, in our discussions of the etheric crystals, we have talked about how these crystals serve as conduits for downloading fifth-dimensional light and energy into the planetary Earth system so that the Earth's planetary meridians can be cleansed. Then certain frequencies of light and information can be held in the energy field of Earth. In particular, we know that there are several power spots on the planet that have the ability to hold certain etheric energies of a higher vibration on Earth.

We know that it is critically important to download fifth-dimensional energy into Earth. Part of the effectiveness of the etheric crystals is to interact with each other, and we have encouraged different levels and ways of interaction. Different Arcturian starseeds throughout the planet have different accesses to these crystals along with different methods of working with the crystals. The basic method is to understand that these crystals are downloaded from the main crystal in the Arcturian crystal temple. Each of the current etheric crystals is a duplicate of the main Arcturian crystal. The subcrystals are duplicates of the downloaded etheric crystals on Earth. You always must work first with the downloaded Earth crystal, and then the subcrystals will support the work of the main crystal. The primary light emanates from the main crystal.

To further elucidate the etheric crystal purpose, the etheric crystals that are now in place help Earth's alignment with the stargate. The function of the etheric crystals is of multipurpose. One purpose is to activate and help in the alignment and the activation of fifth-dimensional light and energy on Earth. The second purpose, however, is to create an energy field that is appropriate and that will allow an attractive energetic alignment with the stargate. Downloading the crystal in Istanbul, Turkey, in June 2009 along the Bosporus Straits brought us one step closer to perfecting the alignment with the stargate. When the twelfth crystal downloaded, we achieved perfect activation of the Arcturian stargate alignment with Earth.

This is very important. The stargate is vibrating and has a certain energetic frequency. You cannot enter the stargate unless you also are at a certain vibrational frequency. Completing the ascension activates you to a higher frequency, and through grace, the ascension helps you to achieve the vibrational frequency necessary to go through the stargate. So when you approach the stargate, remember that you are still coming from Earth, a third-dimensional planet. Part of the energy of the stargate must be in harmony with the planet from which you are coming, and this requires a certain activation of energy from a planet. So when you come from Earth, that higher aspect of the planet Earth has to be in alignment with the Arcturian stargate.

There are many forces that affect the stargate: There is the force of the Central Sun. There is the force of the ascension. There is also the energy field of the stargate itself. The energy field of the stargate is coming more into your consciousness now. You are going to want to work on creating an attractive energy alliance and alignment with the Arcturian stargate. This is part of your ascension work, part of the preparation for the planet Earth that is mainly to be a conduit of light that will allow a transition for many higher beings from Earth's incarnation process to the Arcturian stargate. This work is of the highest spiritual value and the highest spiritual purpose. You will be able to follow the path for your ascension to the Arcturian stargate, providing a link and teachings for others who will follow on how to align with the Arcturian stargate. I wish to let Archangel Metatron speak to you, as he will also be giving you some instructions on your soul journey to the Arcturian stargate. I am Juliano. Blessings. I will return to do a brief exercise with you.

Understanding Holiness

Greetings, I am Metatron. Some call me the "Divine Leader of the Archangels," but I only want to be known as your guide, teacher, and helper. Indeed, the word "angel" in Hebrew is defined as "messenger," and "the Great Messenger" is the way I define my name, Metatron. I am here to give you great news. The great news is that you are holographic energetic balls of lightbeings. That experience of being an energetic field of light can be overwhelming. Some people have gone into the mystical experience and have become overwhelmed by it, losing their sense of perspective and purpose. They have not really benefitted by being exposed to the lifting of the veils; the lifting of the veils by itself can be a rather confusing experience unless you have the proper preparation.

There is a path, a way, and guidance available that can lead you comfortably to your soul's highest evolution and highest travel. Part of that rests with your ability to focus on holy beings—the holy creation and the holiness of Sananda, for example—and your ability to relate to the holiness of the ascended masters. You can call on the *Melech Ha Gadol*. You can call on Sananda and on Archangel Michael. You can call on many of your beloved masters who will gladly, and with great love, lead you to the stargate. With great love they will help your transition to higher spiritual links.

My message to you is focused on understanding and working with the energy of holiness—you might also call it the energy of "sacredness." That energy of holiness and sacredness is not only on the fifth dimension; it is available on the third dimension, and you can create spaces on Earth that are holy and sacred. These holy and sacred places then become conduits of light for the fifth dimension. In fact, that is one of the roles of the etheric crystals: to create a sacred and holy space on Earth. In a sacred and holy space, one can download greater fifth-dimensional energy and light. In the Bible, one example of a sacred conduit is called Jacob's ladder. The corridor is like a ladder. Jacob's ladder can truly lead to the stargate. An interesting fact is that connections to corridors also allow higher beings from the fifth dimension to appear on Earth. This happened to Elijah, who saw fifth-dimensional chariots. You have to understand that when the corridor of ascension is open, then there is up and down movement. That means that many of the Arcturians at this ascension corridor will be coming through the corridor to work with and meet you. The other holy beings will come at the same time. This is one of the great gifts of the ascension—the assistance is going to be overwhelming.

Work on understanding holiness. That is why we repeat *Kadosh, Kadosh, Kadosh, Adonai Tzevaoth*—Holy, holy, holy is the Lord of hosts. Part of the importance of this phrase focuses on the codes of ascension. This phrase is also a reminder to you of the holy space that you are working in. Even in darkness, there is light to be found. There is light to be found in duality and the breaking down of the illusions that have been operating on this planet. You know that we are now directly experiencing the planetary shift, where the illusions that have been operating to keep institutions afloat are breaking down. Truth is coming. The illusions will no longer be powerful enough to cover the truth. That can be a painful energy.

A strong energy is required to break down the illusions. [Sings.] *Kadosh, Kadosh, Kadosh, Adonai Tzevaoth.* Let this place that you are standing on be holy. Your transition to the stargate will be filled with holiness. Let the holiness be a protective force for you. The Creator Spirit has a beautiful evolutionary path before you. It is available to you now. Take advantage of this alignment of Earth with the stargate. Take advantage of the ascension. Take advantage of your abilities to go back to the stargate and of your new freedoms to be able to choose and participate in your future incarnation process that include the ability to go to other planets. This is a great gift. I am Archangel Metatron. Good day.

KEEP YOUR PRESENCE

Greetings, I am Juliano. I have placed a corridor of light around each of you. I ask you now to project your thoughts into the corridor. As you project your thoughts into the corridor, you can project an image of yourself. Create this image of yourself in the highest form, the most beautiful form, you wish of yourself. For example, you can be as thin as you want, and you can have as much hair as you want on your head. You can have the shape you want and the smile you want. Just project that image now. Then, as you project that image, give that image the ability to travel by thought. That image of yourself is traveling through the corridor and through the Arcturian stargate corridor that is now near you. You are traveling there at the speed of thought.

You come to the great garden—you are able to travel instantaneously with thought and are instantaneously in the garden at the stargate. You are with many of your Earth colleagues and group members. Sit in the garden at the stargate. It is filled with light energy, excitement, and spirit. I, Juliano, am there at the stargate with you, and I very gently open up the gate, just a small amount. As I open up this gate, the spiritual force that is there is just indescribable in human terms. The spiritual energy that is coming through the gate spreads a beautiful, etheric blue light into the garden that is so intense and so satisfying to each of you. I open the gate further to allow you to absorb this light. The light that is there is now becoming more intense, and you are still able to tolerate it with full consciousness and full presence. A very important word in understanding your ascension and going through the stargate is "presence." Keep your presence.

Now, that is as far as I can open the gate for you. I will leave this gate open for a few more minutes. We will be in silence as you experience this powerful energy. [Pause.] I will close the door of the stargate now, and you can begin your return now through the corridor. Reenter your body in perfect alignment, bringing with you all of this beautiful spiritual light and energy into your physical body. You can use this for your greater health and greater spiritual light on the Earth. I am Juliano. Good day.

CHAPTER 19

ENTRANCE TO THE
2012 GATEWAY

Juliano, the Arcturians, and Archangel Metatron

Greetings, I am Juliano, and we are the Arcturians. In 2010, we entered the gateway to the 2012 energy field. This gateway is the entrance point at which one can begin to feel the energy and the charge of that 2012 energy field that is a reflection of the interaction of Earth's own energy field with the galactic center. This interactive pattern is setting up a huge field that will result in an enormous energy shift. One of the most important points that I want you to understand is that the energy of 2012, especially on the winter solstice, is resultant from an interaction between Earth's energy field and with the consciousness of humanity. Because it is an interaction, this means that what is done, what is felt, and what is thought by humanity is a contributing factor to the development and the outcome of the 2012 energy.

There is a concept explained in quantum physics that states that the observer influences the outcome of what is observed. In other words, nothing occurs in isolation, even on the subatomic level. Quantum physics talks about subatomic particles—particles that are too small to see. In a similar way, you know that thought and consciousness are immeasurable—the energy of the thought field is even more subtle than subatomic particles—yet thoughts can have a quantum effect on global consciousness and on the 2012 energy field now that we are at its gateway.

All gateways signal major shifts. Even from your personal experience, you know that the energy field of the gateway can create a somewhat chaotic stirring up of all aspects of Earth, all aspects of consciousness, and all systems on Earth, including the geological, political, sociological, meteorological, and other Earth systems. You are beginning to change, and even though you welcome a shift or change, it is still a new energy. This relates to our earlier discussions of evolution and the fact that humans and animals evolve at a point of crisis, at a point of stress. The dividing lines between leaps of evolution and leaps of consciousness are the lines that are drawn from the energies of that crisis.

Gateways can reflect a stirring up of energy on a microcosmic level. For example, if I take the individual systems that are reflected now, then I can tell you that the economic systems are still in flux and that there still is a great potential for upheaval and stress. If I look at the political systems and the political interactions and even the sociological energies in the countries of the world, which have to do in part with political shifts and changes and upheavals, I can say that there are many places on Earth now that are building energy, becoming like powder kegs waiting to explode. If I observe volcanic energies in the Inner Earth and look at possibilities in the energies of earthquakes, I can also report the same thing: There are major shifts and upheavals ahead. [Channel's note: this lecture was given three days before the earthquake in Haiti.]

You remember that the early days of 2010 were dramatic. Even personally, you probably felt a degree of discomfort and possible isolation. Maybe some of the problems and issues that you have been seeking to resolve seemed to be stirred up. Yet this is not a negative thing. This is not a doomsday prophecy, not something where you can say, "Oh, Juliano, does that mean that we are really heading for the cleansing and the major Earth changes?" We don't look at it from that standpoint, although I certainly understand that perspective. We look at it this way: We understand there has to be some sort of crisis, some sort of stress, that will force people—force humanity—to shift. We have been preparing you, the starseeds, for many months and even years to be capable and ready for this shift.

This shift requires that you also be capable of making an evolutionary leap in your consciousness and that you prepare to make this evolutionary leap with the intention of contributing to the evolution of the species. You have been learning the techniques of imbuing the thoughts and the conscious energy field of Earth with fifth-dimensional energy, with fifth-dimensional perspectives, and with higher light. This means that you are able to gain the perspective of the fifth dimension, a perspective that includes multidimensional presence, the evolution of species, and the abilities to ascend. You can open up corridors for energy transfers and higher thinking from the fifth-dimensional realms. Higher thinking can be attuned and downloaded into new thoughts and new techniques for healing, and it can provide new perspectives on old problems.

You Are in Galactic Awareness

There is now also a motivation to begin to act more forcibly and more assertively for change. This means that it is time to work on the energy grid of the etheric crystals. The energy field of the etheric crystals is a dialectic energy field that can be focused on certain changes, such as to modify the power of earthquakes, to attenuate the power of winter storms, and to work on sending energy to world leaders so they can make higher decisions. A wrong decision by a world leader is now going to have much more dramatic effects than it would have had even three years ago, because we are now at a more critical state in the world.

I have recommended a special energy meditation in a twelve-hour period: Each hour, a different group of Arcturian starseeds and Group of Forty members focuses on a different crystal. Then, during the twelve-hour period, all of the twelve crystals will generate a light field. These light fields from the twelve crystals will then be downloaded to the subcrystals at that hour. Let us just say, for example, that we are going to focus on Mount Shasta at 9:00AM California time. Then at 10:00AM California time, or one hour later—it all would be based on the time in Mount Shasta—the energy would go to Mount Fuji. Then an hour later, it would go to Grose Valley. This would create a force field.

Remember, I said that 2012 is an interactive force field: Interactive means that what you are thinking and doing is also affecting what is happening. We want to accelerate, magnify, and increase the power of the twelve etheric and dialectic crystals so that energy field can be projected to the 2012 energy field. In order to understand this better, I will focus on more information about how this interaction can be strengthened.

We have reached the point in humanity of Earth called galactic awareness. This point has been accelerating dramatically in the past twenty-four months. If you look at the whole history of man, you would say that the knowledge that humanity has of the galaxy has been a slow awareness. Perhaps we have seen some bright spots, such as in Mayan understanding. There are other tribes and other groups that have had this awareness of the galaxy and even the interaction of the galaxy with Earth, but the twentieth century experienced a big breakthrough in terms of the understanding of the galaxy. The last twenty-four months in world history have seen a phenomenal leap in the human understanding of our relationship as a solar system and as a planet to the galaxy. Many scientists have now reached the conclusion that there is a total interactive force field in the galaxy that affects Earth. They have discovered how truly amazing and outstanding it is that the galaxy has an interactive force field with Earth—and that humanity and Earth also affect the galaxy and even the Central Sun. The interaction that humans have with the Central Sun and with this galactic force field can be maximized.

I have to explain that this effect can be negative as well as a positive. One example of a negative effect of humanity's consciousness on the Central

Sun and the energetic force field of the galaxy is from the Hiroshima and Nagasaki atomic bombs. I am not making any judgments about the political benefit of ending that war. I am just telling you that those two explosions had a tremendous effect on the energy field of the galaxy and the Central Sun. It aroused many of the higher beings throughout the galaxy, and they have repeatedly stressed to many of us the desire to stop humanity from spreading atomic-weapons' consciousness into the galaxy. They believe that Earth humans could bring that type of thinking and that type of technology into the galactic energy field, especially since not only the consciousness of Nagasaki and Hiroshima but also the consciousness of other nuclear tests and the Chernobyl disaster have affected the galactic-interaction energy field. There has certainly been a reluctance to allow humanity to develop this knowledge of nuclear energy.

At the same time, the Galactic Council recognizes that there are many higher beings on Earth right now. What a polarization! In truth, there are more evolved spiritual beings on Earth now than at any other time in the history of this planet—potentially over 100,000 on Earth now. I am not saying that these enlightened beings are perfect beings on the level of Buddha or Jesus, but I am saying that they are enlightened in terms of consciousness and understanding. Perhaps it could be compared to the Sufi thinking, which is more universal, based on brotherhood. Many of you are part of that enlightened group.

You might say that this is such a small number compared to seven billion people that it is insignificant, but 100,000 enlightened beings is truly a huge number. There are various figures thrown around, and 100,000 is actually a small estimate, because I could say there may be as many as a million or a million and a half that participate in this type of enlightened thinking. Many of those 100,000 may not have the commitment or the understanding of the ascension, multidimensional thinking, or multidimensional thought projections, but the Galactic Council began to communicate with many of the starseeds through the higher beings that this channel, and many of you are now channeling.

As we entered the gateway in 2010, the Galactic Council began making the energy fields easier to access so that more of you could call and begin to communicate with your guides and teachers on a personal level. In fact, it is truly phenomenal how many of you have come into your own channeling abilities. Your abilities to connect with masters and teachers, to download new information, and to maintain your strength and the courage as you do this spiritual work have improved. As you progress, you will need to continue to travel to power spots on Earth and to commit to some new and fantastic spiritual projects.

MULTIDIMENSIONAL REINCARNATION THROUGH THE ARCTURIAN STARGATE

One powerful example of such a new spiritual project was the downloading of the twelfth etheric crystal in Serra da Bocaína, Brazil. The energies of the groups of forty were able to be used to manifest a beautiful tepee there. The tepee wound up being at exactly the center point of the etheric crystal. Each etheric crystal radiates energy, and this one in Brazil is so powerful that it connects all of the other eleven crystals with its force field. It is now continuing to download information and energy that can be transferred, and it has fostered a new, more powerful alignment with the Arcturian stargate.

Ah, yes—the Arcturian stargate. As we go through the gateway of 2012 at this time, one of the major energy shifts is focused on galactic time and galactic energy. Your consciousness of galactic energy and time has opened up your connections to multidimensional reincarnation. There is Earth reincarnation and there is also multidimensional reincarnation. Now that your consciousness has been opened to this level, the doorways of the stargate have come more into alignment, preparing for your entrance. Your entrance into the Arcturian stargate is a way of experiencing multidimensional reincarnation.

Earth incarnation is an opportunity to complete your life lessons and your soul lessons, and then you can move on to the next level. The next level might require reincarnating in another place on Earth. It might require meeting your soul family again in another situation. There are many different possibilities. Eventually you hope and pray that you reach the last lifetime in which you can complete and graduate from Earth and third-dimensional incarnations.

Multidimensional reincarnation is the ability to go into different realms and to go to different planets. You want to go to higher planets. There are other planets that are third dimensional, and it is true that you can reincarnate to them. An example of a lower-energy reincarnation would be, for example, a warrior like Saddam Hussein, who dies and reincarnates on another planet where he continues to be involved in different wars and killings. There are still many planets in this galaxy of third-dimensional density that would be perfect resting places for someone like that, and they would get to experience war and violence over and over again. Maybe at some point they would get to graduate and move out of that situation.

You, however, may not want to reincarnate on a third-dimensional planet. In fact, when I say, "Earth reincarnation," I have to also make a note that in some cases there is cross-planetary, third-dimensional reincarnation. That means that in some cases, people are reincarnating on other third-dimensional planets. Cross-planetary incarnation is actually one explanation for many of the polarized energies you are seeing on Earth. There has been a lot of cross-planetary reincarnation on Earth.

Some of this has occurred from cross-fertilizations and tampering with the birthing of species. This has been documented and has been discussed, for example, with the planetary system Marduk as well as in discussions of the nephilim, the fallen ones in the Old Testament, and also in the concept of the twelfth planet.

That twelfth planet, by the way, is "transdimensional." It is not a planet that is in the third-dimensional path of the gravitational field of the Sun. Many people have thought that this planet goes around the Sun and goes into this elliptical orbit that goes past Pluto, and then once every 2,000 or 3,000 years it comes back and comes closer to Earth and makes its appearance known. Actually, it is a transdimensional planet, and this means that it goes in and out of dimensions. Sometimes it comes into Earth's dimensional field and is seen, and sometimes it isn't. It is not permanently in the third-dimensional energy field. There are people there who are working on that planet who want to reincarnate on Earth, and when the planetary system gets closer to Earth, then they look for ways to come to Earth. Their understanding of why a planet will go in and out of dimensions is still somewhat limited.

I can only compare this to the planet in the Pleiades star field when, through scientific accident, the planet remained stuck on the precipice between the third and the fifth dimension. At that point, the planet was in a similar situation to Marduk, and it was going to go in and out of dimension—not a very favorable situation. The Galactic Council studied the situation, and because there were so many higher beings on the Pleiades, permission was granted for the planet to permanently enter the fifth dimension.

I am just reviewing this with you because I want you to understand that you are evolving toward multidimensional reincarnation. This is the idea of the stargate that you would be able then to control and correct a path that will allow you to incarnate on other higher planetary systems. In order to do that, you need an awareness of the galaxy, that there are other planetary systems in the galaxy. You need an intention of consciousness in the current Earth lifetime as you prepare to travel through the stargate, becoming open to the ascension and to the opening of the stargate. Remember, we are in the gateway of 2012. The gateway for 2012 is also an energy field for ascension. It is not just an energy field for Earth changes and clearings and cleansings. The energy field, remember, is interactive, and so by fostering the interactive energies of the 2012 gateway, you can accelerate the ascension.

THE ETHERIC CRYSTALS CAN HELP YOUR ASCENSION

I am suggesting that as starseeds and Arcturian groups of forty members we begin to activate the ascension energies through an exercise on an hourly basis, activating the twelve etheric crystals with the Central Sun and 2012 energy and to create an interactive force field and reactivate the alignment of Serra da Bocaína, Brazil, with the stargate. Begin to visualize that you are crossing into the stargate. You can do this through thought projections. This gateway represents a newer energy. Until this point, we have said that it is difficult to get too close to the doorway of the stargate and that you have to complete your Earth lessons in order to go through the stargate. Now the doorway, the vestibule, the gateway to the stargate is more open than ever before for Earth beings.

Please meditate with me now and visualize the Arcturian stargate. Visualize, to the best of your ability, that you are at the twelfth etheric crystal at Serra da Bocaína and that you are being elevated up the ladder of ascension. [See the appendix for a map of all etheric crystal locations.] You hear the special sound of ascension, and you are elevated to the Arcturian stargate. Remember that the energy from the twelfth etheric crystal and its alignment with the stargate is also connecting with the energy of the other eleven etheric crystals. The other etheric crystals now are also becoming more open to the energy of the stargate and the concepts of the multidimensional reincarnation.

When I say multidimensional reincarnation, I hope you understand that this means that some of you have obviously been on other dimensional planets before you came to Earth. Some of you have been on Arcturus. Some of you have been on the Pleiades. Some of you have been in Alano. Some of you have been in the Andromedan systems. The question has always emerged: "Well, Juliano, what is going on? If I have been on those other dimensional planets, why have I come back down now to a third-dimensional planet? Why am I not staying in these higher-dimensional planets?"

The answer is somewhat complicated, because I have to explain something about galactic time. The greatest innovation and achievement with dimensional beings has been the mastery of time. The understanding of time travel and its relationship to dimensions has created abilities that are far beyond your imagination. Time travel breaks many rules of your physics and linear thinking. When you look at time as circular rather than linear, you will begin to appreciate that, in certain instances, you can go back in time, and in other instances, you go forward in time. This experience on Earth may be in an earlier time for you. In this view, you are already ascended with us in the future time.

Stay with this thinking. It is very easy to become confused. I don't want to confuse you any more than is necessary; I just want you to understand that multidimensional reincarnation is not linear in the way that Earth reincarnation is. However, multidimensional reincarnation is also cumulative: Reincarnation can be viewed as a series of incarnations. Thus you can have a higher incarnation and then a third-dimensional reincarnation and then a couple higher ones again. Therefore, reincarnation is cumulative, and you are eventually able to totally graduate and not ever have to return to a third-dimensional existence unless you chose to for some special mission. Some of you who are starseeds now have been with me on the Pleiades. Those of you who are connecting with your Arcturian guides have also been with me on Arcturus and have been with me on some of these other planetary systems. If you could grasp this cumulative concept with multidimensional reincarnation, then you would have a better understanding of how it is possible to be in the third dimension again.

The *Kaballah* teaches about the concept of the "lifting of the sparks." The understanding of this idea from the galactic standpoint is that you are lifting the sparks of some of your other incarnations. I could say that you have lifted a spark from your earlier Earth incarnation. You are beginning to grasp the complex nature of yourself: Imagine that you had a past incarnation in a higher planet. Now imagine that you came back here to understand parts of yourself. I think that you are ready to go to this level of thinking.

I will conclude this portion of the lecture by explaining to you that time is accelerated. Try to combine your galactic awareness and the consciousness of the Central Sun with the understanding that you are entering the door, the gateway, to the 2012 energy field. With this awareness comes a corresponding acceleration of time. I believe many of you have already experienced this time acceleration. Hasn't this been a fantastically accelerated time? Haven't many events around the planet occurred already? Don't you feel as if everything is moving so quickly now?

I would like to turn the next part of the lecture over to Archangel Metatron, who will speak some more about the sparks. My dear friends, Arcturian starseeds, and Group of Forty members, we will be with you now, and we will support you with healing light. In particular, I will be sending you protective light and protective energy. You are valuable to the evolution of Earth, of humanity, and also of the galaxy and the galactic consciousness that we are spreading. I am Juliano. Good day.

UNIFY THE SPARKS OF YOUR SELF

Greetings, I am Archangel Metatron. Shalom. I am the keeper of the Arcturian stargate, the protector of the gateway for your multidimensional reincarnation, and also your guide and teacher to help you in your understanding of the raising of the sparks. Many of the Kaballistic masters have talked before about the raising of the sparks. Many have talked about the idea that in the moment of creation, there were explosions of energy and that the containers could not hold the spreading sparks. This is possibly the reason why there is the presence of evil on the planets.

I want to introduce a different idea to you about the sparks. I want to suggest that one of the main missions of your soul life is to raise and to find your own sparks. I want you to consider that you are a complex being and that your energy is now contained in a force field. At one time, you could not totally hold the energy, and it was spread around over many different places in the galaxy and the universe and on planet Earth. These spreading sparks are the fallen sparks that the Kaballists talk about. One of your greatest and most important missions is to gather the fallen and spreading sparks of yourself and to bring those parts of yourself into unity and to heal them. Some of you have parts of yourself from Atlantis. Some of you have parts of yourself from the Maya. Some have sparks from earlier times in Europe. Some of you have parts of yourself from the native peoples in South America and in New Zealand.

You have fallen sparks here on Earth. You also could have fallen sparks in other planetary systems. Consider this idea. Probably many of you have been on Arcturus or some higher planets. Despite the fact that you were on higher planets, you still may have had some fallen sparks representative of yourself on Earth. You have therefore had the wherewithal, the energy, the concentration, and the support of your guides and teachers to come back to Earth now and to heal and to unify those fallen sparks of yourself. *Neshemah*—"light of your holy soul."

Call on all parts of yourself to come into unity. Call on all parts of yourself to be healed. This can be a tremendous period of enlightening energy for you to understand. Many of you have questioned why you have come back to Earth. Many of you have asked: "How could it be that I have lived in other higher dimensions but now I am back here on Earth? Am I being punished?" No, look at this time on Earth as a grace and as a time to gather the sparks. Look at your service to others. Help others find those parts of themselves. Is this not what soul retrieval is—finding the lost parts or sparks of the self? Your purpose is now both to find those parts of self, to heal them, and to bring them back into unity with the whole self. Now you are finding the opportunity to unify with your galactic and multidimensional self.

This uplifting of the sparks also includes the unification of those parts with your greater higher self. It's a two-part process: upliftment and unification. *Yechudim* is the Kaballistic name for this unification. "We ask *Hashem*, the Creator, to give us the power to raise our sparks from our lower selves, from our selves from other lifetimes, and from our selves from other dimensions. Help us, *Hashem*, to raise all our sparks so that we can bring them into unity to our greater, higher self." One of the secrets of achieving unity is to be in service to the light and to the ascension and the planetary evolution. By doing that, you are given special grace and powerful energy to raise all parts of self.

Olam Haze. Olam Haba—"This world and the world to come." There is this world, and there is the world to come. Now we can unify both. In the world to come, you will be unified with your higher self through the multidimensional self. You will be in total healing light in the world to come because of the work that you are doing now. I am Archangel Metatron. *Shalom.*

CHAPTER 20

BRINGING THE PLANET INTO
A NEW BALANCE

Juliano, the Arcturians, and Archangel Metatron

Greetings, I am Juliano, and we are the Arcturians. In this lecture we will continue our discussion of biorelativity and the methods of biorelativity for bringing a planet into a new balance. I want to emphasize that what we are seeking and what you are seeking in respect to working with the Earth is to find the methods, activities, and meditations that would bring the Earth into a new balance.

It is correct to say that the Earth is not going to go back the way it was in 1960 or 1970. It is also correct to say that a new balance or homeostasis for the planet must be sought, one that will take into consideration all of the energies up until this point. The idea is that we will work with you to seek a balance that is in alignment with the highest interest and manifestation of the spirit and life on this planet. This highest homeostasis will be in alignment with the biosphere so that the Earth can continue on its path toward its ascension to the fifth dimension.

It is a law of the universe that everything is in a state of change and a state of motion. This includes you as human beings as well the planets. When you look at the energy and the methods of biorelativity, you need to look no further than to your own body. Ascension is both a personal and a planetary process, and working with the ascension energies will assist you in healing yourself and your body as well as bringing you into a balance for this ascension.

The principles of your physical healings can also be applied to the planet. The most basic principle of biorelativity is that the Earth is a living spirit. You have many names for this spirit: Some call her Gaia. The native people call her Mother Earth. We also use the name Blue Jewel. It is vitally important that you recognize that the energies of Earth are a living spirit, because humankind's knowledge of what is spiritual and what is physical is narrow and often does not include the idea of a planet having a life-form energy. Yet it does! That's why the Earth is so unique—it has this fantastic abundance of life forms. We have traveled through many different areas of the galaxy, and it is truly an amazing manifestation here on Earth. There has been such a bountiful expression of life here.

THE VALUE OF FORTY

I know we have spoken about the numerical values. We have spoken about the values of forty and of the forty groups of forty—equaling 1,600. The method of biorelativity that we are teaching focuses on the numerical powers of numbers as the basis for effecting the new balance. Many people witnessed the powerful earthquake event in Chile and also in Haiti, and they are still speaking of the Ring of Fire and the possibility of another earthquake happening there as well. It was demonstrated, perhaps unintentionally, that a tsunami possibility existed after the Chilean quake, and many people unknowingly participated in a biorelativity event on television. That event consisted of the act of observation through television and waiting for the tsunami on the islands of Hawaii and also in Japan and other areas.

While there was a fantastic energetic connection in this case, it was not an intentional biorelativity event. It was not an event during which people necessarily tried to stop the tsunami but rather an event in which millions of people invoked a collective focus of consciousness and awareness. This event was a demonstration of the powerful effects of television for uniting people in group consciousness that may have also resulted in a subconscious mitigation of the effects of the waves. At this point, I realize that you may not be able to have five to ten million people consciously meditate together and connect with television in this way, but I do know that the imagery that was demonstrated in this television event illustrates an important principle of biorelativity: Images and visualizations are a way to communicate to Earth's subconscious and also a way of communicating with your subconscious.

The power of numbers becomes critical as you work with these biorelativity exercises. You are working with the number forty, and you can also work with 1,600—this means that you are working with multiples of forty. This is an energetic power that is universal: The number forty is a galactic force. The power in that number can overcome other forces, even though forty is numerically a small number. Compared to the population of Earth and to the ten or twenty million people that may have been watching the television at the time of the possible tsunami, even 1,600 people are equivalent to a speck of sand. But while 1,600 people may seem to be miniscule number, it does not matter: They have a force that far exceeds their numerical value.

In order to work with that force and to maximize your small numbers and your power, you have to be more exact about who is in each Group of Forty, who is registered with you, who is participating, and so on. In other words, it becomes really important to know that there are groups of forty people that make up 1,600 people and that they are somehow unified. They need to be connected through some kind of list as well as through a verbal understanding. I know that it seems like a monumental task to try to get the names of 1,600 people in some central location, but I want to assure you that if you find ways to maximize your power and to work in the numerical value, then you can overcome your comparatively small numbers so that your powers will far exceed your numbers: This is demonstrated in stories of the Old Testament in which small groups of Israelites were able to win battles against larger armies. It is also demonstrated in the value of forty as the number of days to spend in the desert to find your soul connection, as well as in the significance of forty years and many other examples of the aspects of forty.

As you might already understand, even the Maya worked with this power of numbers; they worked with the power of the year 2012. You may believe that 2012 is the central year of the gigantic shift, but that is not the most important element to understand. The most important thing is to see that somehow the number 2012 itself represents a powerful numerical energy, just as the number forty and the connections that you have using the multiples of it can far exceed your limited numbers and create a powerful effect.

RING OF FIRE VISUALIZATION

As I continue to discuss methods of biorelativity, let us focus specifically on the energy of the human body and the concepts of healing through acupressure and acupuncture, using that analogy to look at the Earth. You may already have some understanding of Chinese medicine. The ancient Chinese were connected with ancient galactic teachers. In their methodology, the masters understood that when energy is blocked in a meridian in the body, it can result in illness in that body. This analogy is just powerful and true on the body of Earth as a planet. In your meditations and in your biorelativity work, you will want to focus on unblocking Earth energy—and unfortunately, there are many sacred spots on the Earth that are blocked. I do not want to raise alarm and become too focused on the negative aspects of the blockages; I simply want you to just understand the meridians and pathways on the planet Earth.

The Ring of Fire in the Pacific would be a beautiful and simple example of such a planetary meridian. I think you all have seen that image—perhaps on television—where you could see the energy, the pathway, of the Ring of Fire going up around the coast of South America, Central America, across the Pacific coast area of the United States, and on over to Japan. That is one example of a blocked Earth meridian. Already there is much discussion that the next earthquake is going to be further along the Ring of Fire. Some people have already sent this energy and image, but it does not have to happen. I am going to lead a meditation in which we can work with that Ring of Fire energy so that the energy will not be blocked.

Working with the concepts of biorelativity, we believe that the planet is going through a change and an energetic transformation. We are not trying to stop the energy; we want the energy to flow in a particular energetic force. This energetic force can be smoothed and brought into a balance. The idea is that Earth needs to have meridians and pathways that are open. We understand that many of the original pathways, or meridians, were used up between 1988 through 1999. This was one of the transformational points on this planet. Up until that time, the meridians were open, but now many of them have closed. We have introduced the idea of new acupressure points on the planet and of new meridians that could be established that would be totally connected to a fifth-dimensional energy source. These new meridians were not based on the existing pathways but on an interaction with a higher energy force, on downloading the twelve etheric crystals into the Earth.

The twelve etheric crystals can be perceived as acupressure or acupuncture points within the planet. They are then able to establish a positive energy flow between each of the etheric crystal points. I will quickly review the names of those etheric crystal points where this energy has been downloaded: Lago Puelo in Argentina, Serra de Bocaína in Brazil, Copper Canyon in Mexico, Lake Taupo in New Zealand, Grose Valley in Australia, Montserrat near Barcelona in Spain, Mount Shasta in California, Volcán Poáz in Costa Rica, Istanbul in Turkey, Lake Moraine in Canada, the Bodensee (or Lake Constance) in Central Europe, and Mount Fuji in Japan. [See map at the end of this book.] These places are acupressure or acupuncture points for the Earth. These points can be activated through your meditations in what I call a dialectic energy flow.

Visualize that all of these points are connecting and communicating with each other. This connection then creates an energy flow that is more powerful than the sum of the individual ones. Then the dialectic energy flow can be brought into the energy of the Ring of Fire. This energy flow is then sent through the Earth meridian and creates a higher balance or energy, which will help to loosen any blocks so that there will not be another "bump." In your mind, please visualize these twelve etheric points. We have asked that these points be brought into an image of the Kaballistic Tree of Life. The image of this Tree of Life is also a dialectic energy force that increases the power of the energy flow. To the best of your ability, visualize twelve spheres. If you cannot remember the names of each of these etheric points, just visualize twelve spheres shaped in the model of the Tree of Life. I, Juliano, am calling and reactivating all of the spheres.

If you have trouble visualizing all twelve spheres, then go to the sphere that you are most comfortable with: If you are in the United States, you might want to go to the etheric sphere representing Mount Shasta. If you are in Mexico, you might want to go to Copper Canyon. If you are in Central America, you might want to go to Volcán Poáz. If you are in South America, you might want to go to Lago Puelo. If you are in Turkey or the Middle East, you might want to go to the sphere in Istanbul. If you are in Europe, you might want to go to the etheric sphere at the Bodensee or Montserrat. If you are in Canada, you might want to go to Lake Moraine. If you are in Japan, you might want to go to Mount Fuji. If you are in Australia, you might want to go to Grose Valley. If you are in New Zealand, you might want to go to Lake Taupo. Which one do you feel connected with? Go there now in your mind. I am connecting with all of you and all of them. Generate a connection to all of the twelve crystals.

Through our intentions, the crystals create a powerful spiral light that emanates out of the ground and up into the atmosphere. It is now a beautiful holographic spiral of light. Visualize this holographic spiral of light. It is spiraling up to the North Pole, so powerful is this spiral of light. Remember, it is a dialectic force. It is far beyond what each of us can do individually. We are in a group energy field. Some can see this spiral in the shape of a DNA spiral, which is a good image. This beautiful spiraling light comes up from the twelve etheric crystals and is now shaped in the form of the Tree of Life. We have created a dialectic energy force that can be downloaded into the Earth. I want you now to visualize that this great spiral of light has huge powers of balance—huge biorelativity powers of helping energy to flow through the Earth. It has beautiful powers to bring calmness and balance that is in alignment with the powers of peace and calmness on the planet.

THE ETHERIC CRYSTAL MERIDIAN SYSTEM

Now, I, Juliano, with your assistance, will visualize that this dialectic energy force field, which we have just beautifully activated from the twelve etheric crystals and have spiraled through the top of the Earth to the North Pole, is now gently injected into the Ring of Fire, starting right at the base by Chile. I know that there are many aftershocks; I know that there is much instability, but this energy that we have injected in there is calming and balancing. It flows immediately so that we can spread out the major disruptive forces that might have been congregated into that area. It is now spreading gently through the Ring of Fire. Visualize this meridian going up through South America, Central America, and the Pacific coast of the United States. Bring with you the energy of calmness and balance. This is important at this point because we are visualizing a calmness.

We are not activating any new earthquake at all. There will not be a new earthquake for a period. We are activating a gentle and harmonious light that is going through the Ring of Fire, up around Alaska, over to Japan, continuing around all the Asian areas and connecting with Australia and New Zealand. This is a beautiful meridian. We are sending this energy now of balance and homeostasis. We will be in meditation for several minutes as you work with me now. This is a dialectic energy force that we are sending. You will hear me periodically sending tones and chants through the channel as we meditate. Remember, as we are going through this energy field, the Ring of Fire, we are also going through the oceans— the Pacific Ocean in particular. We are working with the feedback-loop system of the ocean currents so that they are coming into a greater harmony with the biosphere. This can create a calming effect on the El Niño energy.

I, Juliano, continue to flow this energy from the twelve etheric crystals that has created a dialectic energy field, and it continues to be injected into the Ring of Fire meridian. Now, let me speak some more about meridians, because, in essence, we have created a new meridian system on the Earth by activating these twelve etheric crystals. To understand this more clearly, think of the concept of bypass surgery. Sometimes when an artery is blocked, instead of trying to open the artery—maybe the artery is so damaged that you cannot work with it—you perform what is called bypass surgery. In bypass surgery, you may take a vein from one part of the body and put it into another part so that the energy flow can continue, bypassing the blocked artery, and the heart can function normally.

Through our biorelativity work, we acknowledge that some of the Earth meridians are blocked, and just as one might do in bypass surgery in a human body, we can work to bypass those blocked Earth meridians. I know this may sound amusing—it is a funny analogy—but it is actually quite realistic. The Earth has a tremendous healing force, a tremendous healing power, just like your human body has tremendous healing powers. The Earth has untold healing powers if they can be activated. Through our work in biorelativity, we have created another meridian system that we have called the twelve etheric crystals meridian system. This creates a bypass so that the energy of the fifth dimension, which is interacting with the third dimension, can freely flow between all of these etheric crystal points.

The fantastic advantage for Earth healing in working with biorelativity is that it accelerates a new etheric crystal flow. In biorelativity, you want to generate a force. The force you can generate is first based on the numbers you are working with, which is the power of forty times forty. The second power is the meridian energy field created from the twelve etheric crystals. You should first work with the power and then with the existing bypass meridian—the system of twelve etheric crystals that we have established. You should then generate energy from there, and through projections and visualizations, you can then direct that energy into existing pathways, creating a greater balance. In other words, it comes back to the new balance; you do not want to generate a balance where everything is static, because you know that the Earth has to change. The Central Sun is influencing the Earth. The Earth has to process all of humankind's energy without breaking down—without breaking the vessels. You don't want the vessels to break; you want the energy to continue to flow.

THE POWER OF CROP CIRCLES ON MERIDIANS

The next powerful aspect to focus on in biorelativity is visualization—the act in which you visualize the Earth and its meridians. This idea focuses partly on the power coming from crop circles. The power and energy of crop circles is a representation of new Earth meridians that need to be superimposed onto the surface of the planet. Crop circles are actually expressions of biorelativity energy from other dimensions that are coming to the Earth. That means that those pathways and those energies that are represented in a crop circle may be beyond the comprehension of a normal human.

For example, think about meridians in the human body such as the kidney meridian or the lung meridian. Visualize a meridian line that moves down through the Earth just like meridian lines move through the human body. Those lines are actually in the etheric energy field of the human body and as well as in the energy field of the Earth. They are not lines that are in the physical, even though they are expressed in energetic pathways in the physical. Thus, because the actual meridians of the human body are in the etheric energy field, some refer to that energy field as the astral, or the energetic, body.

It is the same in the Earth. The actual Earth-energy pathways are all expressed in the astral energy body of the Earth. We are talking about the complex etheric energy pathways of a planet. The energy pathways of a planet are not going to be that simple. We can look at the Ring of Fire as an energy pathway, and most people can visualize this and feel pretty comfortable in working with that image. I am glad that you can do that. There are also other obvious meridian pathways. For example, the equator is another simple pathway. The path between the North and the South Poles represents another pathway.

Now, some of the crop circles you have been seeing represent complex mathematical interactive forces that may be beyond your comprehension. They can provide a healing energy, but remember that these patterns are communicating with the energy fields of the Earth and the energy fields of the Earth understand those patterns. These crop circles are not just to be there for twenty days and then disappear. They are images of meridian or energy lines that need to be worked with on the Earth and somehow coordinated. Crop circles often appear in England, and they may exist for a short period of time. These circles are examples of visualization of how one can be working with meridian lines. We can recommend that someone work with the images from crop circles and understand that these images represent energy pathways that are comparable to meridians that are in the energy field of the Earth. Remember, I said that this is a new balancing process that the Earth is going through. It is a balance that is quite complex. The planetary system of meridians is far more complex than a person's meridians, but these new images can be worked with.

Another biorelativity visualizations would be to look at the storms you have seen on radar in which the storm is dissipating or lessening. I would like for you to visualize the energy of El Niño—a powerful energy source coming from the waters of the Pacific Ocean—and how it is causing great forces of storms across South America, Central America, across the United States and even in Europe. It is powerful. For this exercise, visualize that the El Niño energy is calm. The way we can visualize this is to imagine the El Niño energy spiraling up toward the North Pole and away from the Earth and out into the atmosphere. Just visualize a huge spiraling light. Yes, there will be storms continuing, but they will be modified: They will not be as strong. Particularly the storms around the Haiti area will be modified, so they will not bring as much discomfort and flooding. This will allow people an opportunity to recover somewhat.

TWELVE NEW PLANETARY CITIES OF LIGHT

I now want to speak again about the planetary cities of light because they are also connected to the twelve etheric crystals, and they are part of the new meridians. We can use the metaphor of bypass surgery again, although that is not a total analogy. The planetary cities of light are holding light, but they are also creating vessels that can receive new fifth-dimensional energy and new fifth-dimensional light. It is clear that the Earth cannot go through the changes and balances that are needed without a fifth-dimensional input. This fifth-dimensional input has to be held in some container. It is the same in your personal work. You can download light, but if you don't have a way of holding the light, then personally, you can become disorganized and confused. You have to have a way of either emptying yourself or expanding yourself so that you can process and hold newer energy. That includes expanding your mental body, your emotional body, your spiritual body, and also your physical body.

It is the same way with the Earth. The Earth needs some new way to hold this energy, and the planetary cities of light provide this function. Part of biorelativity is to activate planetary cities of light that hold the energy of your planet. You can now activate newer places, and these places will be another round of the twelve cities of light in addition to the first twelve. I, Juliano, am calling on you to activate twelve more new planetary cities of light. It is time to activate a second level. On Arcturus, we have someone in our temples accessing, coordinating, and working full-time with the energy field of our planet. When you look at the Earth, you might say, "Well, this is a monumental task." It requires that you continually work with this energy. It is impossible to have someone do this full-time, because this is not the way in which your energy fields are set up, and it is not the way your work life is set up.

I know that some people are working on the concept of the twelve planetary cities of light. On certain designated days, you can meditate every hour on one city and then transfer to the next. This is a fantastic way of sharing the energy. This is why I am suggesting that we grow to twenty-four cities of light now. After twenty-four, we are going to go to forty planetary cities of light. You will see another exponential increase of spiritual light on the Earth now. I would say that we have at least another sixty days before we can develop the next planetary cities of light. I encourage you to do the meditations on the first twelve, and then I encourage you to identify the next twelve.

These current planetary cities of light are holding existing energy, but in some ways, we can use the example of the bypass again because some people are saying we need to unblock the energies in certain main cities. Yes, I agree. Therefore, you can work with enclaves within larger cities. You can work with neighborhoods; a small neighborhood within a big city such as Los Angeles can become its own city of light. There are huge energies around such large cities, and it can be difficult to spiritually coordinate such energy when it has so many different influences. You can, however, look at enclaves in existing cities, and I suggest you establish an enclave in Los Angeles, even if it is simply a neighborhood, as well as enclaves in other major cities, thus forming cities of light within cities. You can also work with areas: For example, the idea was suggested to make the whole area of Chihuahua, Mexico a city of light, so you could also establish an enclave in Chihuahua. You will be surprised at how the list of cities of light is going to be growing!

This leads me to the idea of events. You are going to have to work as a group to develop larger-scale events. This means that some of you are going to be able to broadcast and transmit the energy and power of this Group of Forty to make international events. It is true that the channel is in an excellent position because he is able to travel around the world, but others are going to be able to do that broadcasting as well. Work with events. Meet in large groups and hold the energy field. Remember that much of what you are doing is establishing new meridians and new pathways. This becomes the teaching of the methods of biorelativity.

I want to also remind you that Native American traditions have a great visualization tool called sand paintings. For example, sand paintings are used in order to heal. A painting is created that represents a healing force. You can work on sand paintings or images that can be used in healing the Earth—some of you are already receiving images as you are hearing my words today. I now want Metatron to also speak about biorelativity and personal and planetary healing. I love you all. This is going to be an active time, and the Group of Forty is going to become much better known. You are going to be much more assertive in your work now. I am Juliano. Good day.

LET THERE BE . . .

Greetings. *Shalom.* I am Archangel Metatron. *Baruch Hashem*—blessed is the Creator of light. Many of you are becoming the children of light. This means that you are able to be the cocreators of energy for the Earth. This is a big responsibility, and you are all evolving into it. Some of you have come to this Earth at this time to actually be cocreators and to practice in the cocreation of planet Earth. I can tell you that this is one of the reasons that some of you came.

There is much chaos on this planet, but there is also much opportunity for influencing this chaos and influencing the change to a positive outcome. In the Old Testament, this world was created with the words, "Let there be light." *Adonai Elohim, Baruch Hashem* (Adonai is one; blessed be the name) spoke the words and then there was the creation. That was the first example of biorelativity where the Creator's will was manifested by the words: "*Ye He Aur*"—let there be light. And there was light!

Juliano asked me to talk about biorelativity, so let us look at that example, "Let there be light," and say that when you are doing work in biorelativity, you can speak powerful words to the Earth: Let there be peace. Let there be calmness. Let there be balance. Let there be life. Let the meridians of the Earth be open. Let there be. You see, those words, "Let there be," are very powerful words in the understanding of biorelativity.

Another beautiful example of the co-creation and the *B'nai Elohim* light—the work of the children of God—is to powerfully enunciate words and instructions to the Earth about what has to be. So let there be calmness around the Ring of Fire—speak these words with intention and power and speak them in a group. It is as if you are sending a vibrational energy field into the spirit of Gaia. Gaia has become accustomed to the language of humankind. "In the beginning God created the heaven and the earth. . . . God said, Let there be light, and there was light" [Genesis 1:3, KJV]. So say with intent to the Earth: "Let there be light. Let there be peace."

My recommendation to you, planetary healers of the Earth, is this: Acknowledge the power of your words. Acknowledge that you are part of the co-creation spirit and begin to enunciate and send these thoughts, beginning with the words, "Let there be." I want you to generate the thoughts after the statement, "Let there be." You will be surprised, especially when you are using the values of forty, of what can happen when you say, "Let there be." Let there be peace. Let there be light. Let there be balance. Let there be harmony on the Earth. Let the biosphere flow. Let the meridians on the Earth be open. Let the sacred spots on the Earth vibrate with love and light. Let the planetary cities of light vibrate and gain in intensity and power. Let this powerful, healing Group of Forty activate the energy to bring the Earth into the fifth dimension. I am Archangel Metatron. *Shalom.*

CHAPTER 21

BIORELATIVITY AND EARTH CATASTROPHES

Juliano and the Arcturians

Greetings, I am Juliano, and we are the Arcturians. Let us look at biorelativity and the relationship between human-made catastrophes and what would be considered Earth catastrophes. What we call Earth catastrophes are usually the following: earthquakes, volcanic eruptions, storms, typhoons, or hurricanes. These are all events that can create major problems for people living in their path. From the Earth's perspective, some of these catastrophes can be viewed as part of the homeostasis energy. The homeostasis energy refers to balance within the planetary feedback system. That balance allows a variation of energy to be maintained. However, if the variation of energy becomes out of balance, disproportionate or blocked, then a concurrent release emerges that will allow the homeostasis to remain in effect.

The homeostasis that is required for the existence of humans on this Earth is a narrow but obvious band of energy that is part of the biosphere. The biosphere includes energy currents from the oceans, the oxygen content from the atmosphere, and related electromagnetic energy fields. These electromagnetic energy fields are also affected in part by the cosmos. This means that Earth's electromagnetic energy is affected by the Sun, and it is also affected by outer cosmic events that are continually sending energy throughout the universe and throughout the galaxy. These cosmic energy forces are much more difficult to measure, but they do exist—and they are cumulative. Ultimately, from our perspective, we can assert that energy even as distant as the Central Sun at the core of the galaxy does have an effect on the energy of this planet. Some of that energy is much more difficult to measure, as it contains extreme nanoparticles. Nanoparticles can also refer to spiritual vibrations.

We must also say that humankind has been an influence on the electromagnetic energy field of Earth. When we are speaking of the biosphere, we usually describe human activities as affecting the air, the oceans, or the forests. In our Group of Forty discussions, we don't usually mention the effect that humankind is having on the electromagnetic energy field of Earth. There are accumulations of different energy patterns emitted from a variety of sources. These sources include rockets, nuclear energy, high-frequency auroral energy sources such as radar, military activities, and many other sources of electromagnetic energy. Emissions from these sources do accumulate and affect the electromagnetic balance of Earth.

This is already being demonstrated by the fact that the electromagnetic energy of the planet has been and is being altered. The thickness of the electromagnetic energy field has changed, and its composition has shifted. We have also noted that there are null areas, what we refer to as holes, in Earth's electromagnetic energy field. Some of these holes, or imbalances, actually travel around the planet. We would call a huge electromagnetic imbalance or hole a null zone, or perhaps we could even refer to it as a dark hole. One example of the effects of such a null zone is the war in Iraq—and now also the war in Afghanistan. There are many wars, many dark spots, and many energy depletion zones on the planet. These zones are too numerous to list, but these areas, in particular in Iraq and Afghanistan, are prominent zones of energy depletion on the planet.

Sustainable Systems and Planned Shift

A series of energy depletion zones continue to pop up around Earth. I would like to remind everyone that in 2010 we entered a period that we have referred to as the 2012 corridor. The energy of 2012 is a major transformational energy. We have pointed out that Earth is not going to end in 2012, but that this is instead a major transitional point, a major turning point. Moving up to that time, we can observe the faltering of older patterns and older ways. This is occurring on multiple levels—on religious levels, on political levels, and on environmental levels—and overall it is occurring even on the mental level and the belief-system level. The old ways of viewing reality and the old ways of doing business, so to speak, are not going to be sufficient for maintaining systems. Of course, this includes economic systems as well.

It is, from an intellectual standpoint, an intriguing time. It would be interesting to read about this time a hundred years from now in a history course; you could see the transformations occurring in this period you are now living, and it would be of great intellectual interest and excitement. To actually live in this period is another experience that is much more difficult to describe, because there is a great deal of pain and contraction associated with these experiences. It is not overly pleasant to watch the downfall of some of the systems on the planet. These systems have been successful from one standpoint: They have allowed wealth to be distributed, even though that distribution is uneven and disproportionate and unfair. It has allowed a huge technology industry to emerge that has resulted in some amazing inventions, including space travel, computers, and some seemingly huge advances in the health world.

At the same time, these older systems inherently carry the seeds of their own destruction in them because they are based on a model that is not sustainable. There is a new energy, a new way of looking at systems by describing them as sustainable or not sustainable. Those systems I refer to are the religious, economic, sociological, environmental, and scientific systems. They are the fabric that holds together the illusion of your reality on Earth, but in their entirety, they do not inherently contain sustainability and therefore will eventually collapse.

This collapse could be a dramatic, sudden collapse or a planned shift. Such a shift would be preferable, because it would allow ways of making accommodations and changes. The dramatic collapse, which perhaps could best be seen economically, would be much more painful. Remember that the economic wealth you saw earlier on this planet as recently as three to four years ago was based on an illusion that everything was sustainable. That illusion collapsed, but the system remains, functioning on the same principles that led to the first collapse. So now you see the possibility of a second or third collapse.

Again, the reason for this is because that system is not sustainable: Earth's resources are the basis of all economic wealth. When Earth's resources are being destroyed and consumed at such high levels as they are now on this planet, then one can pretty easily see that this system of consumption will not be sustainable. Even the idea of going to other planets or going to the Moon, although interesting and intriguing, would not really answer the sustainability problem: In earlier times, this problem was solved by discovering new worlds and new resources. That was, relatively speaking, easy compared to trying to discover and activate new resources on the Moon or on Mars.

WE STAND AT THE POINT OF AN EVOLUTIONARY CRISIS

As you know, we are students of the galaxy and of planetary travel. It is fairly normal in the history of planetary travel to meet civilizations and races who are seeking to solve their sustainability problems through interplanetary travel. Even in your own literature, including science-fiction literature, there are myths and stories about other planetary travelers who represent a core elite from their planet and who are seeking resources outside their planetary system simply because their own resources have been exhausted. Yet it would be better if the human species would make the necessary adjustments now before exhaustion of resources occurs. We refer to this current period that you are experiencing as an evolutionary crisis. Part of the reason this is called an evolutionary crisis is because of the need for changing models, parameters, and paradigms—because older paradigms will not work to sustain humankind into the future.

We want to relate these ideas to biorelativity. Biorelativity is the idea of trying to influence, communicate, and relate to a planet based on telepathic communications. The interaction of biorelativity with the planet begins by listening to what the need or the energy of the planet is and also by trying to have the planet in some way interact and respond to the needs of the people living on it. Remember, while the planet is a living being, it is not a being like a human being. The planet does not have an ego, for example. You can describe Earth as a living organism, but you can't say that it is a living organism like a human or an animal, because it has an energy that is planetary. It is not humanoid in any way, even though there is a spiritual energy and there are ways of communicating with that energy force. The planet does have an overriding guide. One of the planetary guides is Sanat Kumara, who has been designated as the planetary logos, he who oversees the planetary energy and the planetary functions.

The idea of the biorelativity is that you are trying to develop links—ways of communication, ways of listening to energy from a planetary system (and if possible, interacting with that energy). Now humankind wants to interact with Earth in a way that will increase sustainability. We know that the feedback-loop system has been successful in maintaining a certain balance. At the same time, the feedback system has limitations. You can only add so much alkalinity to an ocean before that ocean reaches a point at which it cannot sustain its currents at the level needed to keep a balance for the biosphere of the waters. There is only so much pollution you can put into the air before it reaches a point where the air cannot maintain the system necessary for human life. At that point, the system can break, creating what I call abnormalities or irregularities in the system. Again, our goal and discussions do not focus on wanting any one system to break; ideally, we want the systems themselves to make adaptations and shifts.

Part of our teaching is to work with the planet and look at the planet as a system. The Earth system functions in a similar way to the meridian system used in Chinese medicine when talking about the human body. This is an analogy; it is not a true similarity because, again, we are dealing with a planetary system. We don't have the vocabulary in your language to talk about planetary systems yet. We are getting close to a better vocabulary. We are speaking of Earth's meridians and ley lines. We are talking about energy spots that are extremely important for keeping the feedback-loop system going. We talk about the need for keeping certain ley lines or meridians open, and if those meridians are blocked, then energies can become disruptive anywhere along the ley line, possibly creating disruptive releases. The volcanic eruption in Iceland is an example of such a release.

BIORELATIVITY AND ADAM RELATIVITY

One question about using biorelativity has emerged: What about using biorelativity to influence humans? What about using the idea of biorelativity to try to change the attitudes of the world leaders, influencing those leaders to create better stewardship for the planet? Remember, the whole concept of biorelativity is contained in the word "bio," which relates to life force and in part to the planetary system as a coherent living organism. It is a good idea to use the same principles in trying to change world leaders and other people who are in control of the environment or the economy.

To work with this idea, we need a modification of the biorelativity principle. We can consider this modification under a new name: "Adam relativity," since Adam was the name of the first human and you are considered in the Galactic Council to be the Adam species. Adam relativity would then be an emerging energy and a new field that would develop principles of energy work to influence and create systems to modify humans in order to prevent a collapse of the biosphere.

There are many other variables to this approach of Adam relativity. First, there is a great deal of genetic storage of information from earlier times on this planet, along with a long history of genetic manipulation and subconscious and unconscious codes that you are still living out. We point out that the scientific technology of humankind is far below the spiritual levels that are necessary. Even so, humankind's spiritual development has not even kept up with the technologies; in fact, your technology is more advanced than your spirituality.

This means that humans have been able to use this technology to further lower the energy that is manifested as wars. The technology of wars has become expanded rather than decreased in the face of the scientific technology. In fact, there has really been no significant gain in the geopolitical world of conflict because of human advances in technology. There are probably more wars and killings going on now than at any other time on the planet. You could say that perhaps the numbers of wars is an equivalent percentage to the total population of previous eras. And while you might say that two thousand years ago, 30 percent of the countries that existed at that time were at war, and now 30 percent of the existing countries in your current time are also at war—therefore making it sound as if we are still in the same place—it is not the same because everything has been amplified. The destruction that is occurring on the planet is far greater than it was two thousand years ago when earlier wars were going on.

So we return to the discussion of Adam relativity. As we offer you some ideas on this topic, it leads us to one of the main focuses of this discussion: the oil-rig disaster that occurred in the Gulf of Mexico. This is a human-made disaster. It is not, at least on the surface, an expression of Earth's imbalances. This fact that it is human-made would also tend to make us look at different ways of intervening: Biorelativity is based on the concept of interacting with Earth and Earth patterns, but here is a human-made pattern, similar to other catastrophic events such as Chernobyl or the use of nuclear bombs, as well as the high-frequency auroral radiation patterns (HAARP).

All these situations are brought about by human actions. Therefore, if you were trying to use simple biorelativity, it would be difficult because Earth cannot respond to these things in the same way as she can to more natural events. For example, if you were talking about a hurricane coming to shore, we might work energetically to diffuse the hurricane so that instead of having 110-mile-per-hour winds, it would have winds that only moved at 80 miles per hour. Using biorelativity, there is a possibility of having a storm become more diffuse. Yet how can you defuse a Chernobyl-type situation when humans who have free will release huge radiation into the atmosphere?

The oil disaster was seemingly a human-made disaster, yet one would have to look at some of the other issues occurring. The first issue is: What kind of forces are we dealing with, energetically in Earth, when humankind decides to go that deep into the waters to begin to drill and take energy from Inner Earth? One might ask, "What balance is being upset by that process?" Within one paradigm, you would say, "Well, the oil is there, and it doesn't matter how deep it is; it is there for us to use." But working from a paradigm that understands the feedback-loop system and biorelativity, you would have to ask: "Is there any necessity for keeping that kind of energy within Earth? Is there is some kind of energetic balance that is important, that is necessary, for Earth? Maybe that energy needs to stay there to keep a balance within Earth." That is a different way of thinking. The next issue to consider would then be: If humans decide to try to get these energies anyway, what kind of force is one tampering with? What kind of energy could possibly be released if there is an imbalance created by removing that oil? To put in another way, could tapping such energy create an imbalance?

The third issue to look at is the polarization on Earth and the electromagnetic changes in Earth's atmosphere. Sometimes when electromagnetic changes occur, people's thinking is not as clear. You could say, for example, that there are periods of enlightened thinking and then there are periods of darker thinking. There are periods of clarity in which there have been wonderful scientific discoveries and great advances, and then there have been periods that you have called the Dark Ages. The energy on Earth right now contains both. You have huge periods of enlightenment, with huge energies of mental clarity. You are also having dark energies. By using the word "dark" I mean "contracted." I am talking about darker physical energy such as the Chernobyl nuclear disaster or the recent oil leak. You have to ask what kind of mental clarity the people have who are operating these oil platforms have.

You notice that I am comparing the oil rig disaster in the Gulf of Mexico to the disaster at the Chernobyl nuclear power plant. The oil spill is a parallel disaster of catastrophic proportions. The polarization and the energies of contraction can negatively affect people who are running these complex things. The people operating these oil rigs and nuclear power plants can make mistakes in part because of negative energies. There might have been only a small mistake at the oil rig, but unfortunately the problem is that when the negative energy we are referring to this intense, any mistake becomes of monumental significance.

LEARNING THE NECESSARY LESSONS

We would like to say that the biorelativity focus and exercise can stop the flow of this oil. This is an unparalleled event comparable to Chernobyl. Actually the damage is going to be perhaps greater to the planet than Chernobyl, as terrible as the Chernobyl catastrophe was. What has humankind learned from the Chernobyl accident? Has humankind stopped use of nuclear energy? Have humans changed nuclear safety regulations? Do humans have the level of intelligence and concentration necessary to hold the operation of these huge projects?

Given the polarizations and the negative energy forces on the planet, can we assume that humans will have the expertise, concentration, and discipline to continue to operate nuclear power plants and oil rigs without accidents? The answer is no. If everything continues the way it is right now, there will be another nuclear accident or major oil spill. It does not matter how much advancement scientists say they have made; they cannot cover all the bases, especially the final base that needs to be covered: the interaction of these complex systems with humans. Humans are affected by energy.

A combination of factors led to this problem. The first factor involved humans dealing with ocean depths and energy patterns beyond their knowledge or ability to harness. Other circumstances would be the electromagnetic energy field around the planet and how it affects people's thinking and the darker forces. Remember that the Gulf of Mexico is somewhat close to the area where the destruction of Atlantis occurred. There is an Earth memory of that time of great destruction, so it is recommended to send biorelativity energy there based on the highest level of cosmic light and higher energy, or undifferentiated cosmic light, that can be sent to that platform area. At this point there needs to be a calming and constriction of the situation, and it needs to come from the highest energy sources that we can bring, because the situation is out of control.

In this exercise, I would like to focus on two lines of thinking, two lines of energy. The first is the energy of cosmic light, undifferentiated cosmic light, the highest healing light we can bring down. The second line is to bring down the highest energy, the highest light to those people who are now working to solve this problem, which can only be looked at in the way you would look at a runaway nuclear reactor. We are aware that people make mistakes. We want the situation to stop being out of control. We want this oil explosion to stop being out of control.

A MEDITATION ON UNDIFFERENTIATED COSMIC LIGHT

To begin our meditation, I would like you to focus on Mount Fuji, which represents on our Arcturian Tree of Life the highest undifferentiated cosmic light that we can bring down from all sources, including the Central Sun. To the best of your ability, please focus your energy now on Mount Fuji and the cosmic light that is there, the light that can be brought down from the fifth dimension. Take the energy we have brought down from Mount Fuji—from the highest sources, the cosmic light—and direct that light from the etheric crystal in Mount Fuji directly to the Gulf of Mexico and to the area approximately fifty miles offshore from the Louisiana coastline in the Gulf of Mexico. With me now, send and direct the cosmic light, the highest undifferentiated light, to that area so that the rupture can be healed. The oil spill area is like the rupture of a blood vessel, a hemorrhage has been created by humans. It can be healed. Send that light now in this meditation. We will be in silence as we all focus on this.

As a second aspect of this meditation, please connect with the highest cosmic, undifferentiated fifth-dimensional light from the highest source. This light is filled with knowledge and new ideas. This light is filled with creative forces that transcend the normal third-dimensional balance and third-dimensional causal links. Send and direct this highest undifferentiated light now to all of the people—all the scientists, all the geologists—who are working to solve this problem of the oil spill. Send this cosmic light to them now. We will go back into meditation and send them that light as a collective.

For the third part of this meditation, send this highest light to all the animals and plants in this area. This is a very biodiverse area, and its energies are being depleted. Trauma is being experienced in this biosystem. Send this cosmic light now to the biosystem of that area of the Gulf by Louisiana, Mississippi, Alabama, and Florida. The oil spill has affected so much in this area, and it needs a boost of light now. Project this light to them.

I, Juliano, align the starship Athena over this area, and I am sending blue light of the highest level into the area of darkness where the oil is spewing out in order to help close the faucet of this hemorrhage. Try to hold this light and energy as best as you can during this critical time now as we move from a major disaster to the brink of a catastrophe of worldwide proportions. Use this focus to send light to the best of your abilities on the three different levels we talked about, sending higher cosmic light and energy to the whole area. Send a high level of cosmic light to those people who are working to solve the problem, as well as to the plants and animals in that area. Then, finally, you can participate as well in working with me as I send laserlike light to help close the hemorrhage of the Earth's body—a hemorrhage that was caused by humans.

CREATING SACRED SPACES THROUGH ADAM RELATIVITY

In conclusion, I will speak some more about Adam relativity. Adam relativity is based on the principles of biorelativity, but it is also based on the principles of the Tree of Life. The Tree of Life shows that there needs to be a balance between the sacred and the mundane. In Adam relativity, we are able to counterbalance with higher light the contracted areas, the unspiritual areas, the war areas, and the areas of destruction. That is why we want to work with the energies of the planetary cities of light. We will soon be developing a time and an energy to activate the additional twelve cities of light. We appreciate very much and are excited about all the enthusiastic response to the cities of light. This is another example of using the energy of sacred spaces.

The creation of sacred spaces is a major Adam relativity activity that will help to shift the consciousness of humankind. The second activity of Adam relativity is going to be the idea of thought projection and remote energy, sending energy to those people who are in positions of decisionmaking. This is much more complicated because we are dealing with ego energy. Ego energy is like a closed faucet at times. We have to work through the leaders, guides, and teachers. There is a way to send sacred energy and create an energy field around the spaces where leaders live through remote thought projection. This would be similar to creating a halo of light around a place. Remember that remote energy transformation and remote energy sending can be effective. Again, we send cosmic light to the area in the Gulf where the oil spill is. Blessings to all of you planetary healers. I am Juliano.

CHAPTER 22

POLARIZATION INCREASES UNITY CONSCIOUSNESS

Juliano, the Arcturians, Archangel Metatron, and Chief White Eagle

Greetings, I am Juliano. We are the Arcturians. In this lecture we will discuss the nature of polarization. You are all experiencing intense polarizations on Earth, and each of you may have different reactions to the process. But I am sure that you have also asked, "Why am I experiencing these polarizations?" and "What benefit is it to my development to be here on Earth during this intense period?" You also know that many of you have actually chosen to be on Earth at exactly this time. You may find that rather perplexing. Why would you choose to incarnate at a time of intense polarization? And of course the follow-up question is why would the ascension and its energies be occurring during such polarization? I will try to answer these questions, but I first want to establish a foundation for exploring the nature of polarization.

The soul has the opportunity now to do an extreme amount of learning during an incarnation when polarizations are occurring. This explains why, from a soul level, you would choose to incarnate during a period of turmoil and polarization. The learning potential is extraordinary, and if you are honest with yourself, you would agree that you have learned a tremendous amount of new information, new ideas, and new emotional aspects of yourself that you never thought could be possible—and this extraordinary learning has occurred in a brief period of time.

It has occurred, however, during a period in which you have experienced a lot of frustration and perhaps some pain and discouragement. From the ego's perspective, it would not be a pleasant endeavor to live and experience so much polarization. However, from the soul's perspective, this is an extraordinary opportunity. Each of your souls is extremely pleased that you have come into this planet at this time, that you are willing to participate in this Earth energy, and that you are also willing to learn. One way to understand this is to refer to the story of Adam and Eve in the Bible; in that story, what is depicted is a descent from unity into duality, a descent into polarization. Duality and polarization are brother and sister.

What the story does not clearly show is what the divine plan was and is. This divine plan is for those souls who want to evolve and who need to evolve. Souls are being offered this opportunity and are choosing this opportunity to incarnate into duality and experience polarization. It is not that a mistake was made; it is not that for some peculiar reason a woman gave in to some kind of sinful temptation. Rather, it is a divine plan, a divine will, that duality and polarization be experienced so that the soul can evolve.

DUALITY PROVIDES AN OPPORTUNITY TO LEARN

Let us look at the experience of polarization and how it is now affecting the planet. The year 2011 exhibits even more polarization than 2010, yet I can see that by July and August of 2011, a period of harmony and greater unity is going to evolve in each country on this planet, becoming a global movement. This prediction is a very positive outcome of polarization, but at the same time, I have to be clear that one of the main reasons why a greater unity is going to occur is due to the intense fractures, the intense Earth changes, and the intense negative results of polarization. Because of such dramatic polarizations on all levels of the planet, many people, many governments, and many leaders are going to see that a unity position must be attempted, as it is in the interest of everyone. Part of this polarization is demonstrated in the phenomena that you call Earth changes. Earth, as a living spirit, has a feedback-loop mechanism that responds to the events, climate shifts, and energy released on all planetary levels. If an imbalance is occurring on one level, then that imbalance becomes a force for polarization and affects an opposite aspect. That opposite aspect is an expression of Earth that shows that she is attempting to rebalance and recalibrate herself to put into effect the nature of the original polarization, the original duality.

Polarization and duality are the cornerstones of the third dimension, and they can occur on multiple levels—on planetary levels as well as in solar systems on galactic levels throughout the universe. The fifth dimension does not have the polarization that we are describing, and of course from your perspective, you are looking forward—and rightly so—to experiencing a dimension in which polarities and dualities are not the foundation of existence. Yet it is important to note that the duality and polarization you are experiencing on the third dimension is also relative. It is relative to the levels of consciousness and unity that you are able to perceive.

Now, I said that the idea of polarization is an opportunity to learn. What I mean by this is that it is an opportunity the soul uses in its evolution, because it offers you the opportunity to understand unity. You cannot understand unity unless you have understood and experienced polarity and duality. This does not mean that you have to participate in the duality, and I know that many of you wrestle with that. Many of you are struggling in the political, economic, and global arenas because you want to identify and work with the most positive, balanced, and spiritual aspects of polarization. In fact, spirituality is driven by polarization and is becoming a stronger and more powerful force because of intense duality. It is true that there are more spiritual people and energy on this planet than during any previous era, yet because of the high population and the many billions of souls who have incarnated, the percentage of spiritual workers is small compared to the overall planetary population.

Polarization always has the seed of unity in it. Who can be responsible for a new unity? What energy is there in the polarizations, in the potential chaos before this planet, that could possibly bring unity and higher perspective to it? That kernel within the duality is the spiritual energy and the spiritual light from the starseeds. How can you hold that perspective? How can you choose to make sense of this duality-polarization, and how can you also work on the side of unity? The answer is that you can hold the spiritual energy, work with the spiritual side, and seek the global perspective. You should continue to hold both sides of polarity in your worldview, your energy presence, your thoughts, and your prayers, as well as in the lightwork that you are doing. Don't become so polarized that you forget or ignore the negative side of duality.

I know that you do not like the negative side of duality. The side that is not spiritually oriented may be against everything you believe, especially since you can see that the negative side is creating more chaos. Yet being aware of it doesn't mean that you align yourself with that chaos. Understand that all you are seeing, all that is occurring on this planet, is part of the unity, part of the process that is going to unfold into greater evolution, greater awareness, and a greater level of support for the fifth-dimensional transition that is before this planet.

Let me give you another perspective: The duality and polarization experience provides the learning tools and steppingstones for your ascension. I would like you to meditate on that. The experiences of polarity and duality are actually, when used correctly, steppingstones for your ascension. This includes both the personal and planetary ascension. The key is that you must find unity consciousness within this duality and have the right perspective.

WORK BOTH DIMENSIONS TOGETHER

We have introduced the Arcturian Tree of Life, which is based on the Kaballistic Tree of Life, but we have expanded it to include some fifth-dimensional aspects that are necessary for the ascension. That beautiful diagram known as the Tree of Life demonstrates balance and counterbalance. The sphere that is representative of the shimmering light and the shimmering energy is a perfect metaphor for duality and polarization.

The skill that is necessary for you to maintain your higher balance is your ability to shimmer. Shimmering is the ability that is based on the foundation of multidimensional presence. You are in your third-dimensional presence. You are also experiencing a particular duality, namely your fifth-dimensional presence. In some ways, you are polarized from your fifth-dimensional presence. You have before you your higher self, which is more connected to your fifth-dimensional presence, and you also have your ego, which is based on the third dimension. You now have the task of unifying your fifth-dimensional presence with your third-dimensional presence.

The primary reason it is so hard to unify these two aspects is because 90 percent of the time, you are conditioned and cultured to remain in your third-dimensional presence. However, the energy of the fifth dimension is now breaking through the third dimension. It is as if there is an intense curtain or veil between the third and fifth dimensions. That veil makes sure that the fifth-dimensional light and energy remains separated. But now you are moving close to 2012. As you enter 2011, you come closer to an energy point in which the veil that separates the dimensions is cracking. The veil is opening, providing access to this fifth-dimensional energy.

I recommend that you use the fifth-dimensional energy as a support, as a tool to multipresence and to increase your ability to shimmer and work in both dimensions at the same time. You will probably notice that there are many mundane things occurring in your current lifetime. These are normal Earth problems that seemingly have no great spiritual significance and are on a rather low vibration. Yet do not let those mundane experiences take you away from the true reality that is right before you. That true reality is you multipresence, your multidimensional existence, and you are already in two different dimensions.

WHAT CAN DUALITY AND CONFLICT TEACH YOU?

You are seeking to energize and to work with linking your third-dimensional incarnation with the fifth-dimension. You are also concerned with what is going on with the Earth changes. You must ask yourself, "What is the lesson I am supposed to learn from this duality, this polarization?" Please ask yourself that question. As painful as it is to observe, there are still major Earth lessons for each of you.

Some of you have seen this type of polarization in other incarnations. Some of you have been on other planets that have experienced these types of polarizations, and some of you have even seen other planets destroyed from the polarizations. Yet here you are again, in a situation where you see a planet on the brink of possible collapse. You see obvious mistakes being made. You see people who are polarized and who are moving in exactly the wrong direction in this evolutionary change. They are moving away from unity and trying to hold their own power base. They are trying to hold their own perspectives and are actually becoming hateful toward those who seek unity. At the same time, there are those who will use the cloak of unity for evil purposes. This is a difficult lesson for everyone involved. This has been expressed even in the ideas of the false leader coming to Earth who preaches unity but really has different intentions.

The identification with your fifth-dimensional body helps you to transcend this drama, but it also allows you to bring in an energy and a perspective that is not possible from your third-dimensional body. Think of how difficult it is to be on the planet. Think of the people you know who are not oriented toward the ascension or toward spirituality. Think of the people who are not oriented toward new spiritual technology, such as the shimmering work we are doing. Imagine how difficult it would be for them to experience this Earth transition without any spiritual tools.

My overview of 2011 is based on the acceleration of the polarizations and the duality that is already present. In many ways, this appears to be a prediction of more difficult times ahead. This includes more Earth changes, volcanic eruptions, more storms, and more earthquakes. This prediction also includes greater divisions politically and economically, as well as the possibility of more conflict, as it looks like the two sides are moving further apart.

Because of this polarized division, the idea of armed conflict becomes greater. I do not see the use of nuclear weapons in any of the armed conflicts that will occur during 2011, but I do see a significant increase of conflicts. It will reach a point at which people on all sides are going to realize that everything is too unsettled and in too much crisis on this planet and that therefore it is in everyone's interest to try and work toward a greater balance.

I am not saying that people are going to love each other, nor are they going to become great brothers and sisters. It's not going to be one unified family in 2011. In fact, you know how hard it is to forgive after there has been such pain inflicted on one another. However, there does reach a point, believe it or not, when each of the polarized camps will realize that survival depends on working with the opposite side. Now, think about how intensely polarized people are in all aspects. Can you imagine what energy and what events will have to occur in order for those people who are so polarized to begin to think that it is in their best interest for survival that they work with the other side? The answer is that the Earth situation will have to become pretty intense for such a working together to occur. There must be some pretty intense shifts and changes in order for opposing people to begin to think this way. Then you will understand the energy in the nature of polarization.

The idea of polarization is expressed in the Tree of Life. Polarization is part of the description of the universe. It is part of the description of the third dimension. The understanding of the nature of the universe is based in the belief that there are other universes; this is not the only universe. We, the Arcturians, know of ten other universes. Some of those universes did have major collapses and major failures in the dimensions. From that perspective, you can understand that universes are on different levels of evolution, just like planets and humans are also on different levels of evolution. But there eventually does come a unity. So I will ask Archangel Metatron to speak to you more on unity consciousness and the use of that energy.

In closing, I want to assure you that your understanding and your ability to bring fifth-dimensional energy back into your third-dimensional body will be invaluable for you to be able to bear, survive, and keep your sanity. Hold your perspective for your fifth-dimensional self and hold your ability to shimmer. Realize that this experience is providing you with the tools for your ascension and that the doorways and corridors of light are going to open up even wider for those like yourselves. Your experience of polarization is also going to intensify your spiritual work and make you more spiritual. You will see others becoming more polarized. The energy of polarization is also making spiritual light more powerful. I am Juliano, and I now turn you over to Archangel Metatron.

ACCELERATION IN THE FREEWILL ZONE

Greetings, I am Archangel Metatron. The good news for you as you approach 2012 is that spiritual energy and spiritual work are becoming more intense, and you are going to be able to make an evolutionary change in your own development that is great. Perhaps you have understood from the 10–10–10 energy that you will be able to accomplish in a short time what would normally take years— or in some cases, lifetimes. This is acceleration. Acceleration is something that you understood when you came into the duality and the polarizations of this third-dimensional energy. When you talked to your guides and teachers between lifetimes, you understood that Earth is the place to be; this is the time to be here.

The third dimension is a freewill zone, and the freewill zone is a dimension of duality, but it is also a dimension of higher learning, a dimension of intense learning. So renew your commitment to unlocking the codes of ascension.

The codes of ascension are within you. They are within your assemblage point. You are able to operate at all levels interdimensionally, but you especially need fifth-dimensional energies for your physical, emotional, and mental bodies. So listen to these sounds and allow them to renew and to open up the codes of ascension within you. [Sings:] *Kadosh, Kadosh, Kadosh, Adonai Tzevaoth.* Let the codes of ascension remain open now.

I, Archangel Metatron call on the omega light to come down on each of you who are hearing or reading these words. Project this onto the screen of your mind: "Let the codes of ascension remain open for me." [Sings:] "Let the codes of ascension be open for me." See those words emblazoned on the visual screen before your eyes. In particular, try to place that screen directly in front of your third eye. Now I send the holy omega light. *Aur Ha-Kadosh.* Omega light, [chants] ooomega liiight. Let the omega light shine on your affirmation now. Remain open for the keys of ascension. The omega light comes down now and emblazons your screen. Let that powerful affirmation drop deeply into your subconscious. We will go into a short meditation as you hold and keep this light in your subconscious with this powerful affirmation.

The omega light is coming from your soul light. The omega light is unifying your soul energy with your third-dimensional incarnational energy and unifying your affirmation into your third-dimensional unconscious. Your higher self and the omega light together are emblazoning down this affirmation and helping you to hold this powerful message in your subconscious. [Softly sings:] *Omega light—Aur Kadosh . . . Aur Kadosh.*

Let the light of Adam activate within you. It is Adam who experienced the fifth-dimensional garden. His experience is part of your genetic codes. He experienced the unity and higher energy known as the fifth dimension, and his experience is in part of your genetic experience. You are able to open to that immortal light known as Adam Kadmon. Adam Kadmon holds all aspects of the Tree of Life within his energy field. You too can activate the balancing of all aspects of the energy field of the Tree of Life within your aura. And we, with the Arcturians, have placed representative etheric energies in all twelve of the etheric crystals that we have downloaded on Earth. In 2011 these energy centers became more powerful and more magnetic. They have been and will continue to be attracting more people as sources of intense healing and balancing energies. The twelve etheric crystals are the foundational energy points that distribute fifth-dimensional light and fifth-dimensional healing throughout this planet. I am Archangel Metatron. I will now ask Chief White Eagle to speak. *Shalom.*

EXPERIENCE HIGHER WISDOM NOW

Hey ya, ho a hey. Hey ya, ho a hey. Hey ya, ho a hey. Hey ya, ho a hey. Greetings, all my relations. All my words are sacred. I am Chief White Eagle. It is time to reactivate your assemblage point—the point in your energy field that is the valve that controls the perceptual fields you are able to experience. You need to be more open to your assemblage points, because the more open your perceptual fields are, the more you will be able to experience higher wisdom. This is the time on the planet when higher wisdom is necessary, when greater chiefs will speak, and when many people will open to hearing the wisdom of the ancient ones. I call on all of you, all my brothers and sisters, to connect to your ancestral lights. I call on all of you to connect to your grandmothers and grandfathers. I ask you to connect to all of the sacred grandmothers and grandfathers in all of the sacred areas of the world. They all want to work with us to help rebalance Earth.

Yes, there will be a rebalancing of Earth. You are seeing this rebalancing right before your eyes. What is different now is that you have the planetary cities of light and spiritual foundations that Earth will respond to. You have unity of all the star families and also the masters and teachers of the ascended races who are willing to work and create a new balance on Earth. From my perspective, I find that joyful. There is a new energy and balance coming to Earth. The galactic kachina is coming. White Buffalo Calf Woman is coming. The entrances for the spiritual ancient ones are opening now. These polarizations are creating a new corridor that will allow all of the great spiritual masters, teachers, mothers and fathers, and grandmothers and grandfathers to come to the planet to merge with the third dimension. [Sings:] *Hey ya, ho a hey. Hey ya, ho a hey. Hey ya, ho a hey. Hey ya, ho a hey. Hey ya, ho a hey. Hey ya, ho a hey.*

The teachings of Earth as a living spirit will become more powerful widely received. The abilities of the ascended masters in relating to Mother Earth, including the teaching about biorelativity, will be welcome. Out of desperation will come a new openness to other perspectives. I see a great opening for the Spirit of Earth to be received into the group consciousness and group energies of the starseeds. I find that to be great news. I find that to be spiritually uplifting for all of my family and all my brothers and sisters. Do not walk in fear; walk as spiritual warriors on this path before you. In some cases, you might think that there will be great judgments that are being unleashed on Earth, but from our perspective, this time on Earth is viewed as a rebalancing for greater unity. The ultimate unity that we seek with you is unity with the fifth dimension. I am Chief White Eagle. All my relations, *ho!*

CHAPTER 23

PLANETARY MERIDIANS AND EARTH HEALING

Juliano, the Arcturians, and Helio-ah

Greetings, I am Juliano, and we are the Arcturians. The concept of planetary healing expressed during the 1980s and 1990s has come again to the forefront in recent years. In the spiritual world, the year 2011 was designated as the year for the planetary healer and, of course, for planetary healing. You as a Group of Forty, starseeds, and lightworkers have incarnated onto this planet at this time to participate as planetary healers—a designation that is well known among the ascended masters and throughout the galaxy. It is a new term for Earth that has only just recently, perhaps in the past six years, emerged in the consciousness of lightworkers. Now as you move through this year of planetary healing and the planetary healer, there will be greater need, visibility, and opportunity to exert your skills and talents for planetary healing.

To explore concepts of planetary healing, we will need to discuss the Earth's meridians. We have compared the way we see Earth to the perspective ancient Chinese medicine has of the human body. We have suggested that there are many parallels between the meridian systems of the human body and the meridian or ley lines of Earth. Some people have estimated that there might be 3,000 major and minor meridians in the human body. While there are several major meridians in the human body that are well known and usually used for introductory and basic healing, as you get to be more specific and more knowledgeable in Chinese medicine, you sometimes go into a more specific healing and a more specific meridian. Let's look at the human ear from the perspective of Chinese medicine, for example. The human ear occupies one of the smallest portions of the skin of the human body, yet it contains numerous meridian points. There are even some aspects in Chinese medicine that focus solely on the ears to effect changes in the energy system of the whole body.

THE NEED TO HEAL BLOCKAGES IN EARTH MERIDIANS

I bring up this point as a comparison to the Earth meridians. When you look at a planet as large as Earth, you might become overwhelmed by the size of the meridians and concerned about how one might be able to travel or work with those meridian lines that go from the top of Earth all the way to the bottom. Further complicating this situation, some of the meridians are over the ocean. As you know, much of your planet is covered by water. This means that some of the necessary work might require people to go into the ocean which, of course, would be impossible or extremely difficult. There are similar issues caused by the fact that some meridians go through deserts or through countries where there is warfare; lightworkers might not have access to these areas.

These are not insurmountable problems. However, they do indicate that we need a different way of looking at planetary healing using the meridians. If there might be 3,000 meridians in the human body, how many could there possibly be on the planet? They would be too numerous to easily count, although we might say without exaggeration that there are over 100,000 meridians on Earth. And even if you were to only focus on the primary meridians on Earth, you would find that they also are very numerous. There might even be disagreement among lightworkers about which meridians to work with first.

Of course, all of this is based on the hypothesis that the Earth's energy channels are similar to the human body. Remember, the basic assumption in Chinese medicine is that when the meridians are open and there is good flow, then there is health. When there are blockages or congestion in these meridians, then there is illness. In Chinese medicine, restoring health involves unblocking congested areas. As you know, this can be accomplished through acupuncture or acupressure in certain areas.

This analogy of meridians and blockages in the Earth is only an analogy. I am not saying that it fits exactly, but it is a close approximation to the reality of Earth energies. Let's look at some of the ocean currents as an example, which most certainly represent meridians on the Earth. We should be concerned about blockages in ocean currents caused by pollution or congestion (sometimes called conveyor-belt flow) related to oil discharges, especially since there have been numerous oil spills in the oceans like the one in the Gulf of Mexico and some of that oil has moved into major ocean currents. This oil definitely has the potential to create partial blockages in Earth's energy channels.

Just as the human body tries to rebalance and heal itself, the Earth also works to heals and rebalance itself. The Earth is an energy system, a living planetary spirit. The planet has a complex feedback system. As a living planetary spirit, it has achieved a high energetic charge that allows human life to exist. We know that there is a definite balance that the planet must maintain in order for human life to exist upon it, and we can assume that the Earth as a planetary spirit wants to hold the human life on its surface. The Earth therefore self-regulates to maintain the narrow band of climate required for human life. This self-regulation includes many complex factors, such as keeping the oxygen and nitrogen levels in the air in correct balance. There are many planets in the galaxy that have life, some far less evolved than life on this planet. The fact that Earth has achieved this status puts the Blue Jewel in a highly elevated position. Not only does the Earth have this fantastic ability to self-regulate and sustain multitudes of different types of life, but it also can sustain human life. This is a fantastic achievement for a planet.

Yet self-regulation has limits, and the many different problems on Earth affect those self-regulation systems. The Earth only has a narrow band of regulation that it can hold in order to keep the life forms here, but it, too, can reach a point where it can't maintain this necessary balance. How close are we to going over the top and breaking that self-regulation capacity? How close are we to a point where the Earth as a living spirit cannot self-regulate to maintain life? How close are we to the limit, the threshold, of Mother Earth? If Earth were to pass that threshold, then the Earth would not be able to sustain the necessary climate to sustain life. Therefore, in all of our discussions of planetary healing, we come to this point: The planet is in crisis. The Earth is closer than most people want to acknowledge to the threshold of collapse. At the point when it crosses that threshold, it could require centuries for the balance to be re-established.

Yet Earth does have the ability to recalibrate to sustain life. Humanity may force Earth to the point at which life as you know it could end on the planet, but that would not mean that all human life in the future would disappear. Some of you have read books and predictions from prophets about future life on Earth. There are people who have seen life three of four centuries from now. Some predictions portrayed people living a very primitive life. Although Earth does have the ability to recalibrate herself, the process could take centuries or longer.

Planetary healers seek to understand the rebuilding process. They seek methods to recalibrate and reconstitute the feedback system before true disaster strikes, and their efforts will help the biosphere so Earth can avoid a total collapse. Planetary healers work to treat and heal the Earth so she can maintain the self-regulation system necessary for the balance of human life. Continuing this comparison of Earth's body with the human body, planetary healers know that one way to improve the self-regulating system is through working with the Earth's meridians. The next obvious questions relate to which meridians the planetary healers should work with and how they should proceed with the acupuncture work on the Earth's meridians.

Earth Meridians and Energy Points

To address the question of the meridians first, in our review and scientific research, we have come up with a new system to implement on Earth. This new system is based on a new meridian system: We know that in acupuncture, the energy flow of meridians is often seen to be in the etheric energy field of the aura. It is in fact the source, the origin, of the energy flow. That energy flow from the aura is manifested in the energy flow of the body, and you can trace the lines of the meridian flows by touching the human body itself.

The human body is multidimensional—both third- and fourth-dimensional—and its system is based in the aura. The fifth-dimensional body is what we want to work with in quantum healing, because higher-energy acupuncture occurs in the etheric bodies. In healing work, we, the Arcturians, are seeking to help you bring down the fifth-dimensional energy into your third-dimensional body. To that end we have done specific exercises with you, including shimmering. We can also work with acupuncture energy-work systems for healing. That is certainly an avenue we are willing to explore with you because we know lightworkers need higher-level fifth-dimensional quantum healing.

Now, let us use this information about the human body to talk about the planetary healing of Earth's body. We are working with the Earth's meridians from a fifth-dimensional perspective, and we have downloaded twelve etheric crystals into Earth. Those twelve etheric crystals represent the source points—the feed lines or the new meridian lines for the new fifth-dimensional Earth and for the healing of the third-dimensional Earth. It is not necessary to learn where the old meridians of the planet are. I am now suggesting to you a simpler and more direct way of doing the planetary healing work. We have introduced this potential to you over the years in a specific and deliberate way, focusing on those twelve powerful energy points where we have placed etheric crystals. [See the map in the back of the book.] We are suggesting that new energy meridians for Earth can be created by connecting these twelve crystals.

People have suggested to us and to the channel that these twelve crystals are not equidistantly placed around the Earth, and that are other powerful points that are not included. They ask, "How can it be, Juliano, that these twelve specific etheric crystal points you have set can be so powerful and representative of the twelve etheric source lines necessary for the planetary healing?" In response, I need to point out that we are working in holographic energy and doing specific holographic work. We have chosen these sites for their particular quantum access to the whole planetary energy paradigm. When you do meridian work on a human body, you often go first to a point that has a positive flow of energy and then bring down the energy from there into the blocked area. In other words, you don't start in the area that has the most congestion. That is the area where you are not getting energy. You go to an area close by that has more energy flowing and send that positive high energy into the blocked area.

If you look at the etheric crystal at Lago Puelo, Argentina, you can see that this area represents one of the purest energy points on the planet. If you are going to do meridian work and want to send energy out to a ley line, this would be a wonderful place to start. It is an ancient site, one that does not have a lot of "baggage" in terms of misuse. There is not much pollution in Lago Puelo, for example. Thus is why we have downloaded an etheric crystal from the crystal temple into Lago Puelo. Every one of the twelve points has similarly pure energy. The points have all been chosen because they represent high clarity and energy. One of the main goals of our work with these twelve etheric crystals is to establish a base in which these points continue to be protected. They will remain activated because many lightworkers have access to these points and continue to visit and work with these areas.

Now we can start, with your help, to create new energy lines from there. Say, for example, we wanted to send out an energy line from Lago Puelo to the Bodensee crystal, located in central Europe at the juncture of Switzerland, Austria, and Germany. What I would like you to visualize is that there is a new fifth-dimensional meridian connecting Lago Puelo to the Bodensee. The meridian is interactive with the third-dimensional meridians on Earth. You can make that connection by creating a powerful, flowing energy channel. Let us visualize another new energy connection. This time you want to go from the Bodensee to Montserrat. Create and visualize a new energy flow line as before. Now if you want to go from Montserrat to Mount Fuji, you create another line. You can create lines connecting each etheric crystal area to another.

Sending Energy to Jerusalem

We want to introduce another idea. The next step in the new meridian line can be from Lago Puelo to Jerusalem. It is true that there is no Arcturian etheric crystal in Jerusalem, yet we know that in many ways Jerusalem represents one of the highest spiritual points on the planet. The energy from Lago Puelo can create a new meridian that would bring fifth-dimensional energy and light to the Jerusalem area. Let us say, for example, that we wanted to send higher energy to Jerusalem. We particularly wanted to focus on peace or calmness with fifth-dimensional balance in Israel and in Jerusalem. Then we can take an energy point from Bodensee, from Mount Fuji, and an energy line from Lago Puelo and channel that line of energy to Jerusalem. I am asking you now to visualize that energy line and that the first level of that energy line is going through the etheric Earth energy field.

As you know, acupressure works with the etheric energy field of the human body, and that field can be seven to eight inches away from the body. Now, we can visualize that the energy field of Earth also is a certain comparable distance away from the planet. If the human body's energy field is seven to eight inches away from the human body, then how distant might the etheric energy field be from the Earth? Even though the energy field of the Earth can sometimes extend fifty to sixty miles above the planet, for the official work that we are doing, we will choose a distance of one mile above the Earth as representing the etheric energy field.

Some people might ask what path to follow through countries or across oceans. Remember, the fastest speed in the universe is the speed of thought. When you project a line, especially an energy line that is in the etheric world, you do it at the speed of thought. The line automatically follows the route that it needs to follow. There may be congested points that block the flow of light and energy. Say, for example, you are in the Bodensee area and you become aware of people who have thoughts about creating unrest, so they form a blocking energy field. You can create a counterbalance from that blocked energy. This is a key point. We are not suggesting that the old energy is going to be wiped out or that the old lines are suddenly going to be erased. What we are suggesting is that a newer fifth-dimensional energy line is created, and in some cases this new line will be a counterbalance to the old, blocked lines.

Remember, we are talking about the new age and the new fifth-dimensional Earth. A new energy line possesses a quantum power that overrides lower energy and therefore instills a newer light field into the place. I began working with you on the direct meridian to Jerusalem and I also suggest that we work primarily with the four crystals in Lago Puelo, the Bodensee, Monserrat, and Mount Fuji. Using thought projection, you can also go to the crystal closest to you, and from there you can project a new meridian line to Jerusalem. Please hold that thought for a moment or two.

There are two key points of which we need to remind you. First, there are ways to accelerate these energy lines and make them more powerful. One way is to have a group of people in Jerusalem who know how to receive this energy frequency. It is important in sending energy that there is someone on the other side who knows how to receive it. That is one factor that makes the energy more powerful. Second, it would be wonderful if there were a group of people, say in Lago Puelo, who gathered to send energy at the same time the group in Jerusalem would be receiving it. This would make the process more powerful. Of course, we know there are many issues in organizing people for such events, but you are planetary healers, you understand about how this process works, and you have the ability to organize these exercises throughout the year.

There are other areas on Earth that need this type of work because of great energy leakages that occur in the Earth's energy field exactly the way they do in your human energy field. Some of you may have worked with people who have holes in their auras or on their meridians and suffer from serious deficiencies. Quite frankly, almost every part of the Earth has some type of deficiency in its energy system. I don't need to go through all of the issues that confront the environment. Some are caused by humanity—in particular through pollution and radiation leaks—some are caused by extra-solar energy sources that can seriously deplete Earth's your energy field, and some are caused by the electromagnetic energy and high activity of the Sun. Part of the energy work for the planetary healers to close those leaks, and this can be visualized directly. The obvious holes right now are over Iraq, Afghanistan, and that whole area. We know there is a hole there because tremendous resources and effort are expended there and nothing is accomplished. That tells you that there is an energy hole there and that hole needs to be closed.

The exercise we just did with Jerusalem could also be done with Afghanistan and Iraq. The nature of the human mind is such that when humans see a hole, they want to put more wood or more paste or something to block the hole. If you are on a ship and there is a hole, you keep on trying to fix it. Yet once the hole starts leaking too much, patching may not work. That is a hard lesson for humankind, and that is why we have pointed out on numerous occasions that intervention energy must come from the fifth dimension. There is not enough third-dimensional energy to accomplish the task; third-dimensional energy is not going to work to heal the Earth. If it could, it would have by now. A more powerful intervention is needed! Healing requires fifth-dimensional downloading.

You might ask who is in place in Afghanistan to receive fifth-dimensional energy. There may be no one, so you need a more intense fifth-dimensional factor in planetary healing in such a situation. For that explanation, I would like Helio-ah to speak with you, and she will talk with you about the Iskalia mirror. Blessings to you all in the year of the planetary healer. I am Juliano.

Using the Planetary Healing Chamber to Imagine a Better Future

Greetings, lightworkers and Group of Forty members. I am Helio-ah. Blessings to you and to all of my friends throughout the planet who are so dedicated to holographic light and healing. We are excited that there are so many of you now who understand the nature of holographic healing and that you want to apply these principles to planetary healing. We have described the holographic healing chamber, a fifth-dimensional healing vessel available now to all starseeds for personal healing. These small personal healing chambers look something like a telephone booth. You go into the chamber and you see a highly advanced computer that contains images and events of your current life on Earth and also all projected events for your future life on Earth. In its advanced format the computer contains previous lifetimes, past incarnations, and—in the more advanced models—the energy for life-between-life work. Those who have had the opportunity to work directly with it have benefitted greatly in being able to do their personal healing in the holographic healing chamber.

The holographic planetary healing chamber is based on the principle of the personal healing chamber. We described the personal healing chamber first to familiarize you with the process. Now you can apply the principles of personal holographic healing to planetary healing. The personal holographic healing chamber has one seat for one person, and it has a dial. When you turn the dial to the left, it goes into the past, and images of the past appear on the screen. When you turn it to the right, images of the future appear on the screen. For holographic healing, you can borrow energy from your future self and download it into the present self. In the future self, you are all ascended masters. In the future you have all been healed. Now you can bring the energy and light from your future self into the present.

This can be done because basically the past, present, and future linear time frame that you are using to function in the third dimension is an illusion. The true reality is that your future, your present, and your past are all interacting and it is more like a circle. You can connect with different parts of the circle and bring that energy into the present. Remember, one of the beautiful techniques for holographic healing focuses on visualizing healing your traumas from the past. These past images can be recreated into positive healing images. For example on a personal level, if you had a past, we can create an image where an angel comes in and helps you, creating a new harmony and an image of balance and healing. Then we download that image into your subconscious so that you actually have a new healing image from the past.

In planetary healing, we set up the chamber exactly like the personal chamber. I want you to imagine that the planetary healing chamber is in a large auditorium. This auditorium would have to be the size of a large theater—in some cases, it could be a gigantic theater with a screen a mile wide. The holographic healing chamber on our starship Athena is exactly that size, and while I am not suggesting that you try to build this holographic healing chamber on the Earth, models of it could be duplicated in movie theaters on Earth.

Like the personal healing chamber, we turn the dial to the right to go into the future. We can work with the future in two different ways. One way we could look to the future is to see many dire predictions, for example for December 21, 2012—this is a favorite future point for many humans. You see many images on television depicting that day with volcanic eruptions, violent overthrows of governments, tsunamis, and many other things. Those images are actually going into the unconscious and the subconscious of Earth, which is unfortunate. Yet if we look a different way and create new images of December 21 to 22, 2012 in the holographic planetary healing chamber, these images could begin to affect the future.

Let us visualize December 22, 2012, as a new dawning of understanding and a new balance. Let's visualize a change in how people deal with polarities. We see changes in how people deal with pollution, clean up the environment, and remove nuclear dumpsites. Holes in the aura over Iran, Iraq, Afghanistan, and even over the United States will be healed and sealed. You can project and create those images on the screen, and those images can be shown in theaters around the planet. Imagine planetary healers beginning to submit these images to theaters and these new images being put into films. Now imagine that millions of people see them. In the planetary healing chamber, many people then project themselves to the Starship Athena and begin to hold that image and bring that energy from the future into the present. Oh, my friends, there is so much more to explain on this. I am so excited that you are beginning to activate your planetary healing abilities. There is so much work to do.

Finally, I want to explain to you again about the Iskalia mirror. The Earth has a main meridian point that connects her with the galactic sources is the North Pole. In Chinese medicine, the crown chakra connects to the higher universal light. The crown of Earth corresponds to the North Pole. We have described that when many of you are ascending, you travel etherically to the North Pole. We have placed an etheric mirror there. That mirror varies its altitude over the pole. Sometimes it is several miles above it and sometimes it comes closer. This special mirror brings down higher galactic light, especially light from the Central

Sun. It is like a collector that intensifies the light. You can direct light from the Iskalia mirror to different areas on the planet and into different etheric crystals to increase their power. We will be working with you specifically to accelerate your planetary healing skills and direct you in new activities for planetary work. I love you all. I am Helio-ah. We are the Arcturians.

CHAPTER 24

STABILIZING ENERGY AFTER EARTHQUAKES

Juliano and the Arcturians

Greetings, this is Juliano, and we are the Arcturians. There are a great deal of Earth changes occurring in all directions, both on the political and on the geological levels. In this biorelativity exercise, our focus is to provide energy stabilization and light to Christchurch, New Zealand, due to the devastating earthquake that recently occurred there. To this end, we are going to connect to Lake Taupo on the North Island, which is the home of one of the beautiful crystals—a very powerful crystal.

New Zealand is itself a very active geological area in the world—very close indeed to Mother Earth, to the Inner Earth, and to the primordial energies that are connected with involvement evolution of Earth's crust and energy field. Given the closeness to which New Zealand lies to this energy, it serves a much higher purpose for the overall geological evolution of the Earth. Please also remember that New Zealand contains some of the purest waterways that are home to many great fish species, and there are many protective coves and waterways that are sacred in these two beautiful islands that compose New Zealand.

FORMING A POWERFUL TRIANGULAR CONNECTION

Today we are going to focus directly on Christchurch. I, Juliano, call on and raise the etheric crystal at Lake Taupo on the North Island. At the same time, we will raise the etheric crystal at the Grose Valley, Australia, along with the crystal at Mount Shasta, California. These three crystals are now above their respective areas at a distance of at least one to one and a half miles. The crystal at Lake Taupo is one and a half miles above the lake, giving it a direct route to shine the energy of harmony and stabilization to the Christchurch area. The crystals of Mount

Shasta and the Grose Valley will act as supportive crystals, supporting the intense energy going into and emanating from the Lake Taupo crystal.

Using the highest arcan power within you, now send an energy of stabilization, harmony, and divine healing light. Send this energy to the Lake Taupo crystal directly from your third eye at the level of eight to ten arcans of healing thought power. Direct that healing arcan energy and thought healing energy to the Lake Taupo crystal now. [Pause.] The light that is emanating from the crystal is being amplified by your thoughts and by your arcan energy, and it is now being downloaded into the center of Christchurch—right into the center of what is called Grand Hotel Chancellor, right into the square by the cathedral that has collapsed, and right into the center of town. This energy from the crystal at Lake Taupo is very powerful. Continue to send your healing energies of arcan light and power from your third eye to the Lake Taupo crystal.

Now let us focus on the light from the Mount Shasta, directing our thoughts to the Mount Shasta crystal for a brief moment and sending the same light to this crystal. You can feel the reflective power coming from you to the Mount Shasta crystal. That energy of arcan power, healing, and stabilization is now doubling as it goes through the Mount Shasta crystal directly to the Lake Taupo crystal and from there is downloaded to the Christchurch area I have mentioned. Now send healing thoughts from your third eye to the Grose Valley crystal in the Blue Mountains near Sydney. That healing thought is coming into the Grose Valley crystal at ten arcans of thought power. It is being reflected now from that crystal at a higher amplification back to the Lake Taupo crystal and then downloading from the Lake Taupo crystal right into the center of Christchurch where the earthquake occurred. The light is percolating the whole Inner Earth in a circle underneath the whole city, stabilizing and diminishing the aftershocks.

It is also creating a great source of light energy that encircles the whole city so that its people feel the upliftment of this light. The people of this city show courage and great fortitude as they work to complete the difficult tasks ahead: rebuilding their beautiful city, rescuing those still alive, treating the injured, and restoring the city economically. They approach these tasks with high strength and bravery in the great Kiwi tradition. The power of the whole country is being unified and strengthened by this tragic event. Once again, the light from the two crystals is bouncing back, reflecting back into Lake Taupo and then spreading around the whole island—the southern island particularly—and filling up and stabilizing the energy forces in Christchurch.

Telepathically, simultaneously hold both that thought and the light again. Not only are you multidimensional, but you can multitask, sending out of one part of your third-eye thought energy right to the Lake Taupo crystal and sending light to the crystal at Mount Shasta with a second part of your third eye. That light is reflected back to Lake Taupo. You can also simultaneously send light and high healing thoughts out of a third part of your third eye to the Grose Valley crystal, forming this powerful triangular connection of high-frequency healing and stabilizing light, filling the area, the people, and the atmosphere with light. You can see that the atmosphere is holding beautiful weather patterns, and you also personally experience a powerful upliftment through this multitasking with your third eye. So you are very active, sending out high arcan healing power. As your third eye opens up more, you can also download light through your crown chakra, if you allow it.

CONNECTING WITH ANCIENT ENERGY IN HEALING

I am Juliano, and I am in the starship Athena above Christchurch. We are soothing all those who have passed on to other realms from this quake, helping them in their transformation and transferring of all those souls who need to pass on. There is a great awareness of the ancestral energies on the islands, and the great healing spirits of the grandfathers and grandmothers are also powerfully activated now.

I am directing the entry level of this light, and I am connecting with each of you now telepathically in your lightwork, in your work of biorelativity, and in your desire to send healing and light of harmony to a place in great need of upliftment. At the same time as this earthquake has occurred, a great opening has also been forming, creating a dimensional shift in Christchurch that is opening up great dimensional light from the higher levels. What is so beautiful about this event is that the Christchurch area is receiving a powerful energy and powerful healing. There is a great openness now that this light is spinning around the whole country, not only in Christchurch and the South Island but also in the North Island.

Direct your attention now to Lake Taupo in the North Island: The crystal light is now an omnidirectional, omnipresent light that is not only going directly to Christchurch but is also being transmitted omnidirectionally around the whole two islands, simultaneously bringing in a spiritual light stream of higher dimensional accessibility. It is a wonderful experience for all beings in this deep connective exercise. This biorelativity healing light is not only activating and helping to heal and stabilize Christchurch and the energy in the South Island but it is also activating each of you as participants in an international and powerful biorelativity healing exercise.

Each of you feels the power of your third eye and the increased arcan power of your ability to amplify your healing thoughts and healing energies. You feel a special connection to the primordial Earth energy field that is there in the South Island and in all of New Zealand. This is deep, ancient energy we are connecting with that is millions of years old. We are helping to calm the energy down in a miraculous way—in a quantum way.

A Golden Halo of Light

I, Juliano, send quantum healing light into the Lake Taupo crystal. [Tones:] *Ooohhh.* I send the omega light; the great healing higher omega light is now being downloaded into this Lake Taupo crystal as well. It is activating what I call "backscatter." The healing light and the healing energy that is being emitted by the Lake Taupo crystal is so intense that there is a backscatter of light frequency coming back and returning into these crystals from Mount Shasta and Grose Valley. From those crystals, the backscatter is also coming back into you. Continue this great stream of connective light. More light is being committed for you and the crystal to be received in Christchurch, and the backscatter is sending more light back into the other two crystals and then coming back into you. This allows you to be able to increase the arcan power of your healing thoughts from ten to fifteen arcans of light.

A golden halo of light—a ring of light—is now over Christchurch, and the inhabitants of that city may even report that they see a golden ring of light around the Sun as the sunset approaches. The ring of light will create a beautiful, fine sunset and sunset halos around the city in many different sections of the sky. This is the aftereffect of our work of sending this light of healing energy. Visualize the beautiful sunset now coming here with its golden halo and beautiful rings that appear in the sky at night. This will signify that traces of the healing energies and healing light that we are sending there now are still in the area.

I will leave the Lake Taupo, Grose Valley, and Mount Shasta crystals up for the next thirty-six hours so that they can continue to be supporting to this area. Remember that when you are doing these healing exercises with these crystals, it is always useful to bring the crystals up in threes so they can form the powerful triangular connections that we have all used and benefited from this afternoon. This healing energy is directly going deep into the Earth at Christchurch. The beautiful cathedral will be rebuilt again in honor of those who have passed on and in honor of the great spiritual light and energy and the great spirit of unity and unification that is coming to Christchurch and that has already be activated. I am Juliano, and we are the Arcturians. Blessings.

CHAPTER 25

HEALING ENVIRONMENTAL WOUNDS

Juliano and the Arcturians

Greetings. I am Juliano, and we are the Arcturians. The state of the environment and the biosphere stems from an interaction between humans and Earth. We have noted that humankind is the only species on the planet that controls all of life and has influence over all life on this planet. Never before in the history of Earth has one species had this much power to control and determine who will survive on this planet—and this includes the animals and the plants, all mammals, all fish, and all insects.

So now as we are looking at this catastrophe in Japan (and I am referring to the nuclear catastrophe), we have a greater awareness of how humans can destroy life and the biosphere on the planet. It is imperative that we try and use our powers of biorelativity to bring together all of the energies, all of the spiritual powers, and all of the thought powers of the starseeds so that this catastrophe at the nuclear plants does not worsen, does not increase, and does not emit more harmful radiation. It is our understanding that nuclear energy and nuclear radiation has the potential for creating a rift or a separation in the fabric of the third dimension. This rift in the fabric of the aura of Earth can cause a leakage in the life-force energy of the third dimension. It has to be corrected. It must be sealed so that the powerful third-dimensional life forces and the life-force energy that keeps the third dimension alive can remain intact.

I, Juliano, call on the etheric crystal of Mount Fuji as well as the other eleven etheric crystals to remain in a high position above their respective geological places. I have asked that each of you continue to send your powerful telepathic thoughts of cooling the nuclear reactors, bringing them into a stasis, bringing them into a state of rest and a lower energy vibration so that this nuclear energy of the reactors can be calmed down greatly. It is incredibly vital that you do this, for the potential of the disaster from the nuclear reactors is greater than the terrible tsunami and the terrible earthquake.

It is important that we understand that the disasters that come about from human action can often create situations that will make the naturally occurring disasters on Earth worse. So I ask that each of you send your powerful thoughts of healing, calmness, and cooling to the reactors. Send those thoughts and that power to the Mount Fuji crystal, and then the Mount Fuji crystal will be able to amplify your powerful thoughts. At the same time, I am using the Arcturian crystal in the fifth dimension above the Arcturian lake, with the Arcturian temple as a second balance. I am also using the Mount Shasta crystal as a third balance so that you can use these three crystals in your multidimensional thinking—the Arcturian etheric crystal in the crystal lake, the Mount Shasta crystal, and the Mount Fuji crystal—and forward your thoughts of healing and the balance to these nuclear reactors so that they are calmed down and brought under control. Use this terminology today: "Allow the reactors to be brought under control now." [Tones:] *Ooohhhmmm. Ooohhhmmm.*

I, Juliano, am also sending omega light into the Mount Fuji crystal to intensify the arcan energy of your thoughts and to intensify the light, and I am also sending omega light directly into northeastern Japan to create calming energy. *Oommeeegaaa liighhht, ooomeeeegaaa liigghht, ooomegaaaa liiighhht.* This is a special vibration of omega light, because that omega light is a fifth-dimensional light and energy that transcends the normal logic of the third dimension. So remember that if you hear any reports of dire consequences and inabilities, this is all based on third-dimensional thinking. The energy we are now sending directly through the Mount Fuji crystal is the omega energy, a fifth-dimensional energy that transcends logic and all normal rational thinking and allows what you might call a miracle. I call on that quantum healing light. Now the omega light is being transmitted through the Mount Fuji crystal directly to all of these reactors and to all of the areas in northeastern Japan and all over Japan that are affected by these catastrophes. [Tones:] *Ooomeeegaaa liiighhht. Oooooooooomegaaaa lighhht.*

The crystal at Lago Puelo is sending a powerful healing force of light directly now to the Mount Fuji crystal and to all of the other crystals, and they are all interacting and connecting in a very powerful way. I, Juliano, am now aligning our starship Athena directly over the nuclear energy plants, and we are sending the quantum healing light to all of the workers, all of the scientists, and all of the physicists who are working to solve this problem and to bring all of the nuclear reactors under control. Send the quantum healing light and the omega light now, as we go into a deeper meditation. The omega light is also filled with quantum healing light that transcends the third dimension and the logic of the third dimension so that the divine intervention and the divine miracle of light energy fills this whole area. It is filling the nuclear reactors and all of the people who are trying to solve this problem. [Tones:]*Ooomeegaaa liggghhht.* Hold this energy. You are doing this well—hold this light. Now Chief White Eagle is also going to join in this powerful healing circle of biorelativity. I am Juliano.

CALLING ON ANCIENT POWERS OF WISDOM AND KNOWLEDGE

Heya hoya hey. Heya hoya hey. Heya hoo. Hey ho. Greetings, I am Chief White Eagle. I meet you with an open heart as we all share in this powerful energy in the powerful energy of Earth healing. We all share in our desire to see this dangerous situation in Japan brought under control immediately. The grandfather and grandmother spirits, the ancient spirits on Mount Fuji, are all joining us now as we sit in a huge etheric circle above the northeastern area of Japan. We are using our healing powers to bring the Earth energies there into a calmness. I, Chief White Eagle, am now going to say a special prayer for the healing of this area.

Father/Mother Creator of All, we are gathered here at this time to pray for the divine intervention of the highest spiritual possibilities to bring this situation into balance into a harmony and into a control. We are praying for wisdom and abilities for all who are working now to solve this problem for the greatest good of Japan and the greatest good of planet Earth, for we know of the dangers before us, but we also know of the great healing abilities of the ancient ones and of the great healing abilities of the planet. So we call especially on the higher powers of divine wisdom and great knowledge. We call on the crystal of the Bodensee, which is filled with wisdom and the divine energies of higher knowledge. We call on Lake Moraine, the holder of great knowledge and great reason, and we send the energies directly into the Mount Fuji area so that Mount Fuji can send divine wisdom and divine knowledge to all who are working to solve this difficult problem.

Mother Earth, we are going to work to correct and to hold powerful biorelativity healing light over northeastern Japan and all of Japan that is now suffering this great tragedy and catastrophe. *Heya ho. Heya ho. Heya ho. Heya ho. Heya ho.* White Buffalo Woman is here and will speak a few words with you as the powerful healing energies and light bring forth many great masters and teachers and prophets to help in this situation. Make no mistake, this is a very dangerous time for the entire planet, so let White Buffalo Calf Woman speak with you.

WHITE BUFFALO LIGHT

Greetings, dear ones, lovers of the planet of Earth. You are all coming into an understanding of the power of your energy, helping to bring down many powerful teachers, masters, and spirit guides in all of your work. And now at the height of a dangerous time on Earth, we are working with you to help rebalance the energies in northeastern Japan and all of Japan, for it is crucial to the balance of our beloved planet that these nuclear accidents be brought under control and into harmony with Earth.

I, White Buffalo Calf Woman, send the white, etheric light of the buffalo directly over northeastern Japan now. The powers of white buffalo contain a divine healing light. See and visualize a white buffalo in the ether over northeastern Japan now. Visualize the white buffalo transmitting powerful light to help balance the Earth. These Earth energies can assist in bringing this nuclear problem under control, so we will go into meditation and visualize the white buffalo and her energy field over northeastern Japan now. [Long pause.] The white buffalo is transmitting a powerful healing white light all over northeastern Japan and especially directing a calming energy to these nuclear reactors. The energy of calming is filling the area with the white buffalo light. [Tones:] *Hey ya ya ya. Ola himala koye yesh mo-ish la.*

I, White Buffalo Calf Woman, am sending this white light to help to seal the rift that has formed above northeastern Japan now because of the nuclear problems. We are sending this light to hold the biosphere intact so there is no leakage from the biosphere over northeastern Japan. All needed healers on this planet are rising to this call to send their powerful healing energies. All shamans and all native peoples are hearing this call to send their powerful healing thought and energy to this area now so that this disaster does not worsen. I am happy that you are joining us and using your healing powers, and I am glad that the white buffalo is becoming known to all of you as a healing force for Mother Earth. That is the true meaning of the arrival of the white buffalo—a new healing light is available and can be used by the great peoples who desire a new harmony and balance to come to your beautiful planet. I am White Buffalo Calf Woman. Archangel Metatron will now speak briefly.

VISUALIZATION FOR HEALING ENERGY

Greetings, I am Archangel Metatron. I am sending the healing light, and I am also sending the sacred energy of the prayer *El na Refa na la* to Japan. Join me in thinking and hearing these words. Sending these healing words will set into motion a powerful healing vibration to this area, particularly to the nuclear reactors and the whole area around these reactors, around this nuclear area that is in a vibrational distortion. We must bring this whole area into a vibrational harmony. [Sings:] "*El na Refa na la*, Japan. Let the healing begin now. *El na Refa na la* to Japan." [Tones.] This situation will be brought under control with the minimum amount of harmful damage possible. The biosphere will heal itself. There are many guides and teachers overseeing the situation and the recovery as well. I am Metatron. I return you to Juliano.

✳ ✳ ✳

Greetings, I am Juliano again. Know that the etheric crystal will continue to send energy and light for the next twenty-four hours. Use the power of this energy, of these crystals, of the white buffalo, and of the omega light. I am also activating the ring of ascension light to be in alignment over Japan right now in order to maximize the healing thoughts and the healing energy of the ascended masters and all of you planetary healers. So now the maximum energy and spiritual light, the most divine telepathic healing light, the omega light, the quantum healing light, the light of the wisdom, and the light of the knowledge is filling all workers who are working to solve this nuclear problem. Let their work lead to the quickest solution and pray that this solution comes into effect as soon as possible, transcending all normal logic. We are bringing higher fifth-dimensional light to the solution. Continue sending your thoughts to the Mount Fuji crystal and visualizing all these exercises that we have performed. I will be working with you soon again. Blessings, planetary healers, holders of the light of biorelativity, and keepers of the healing light of Mother Earth. I am Juliano. Good day.

CHAPTER 26

ATTRACTING
FIFTH-DIMENSIONAL ENERGY

Juliano, the Arcturians, and Tomar

Greetings, I am Juliano and we are the Arcturians. Let us look at the concept of attracting fifth-dimensional energy and fifth-dimensional light both to yourself and to the planet. The main purpose of our working together is to focus on the fifth dimension and on bringing fifth-dimensional energy to you personally as well as to the Earth. There is personal work, personal technology, and planetary technology. When we look at planetary technology, the third and fifth dimensions are close to each other. We have been clear in our assertion that the Earth and third-dimensional energies must be accelerated. An attractive energy force must be created to bring the fifth dimension into the third dimension. This will allow fifth-dimensional energy to be downloaded into the third dimension.

The downloading process occurs first on a personal basis, and so we would like to first discuss in more detail how you bring fifth-dimensional energy into your personal life. Then we will discuss how you can bring this energy into the planet. After that, we will work with the activation of the ladder of ascension in Australia, and then finally, we will work with the activation of a new planetary city of light in Nelson Bay. The activation of these ladders of ascension and planetary cities of light is exactly what needs to happen to attract fifth-dimensional spheres and fifth-dimensional light to the planet Earth.

ADAPTING THE PHYSICAL BODY TO EARTH CHANGES
First I want to look at you as personal beings incarnating on this planet. Many of you want to know how to make your lives better and how to improve your situations. Everyone is aware that this planet is becoming more difficult to live on. Earth changes affect everyone, no matter where you are. Many people have asked

225

where they can be protected from the Earth changes, but every place on this planet is vulnerable, and it is difficult to find any place that will not be affected by the Earth changes. It is clear that these changes will make your lives more difficult, yet at the same time, connecting with this fifth-dimensional spiritual technology can improve your life and help you to cope and adapt.

One of the main adaptations that can be made is in the physical body. When you consider these Earth changes, you have to understand that the immune system has to be recharged and needs to interact with fifth-dimensional energy to do so. There must be a greater understanding of clearing and re-patterning your immune systems. This can be done through vibrational energy work and vibrational medicine, two fifth-dimensional technologies that help the physical body. In many cases, this work is more effective in bringing health to the body than some of the traditional techniques of the Western world.

The physical body and the aura are important factors in connecting with fifth-dimensional energy on a personal basis. In order to connect to this energy effectively, you need to become more aware of yourself as a vibrational energy force and you also have to work with your aura. One of the best ways to do this involves using the concept of the aura as a cosmic egg. As you continually update your aura, work with the pulse of your aura, and connect your physical body with the fifth dimension, you will work with vibrational energies and the pulse of your aura.

The pulsing of your aura can be compared to with the pulse of the human body. If your physical pulse becomes overly active or too rapid, then this could indicate a problem. Paradoxically, when the human aura pulses at a higher speed, you are approaching fifth-dimensional light and energy. In fact, in our exercises with shimmering, we have introduced the concept of pulsing the outline of your aura as the introductory step toward interacting with the fifth dimension. When you encounter people in a lower energy state, you understand that their auras are pulsing at lower rates. A spiritual problem develops when a person in a lower vibrational state tries to bring down a person in a higher vibrational state. Because of this, you have to protect yourself so that people with a lower vibrational pulse do not cause your aura pulse to decrease. Many of you are already protecting yourselves with the work that we are doing.

RECEIVING FIFTH-DIMENSIONAL ENERGY THROUGH THE EMOTIONAL BODY

Let us look at the second level of how to bring down fifth-dimensional energy into your personal lives: using your emotional bodies. The emotional body must be activated so that it can receive fifth-dimensional energy. There are many new energy techniques for healing the emotional body. Advancements have been made in spiritual and soul psychology to aid the release of old aspects of the self and integrating the self with higher energy. These advances have been truly monumental. One newer level of emotional healing focuses on soul psychology and awareness of previous lifetimes and your soul mission. You are incarnating here to work with emotions, because Earth has a unique ability to offer emotional experiences. Many extraterrestrial beings are trying to understand this emotional energy. We have mentioned the Grays before in this context, those beings who have no emotional body and wish to transmute the emotional body of the Earth into their genetic structure.

As you work with your emotional bodies, it is particularly important to focus on the fifth-dimensional emotional perspective. This perspective works with certain higher vibrational energies, including love, compassion, understanding, and acceptance. These are higher-level emotions. It is challenging in this time to experience higher level emotion, especially when you see the destruction, suffering, pain, and illogical actions of humanity. You do not want to experience lower third-dimensional emotions like jealousy, rage, anger, and so on, but how can you maintain the higher emotions? You can connect with your higher selves in the fifth dimension. Higher aspects of yourselves are already there, and these higher aspects can give you a fifth-dimensional perspective.

What is that perspective? What you observe on the Earth is a drama, both on the Earth level and the galactic level. Clearly there are many different genetic sources, races, energies, and patterns commingled on the Earth. That mixture reflects remnants of prior civilizations that came to the Earth and were downloaded into the genetic codes and structures of humankind. The multiple religions, languages, and races on Earth are representative of a galactic drama. This mixture raises the question of personal and cosmic karma. Many conflicts are based on interactions that go beyond normal cause-and-effect relationships that you see on the Earth. One cannot comfortably justify the range of suffering and destruction.

These problems challenge the emotional body, and those emotions can override all of the higher vibrational healing. To avoid getting stuck on the lower vibrations of fear and of anger, you need to get a different perspective. The solution from the emotional body's standpoint is detachment—a special kind of detachment that allows you to care and feel. While you don't want to see any this destructive action currently playing out on Earth, you also understand that this is only a drama you are experiencing, and you have to see this drama because you are being trained to become ascended masters. You are here to learn because you are going to go on to other planetary systems and other realms. This experience is invaluable, yet you must try to maintain the higher vibrational energy.

Therefore, we particularly recommend that you work with heart energy. Keep your heart chakra open and clear so you connect with higher masters who are experts in working with the heart energy. Fear is a big issue at the root of many of the emotional and spiritual problems on the planet. People are feeling isolated and alone. The answer to that emotional issue is to work with the heart energy and to realize that there is a greater dimension and a greater interaction. People need to experience the higher dimension emotionally.

MAKING A SPIRIT-BODY CONNECTION TO THE FIFTH DIMENSION

The last body we have to look at is the spirit body. How do you connect the spirit body to the fifth dimension in order to attract fifth-dimensional energy? This is what we mean when we speak of multidimensional presence. Humans are multidimensional. You have an existence in the fifth dimension, and you can access that fifth-dimensional body with your spirit. When you project yourselves and link to the fifth dimension, you then bring fifth-dimensional energy back into your physical bodies. This process represents a spiritual evolution for humankind.

We have continually said that humanity has reached an evolutionary brink or crisis and must go to the next level. A core group of people must make the change to ensure that all of humanity can evolve. We have referred to this as the hundredth-monkey effect. This is a term that an Earth anthropologist (Ken Keyes Jr.) developed to explain how a large group of monkeys on an isolated island learned a new behavior. After the hundredth monkey learned the behavior, the entire group, including monkeys elsewhere, knew it as well. For humankind, there needs to be such a core group who are spiritually awakened.

We are aware that science has advanced more rapidly than spirituality. To help humanity evolve spiritually, we have introduced a new spiritual paradigm called the sacred triangle to unite galactic thinking, mystical thinking, and Native concepts. Unity of spiritual thinking gives you a special perspective. One of the keys to acquiring this perspective is through the existence of higher-dimensional beings. Humanity has a rich source of mystical teachings in all of Earth's religions, and many of these teachings originated from galactic sources. Each Earth religion has links to galactic energies, and each prophet has had communication or direct contact with higher-dimensional beings. Native connections to the Earth are a key component of this new paradigm uniting Native perspectives with sacred-triangle energy.

This connection leads us directly into our planetary work. Your task as planetary healers is to connect yourself and the planet into the fifth dimension through the planetary cities of light that are being protected and activated by the Arcturian lightworkers to hold fifth-dimensional energy. There are currently forty-two planetary cities of light participating in this Arcturian project. Other efforts that help move Earth to the fifth dimension include using etheric crystals and downloading ladders of ascension around the Earth. In other words, there is planetary healing technology that can attract and hold fifth-dimensional energies. As Arcturian starseeds and planetary healers, using that technology is one of your main missions. You have incarnated so that you can introduce and use this planetary healing technology on Earth.

Become aware of your aura, shaped like a cosmic egg. There is a solid deep blue line around your aura. That line is pulsing in rhythm with your own energy field. Become aware that you can increase the pulsing energy of your aura. Listen to the tones of my voice coming through the channel. As the tones increase in vibration, you can increase the vibrational pulsing of your aura. [Tones:] *Tat, tat, tat, tat, taaa* . . . Sense that your aura is now pulsing at a higher speed. As it opens, you are opening your mental body, spiritual body, physical body, and emotional body to fifth-dimensional energy. Now, as you pulse at the higher speed, you are opening yourself up to fifth-dimensional energy, and you are opening yourself to the planetary mission.

THE FOURTH LADDER OF ASCENSION AT NELSON BAY

If a core number of people can achieve fifth-dimensional awareness, then humanity, the Adam species, can achieve evolutionary change. A core number of planetary cities of light must be created and activated on the Earth, as well as a core number of ladders of ascension. Twelve etheric crystals have already been downloaded. As more and more people participate, the spiritual light quotient, or energy of the Earth, is raised. This will help attract fifth-dimensional energies to the Earth. One of your missions is to help make the Earth more magnetically attractive as a link. The Earth has an electromagnetic aura, and that aura must be in resonance with the fifth dimension to allow interaction. The resonant frequency of light is coming to planetary cities of light, ladders of ascension, etheric crystals, and the energy patterns related to biorelativity and the Earth's energy field.

How can you raise the pulse of the Earth? How can you shimmer the Earth? I am happy that we have activated Nelson Bay, near Sidney, Australia, as a planetary city of light. The lightworkers there have been able to create a vibrational field around the city, and they have placed crystals in key points around the city. They are willing to enhance and protect the energy field to ensure that only higher energy thought waves work through all participants. Think of this beautiful city on the bay. Maybe you can visualize it. I, Juliano, see a great etheric light basket beneath the entire city. I have raised the basket and the Nelson Bay etheric energy so it is directly connected to the fifth dimension and to other planetary cities of light on Earth and throughout the galaxy. Let us hold this vision of Nelson Bay as a planetary city of light.

At an earlier time, the lightworkers in Nelson Bay spoke to each other about visions of beauty in Nelson Bay and how it is becoming a fifth-dimensional city. They visualized the energetic ring of light around the aura of Nelson Bay and raised its vibrational energy. They all sent beautiful energy and light to Nelson Bay and I, Juliano, lowered the basket back down to the Earth. It is so beautiful that Nelson Bay is also the home of the next ladder of ascension. The ladder is on a beautiful promontory called Tomaree Point. The channel and his wife, Gudrun, with Caroline from the Group of Forty in Australia have previously gone to the top of this point. They immediately understood that it is a sacred area with links to many ancient energies of the Pacific—dolphins, whales, and clear, pristine Earth energy force. We have prepared the fourth ladder of ascension on Tomaree Point. Tomar, our Arcturian guide and friend, oversaw the downloading of the ladder of ascension at Tomaree Point. I am Juliano. Good day.

Record of the Activation of Tomaree Point Ladder of Ascension

Greetings, I am Tomar. I love your spiritual energy and commitment to upgrading and connecting the beautiful Earth to the fifth dimension. I am moved that you are so dedicated to your planetary work. We on Arcturus love our planet. We are all trained as planetary healers. I think part of your interest in us is that you want to learn more about planetary healing, part of our regular educational curriculum. Can you imagine a new curriculum in your high schools called planetary healing? This is going to come.

I am especially connected to Tomaree Point and Nelson Bay because this is an area of deep connection to ancient mammals, the seas, and the Aborigines. Tomaree is an aboriginal word. Long ago the Aborigines connected to the Arcturians, and I have had connections with them. In their dreamtime, they have connected to their star brothers and sisters. They have used Tomaree Point to look at the stars and to connect with the Arcturians. At the top of Tomaree Point, they sought and received visions and messages from star brothers and sisters.

I, Tomar, am activating Tomaree Point. I am aligning the starship Athena with Juliano. I am opening up a light corridor. Those who are there at Tomaree Point may be able to see a blue beam of light directly over Tomaree Point—a brilliant, blue-white light. I now set up a corridor of light over Tomaree Point, a fifth-dimensional corridor of light. The lightworkers who are there are helping as I get ready to download this ladder of ascension. You who are there at Tomaree Point are there to receive, and you will feel a new connection and access to the fifth dimension. I, Tomar, bring down the fourth ladder of ascension onto Tomaree Point now.

There is a great activation of the ancient aboriginal spirits here; the grandmothers and grandfathers of the aboriginal leaders feel joy and happiness at this acknowledgement. They are happy that we acknowledge and bring more sacred awareness to Tomaree Point. The ladder of ascension is now downloaded on this beautiful promontory. There will be sightings of dimensional ships here, for this ladder of ascension is linked to the fifth dimension, to other dimensions, and to higher-dimensional beings. This will allow higher-dimensional beings and ascended masters to interact and to visit Nelson Bay. We are happy that this ladder of ascension is in the city.

We realize that Tomaree Point is in a suburb outside of Nelson Bay, but we are considering the whole area as the planetary city of light. Those in Australia working with this city, please consider the whole Nelson Bay area as a holder of the planetary city of light—and Tomaree Point as the holder of the fourth ladder of ascension. The ladder of ascension is now downloaded, and so I would like all of you to visually connect and send your blessings to Tomaree Point.

Now send blessings to the ladders of ascension on Mount Fuji, in Sedona at Bell Rock, and to the Dome of the Rock in Jerusalem. Know that these four ladders are connected. They form an interactive magnetic link, part of a great attractive force to raise the spiritual light quotient and magnetic attractive force of the Earth. Now the Earth can hold and attract more fifth-dimensional energy. You are preparing for your own personal ascension. You are also preparing for planetary ascension. I, Tomar, have seen other planets ascend, and it is such a moving, overwhelming joy to work with and be on a planet that is ascending. Blessings to you. I am Tomar. We are the Arcturians. Good day.

CHAPTER 27

SOUL EVOLUTION AND THE SUPERMIND

Juliano and the Arcturians

Greetings, I am Juliano. We are the Arcturians. Today we wish to talk about the soul journey and the way the soul comes into the Earth plane. One interesting observation on that topic is that on entry into the birth corridor, you experience a memory loss both of past-life experiences and also information related to discussions that you have had with your guides and teachers. This is all valuable and important information. You would think that it would be necessary to retain the memories of your past lives and also the guidance and wisdom from your teachers, as well as your precognitive knowledge of events that will transpire when you enter your physical incarnation on Earth. Yet despite the importance of all this information, you go through an experience of memory loss.

It has been described that your master guide and teacher touches your forehead—usually around the area of your third eye—right before you come into the birth corridor. This action erases those memories. In actuality, "erasing" is not the correct word, for the memories are placed in a special compartment in the superbrain, or the supermind. In the supermind, that information and that energy are accessible. The lost information is only accessible through certain methodologies and through certain spiritual practices; it is not immediately accessible. This also implies that your mind has many levels.

Your mind contains the Earth mind, which some people also call the ego mind. Your mind also has what I call the supermind, which is connected to vast pools of information about your soul and about past lifetimes and future lifetimes, as well as about many other aspects of the dimensions and the expansions and evolutions of the dimensions. The supermind also contains relevant and necessary information about how to connect to the Creator light and how to make the highest contact with your soul.

The Amazing Appeal of the Freewill Zone

The supermind has all of your soul information. When you come through the birth corridor, when you come into the Earth plane, you lose this contact with the supermind and you lose the ability to access it. Therefore, that ability to access the supermind must be relearned. Equally important is the fact that Earth civilizations and Earth cultures are not currently encouraging teachings on how to access this vital and important information from the supermind. In fact, exactly the opposite occurs. That is to say, such psychic or spiritual information and abilities are actually discouraged in the existing predominant cultures and civilizations on your planet. This act of discouraging the development of such spiritual abilities is a reflection of a lack of intense spiritual development on the planet. There are, of course, exceptions to this culturally discouraging attitude toward spiritual connections on Earth; certain "primitive" tribes and cultures working to allow their children to report prebirth spiritual information.

Remember that when you come through the birth canal and the birth corridor, your memory of your former existence is put in a special place in the supermind. You also lose your previous language abilities as well as access to all of the higher functions of the mind that you had before you came into the Earth plane. Essentially, you come into the Earth plane with what you call a *tabula rasa*, or blank tablet, in your mind. One of the necessities for soul development is that entry into this third-dimensional reality requires this blank tablet, or blank mind. There are several important reasons for this. We all understand the importance of having this soul information and connection with soul memory, but the main reason you begin your life here with a blank mind is to have an opportunity to start in a new energy. You are given this new life in the third dimension as a gift for your soul development. From our studies and our deep spiritual exploration, we have learned that the soul is involved in an evolution, and one vital part of that evolutionary link occurs in the third dimension.

So the reason why the third dimension is important is precisely because when you incarnate here, your memory is—for the most part—blank. Any past mistakes, any past inclinations, or any past errors can be reassessed and realigned under the third-dimensional Earth energy field that we call the freewill zone. I cannot overemphasize the importance of Earth as a freewill zone for your soul development and evolution. Yes, being in a freewill zone comes with many problems, but the experience is vital in order for you to learn the soul lessons and do the soul work required. It is utterly necessary that you do your soul work in the auspices of a freewill zone such as Earth.

This is why so many souls are lined up to come into the Earth plane; they want to be in this freewill zone. These souls see all the suffering happening on Earth, yet they are lining up. They see all the problems, but they are looking at it from a much higher perspective—from the perspective of the supermind. They know that being in this energy of the freewill zone is a great boost to the possibility of soul evolution. Can you imagine these souls waiting to come to some of the poorest places on Earth, knowing that they will be born into poverty and knowing they will die from sickness? Yet they understand that there is a huge benefit from the soul perspective that is gained by coming into the third dimension. This is why it is so important and so vital for the souls to come to Earth and why souls will line up, even when they know they will only be on Earth for nine months.

FREE WILL VERSUS PREDESTINATION

I want to look at this concept of the freewill zone because it is related deeply to the whole issue of losing your contact with your soul masters, guides, and teachers when you come in, as well as losing the awareness of your past lives. In higher civilizations such as those on Arcturus, we encourage and promote accessibility to past lives and to discussions of masters, guides, and teachers as soon as is possible. Yet Arcturus is unlike Earth, and many of you have had to wait for fifty years or more in order to get this information—in terms of Earth life, this is often considered the final third of your life. This final third of your life is when you can do what is perhaps some of the most important soul work. Yet isn't that waiting a long time—waiting for two-thirds of your life to pass—before you can begin your most vital work?

Advanced spiritual civilizations like the Arcturians work so that the people can have access to their past lives as well as their future lives. Our work with you in the holographic healing chambers is an expression and an example of how we approach many of these issues, such as talking with guides and teachers, life-between-life energies, working with the past, and working with the future. Every action we want to take we evaluate in terms of the future as well as the past, because we know that the past influences the present. But we also know that the present influences the future and that even the possibility of future events influences the present. If you were going to go on a trip somewhere, you would consider and want to know what the effect of that trip would be on those future events. What karma might you create? In this example, we actually would spend a significant amount of energy in the holographic chambers on future events. This may seem surprising, but when you look at Earth and Earth changes now, one of the lessons that emerges for you as its inhabitants is that you must take into consideration how present actions will affect the future of the planet. This is one of the big lessons the planet is having to deal with now, and even we are dealing with it on an individual, personal level.

The question of future events always involves issues of free will versus predetermination or predestination, and the argument of predetermination versus free will has been debated by many philosophers. Predetermination implies lack of choice. The argument is that everything is set up in advance. Lower consciousness is without awareness of the interaction of past lives and lacks integration of soul lessons. It also lacks interaction of the higher mind. Therefore, using lower consciousness in those circumstances usually means that there is more of a sense of predetermination; it looks as if everything is set up and destined to happen.

There is some truth to predetermination, especially when you have been exploring your relationship with your past lives and your relationship with your birth. All of you have been shown a holographic image of what is going to happen to you in this lifetime. You are shown which parents you are going to be with, which friends you are going to have, and what work you are going to have. You have even been shown how you are going to die. You have also been shown what lessons you are supposed to learn. Your guides and teachers discussed all of this with you before you incarnated, and you were in agreement when you came here that this was what was going to happen.

It appears from this perspective that your life is cast in stone. From the supermind's perspective, these are experiences that need to happen and issues that need to be resolved for your development. Remember, the supermind is not influenced by the lower emotions of loss or sadness or even death. It would look at all these things and not react emotionally to any choices made. This is hard for many people to grasp, for you might say, "Why did I choose to have this bad experience? Why did I choose to have parents who were abusive to me? Why would I experience or want to have this disease?" It is difficult to explain it to the lower mind because the lower mind doesn't have the perspective of the supermind.

TRANSCENDING PREDESTINATION THROUGH AWARENESS

The good news is that predestination has a counter, an opposite. Predestination has an antidote so that those things that seem painful and seem like they are destined to happen don't have to unfold in exactly the tragic or painful way that appears to be predestined. What is the antidote? There are actually two or three antidotes. The first antidote is what we call awareness. Awareness has become one of the major psychological advancements in the twentieth and twenty-first centuries. Awareness includes knowledge of the soul process, a perception of karma, and cognizance of how things were set up for you to have such limitations or experiences.

Awareness has become the antidote for dissolving the predetermination aspect of the situation. It encourages the connection to the supermind. Anytime you can connect to your supermind, you are able to bring down energies that transcend third-dimensional logic and open up a vast possibility of changes. This connection to the supermind opens up new ways of dealing with karma and new ways of transcending karma. The supermind can offer new ways of overcoming illnesses and even new ways of really changing and shifting the planet through awareness.

The attribute of awareness is part of the evolution of a species. Awareness is what distinguishes humans, or the Adam species, from the other animal worlds. It isn't awareness in a selfish way or a narcissistic way. You can have awareness of this greater supermind and this greater connection from the supermind to the soul. You can use that awareness in a holographic way to change and work with past karma and future karma. Working with past karma in the holographic healing chamber will have a tremendous effect. In the holographic healing chambers, you can shift the energies of past abuses and of past wrongdoings. You can even undo energies of wrongs you have done others, and then you will have a tremendous unfolding benefit in your karma.

I want to point out something about the holographic healing chamber. When people work with us on holographic work, many will always want to go back to where they were hurt or damaged. They want to correct the images and the problems that arose because of the pain and suffering. I have worked repeatedly through this channel in many healing experiences where people were wounded, severely damaged, ridiculed, or even put to death for certain spiritual reasons. But we all know that everyone, or most people, have been warriors on this planet, and I have not worked through the channel with anyone who said that he or she would like to correct the wrongdoings that he or she did to others.

I do want to make an addendum to that statement in that there is one glaring exception to what I just said: Some of you were scientists and high-level people in Atlantis and other areas where there was high technology. Some of you suffered because you allowed your intelligence and your abilities to be used for purposes that eventually led to the destruction of your civilizations and many deaths, and there have been some who have come forward and worked with us wanting to clear that energy.

When you do the holographic work from the past, including from past lives, then be open to going back to karmic things that you have done. The healing process from past lives is similar to alcoholic recovery. During the part of the process of alcoholic recovery when people realize they need to make amends—when they gain the awareness of what harm they may have caused others—they want to apologize, to say they are sorry to those they have hurt. This is an important part of their recovery because they have gained awareness, and now they want to remove the energy; they want to remove the karma.

You see, you can remove the karma in this lifetime. That is another powerful reason why everyone is lining up still to come into Earth—because of the opportunities to remove karma. No one, when going into his or her supermind, really wants to have any karma on the soul that would necessitate having to reincarnate again in the third dimension. This is a time on Earth where awareness is possible. So many people are coming into the Earth plane knowing they have an opportunity for this awareness. And with awareness, you have an antidote for karma.

THE GRACE OF ASCENSION IN SOUL EVOLUTION

The second and equally powerful experience, opportunity, and technology for overcoming predetermination is the ascension. Ascension can overcome the necessity for karma and living out certain karmas. Ascension also brings an accompanying grace that helps to overcome karma. There are certain eras, astrological passages of time, and planetary systems within the solar system that are measured in the distance that the solar system is traveling around the galaxy. There are certain passages in the space-time continuum when the energy of grace becomes more accessible and more powerful. At that point of the energy of grace, if the soul is incarnated in that place, it has the opportunity to make huge advancements and overcome or wash away and resolve huge karmic issues. It is such a time right now, and the experience of grace is available. This grace from the ascension is an antidote to karma, and it allows huge soul gains. This time is excellent for the evolution of the soul here on Earth.

Your soul knew that when it came to Earth. Your soul knew that there were powerful opportunities in two powerful avenues. The first avenue was the avenue of the awareness, an opening of spiritual energy on the planet. Equally or perhaps even more importantly, your soul knew that this was going to be an opportunity to experience an unbelievable grace energy that would lead to the ascension. Let us be clear: The ascension means that you have cleared your Earth karma. In certain circumstances, people have five to eight lifetimes of experiences in a very short lifetime here on Earth because of the acceleration of the space-time continuum. This is a fantastic opportunity from the supermind.

I want to return again to this idea of soul evolution. It is difficult to discuss soul evolution in third-dimensional terminology because you correctly view the soul as perfect and eternal. So why would the soul have to evolve? In the fifth-dimensional perspective, there is no evolution as you have it in the third dimension, because that implies lack of perfection in some way—we can't really speak logically about this; I can only try to talk about it or around it so that you have some idea. But the idea is that the soul needs a certain type of experience. The soul has been on many different planes and on many different planets. Some souls have only been on one planet, Earth, but most of you with this group have been on many different planets. I have talked to many of you through this channel, and I know that most of you have had different lifetimes on other planets—not just on one planet besides Earth but on several planets. When you open yourself up to the supermind, you will be pleased to know that you have had many different experiences.

Some of you have had other third-dimensional experiences on other planets. I have worked with some of you who have been on planets that were destroyed. I have worked with some of you who have had experiences in Atlantis where you saw a whole civilization destroyed. Some of you have actually seen an entire planet destroyed exactly at the same level of energy that Earth is going through now. From your perspectives, all of the things going on probably look familiar—hauntingly familiar, I might add. I realize that what is going on on Earth now is traumatic and is causing a great deal of emotional trauma for all of you. Not only is it causing trauma because of what you are seeing, but it is also reactivating the earlier memories.

The soul wants to clear the karma. The soul wants to drop it or resolve it; therefore, coming here is a wonderful opportunity. It is fair to ask the question, "Juliano, how is being here on Earth now going to help my soul evolution, especially in the face of all this destruction?" The answer again is complicated, and it doesn't make total logical sense on the third dimension. There are so many things that have occurred on the third dimension that are not logical. We cannot logically explain many events, and therefore explanations must be turned over to this realm that I call cosmic karma. I will offer some lower-Earth logical explanation that won't totally encompass the right answer, but it will at least put you in the right direction.

THE FACTOR OF UNKNOWING

One of the most important soul lessons for everyone is to learn that there is a unity and a connection with the Creator light and that there is always a connection with your soul and the supermind. You are given the task and have all the tools to connect with your supermind. That lesson has to be learned over and over again, even in the face of a planetary crisis. The second lesson is that there are ways to transcend karma. Look at all of the things you have done in all of the lifetimes that created karma. For example, in one lifetime, you may have abused people, and then in another lifetime, you may have been a victim. Maybe some of you were soldiers in fifty lifetimes. Does this mean you have to have fifty lifetimes in which you are slaves? The answer is no.

The soul can learn ways of overcoming vast accumulated karma. For example, there are amazing medical practitioners and healers on this planet now. I am not just talking about traditional medical doctors—bless their hearts; they are trying to do the best they can sometimes—but there are also other high spiritual healers. In a single lifetime, a healer may be able to heal 1,000 people. Think of how much karma that healer is erasing, then think of the actions that person might have committed in other past lifetimes—either here or on other planets—that may have created karma that needs to be released. It is a fantastic opportunity for the soul to be able to heal 1,000 people. It is an unbelievable number, and certainly it is worth it from the supermind's perspective to come to Earth. It would be worth coming to Earth even in consideration of the suffering you might have to experience to come here.

You might ask the follow-up question: "Why would I come here to suffer? Is that some of the karma I would experience for something that I did that was bad?" Again, the answer is not simple, and it doesn't make total logical sense. Every lifetime has certain risks. You meet with your guides and teachers to have a preview of your life before you come. It is not an exact play-byplay, minute-by-minute report. Think of it as being psychic. You see what the events are that could happen in the future, based on all the most accurate information available from the soul perspective, but that is still not all of the information. This is something I want you to completely understand. If all of the information were available and you saw it, then you would know everything as predestined.

There is a factor of unknowing, however. This is now demonstrated even in quantum physics. When scientists study the subatomic level, there is what is called the uncertainty principle. Simply put, the Heisenberg Uncertainty Principle means that on a subatomic level, there are certain factors that make particle exploration and determination uncertain. Scientists cannot predict with equal certainty where subatomic particles are going to be and their corresponding velocities. This is in direct contradiction to the logical Newtonian laws of motion in which everything should be orderly and predictable.

The reason I am bringing this up is because the Heisenberg Uncertainty Principle also applies to knowledge when you are coming into the Earth plane. You are given a general detail, a general overview, of your life. But there are things that are uncertain that you would not know at that time. The overview you are given is the best possible overview based on available information. People sometimes ask the Arcturians: "Don't you know everything that is going to happen from your perspective on the fifth dimension? Don't you know everything?" The uncertainty principle exists in all dimensions. The study of galactic *Kaballah* has come down to the Earth plane from the work of the Jewish mystics and others who have studied the *Kaballah*. From this work, an important principle has been demonstrated. That principle is that the Creator cannot be totally known. What is possible is that you can experience an aspect of the Creator.

My friends, each planetary incarnation, each position in the galaxy, and each position in the solar system provides another unique aspect of knowing the Creator. You might say from the soul perspective that one of the highest soul missions is to know the Creator. In the *Kaballah*, it is believed that you know the Creator by knowing creation. Because the mind of the Creator—if you can even say Creator has a mind as you understand it—is not known, then all of the information, even in an incarnation on Earth, is not totally known. Therefore, sometimes when you are choosing an incarnation, certain aspects of it could occur that you didn't plan on. These aspects can wind up being painful, and you might think that you are being punished, but it is not always the case that an illness, for example, is a punishment. In some cases, illness was one of the prices you had to pay to have this body in this incarnation at this time.

It is generally known that there are a lot of uncertainties in coming into the Earth plane with all of this density. It would be easier if you were incarnating on Arcturus or on the Pleiades. Then you would know that there would be less intervening variables in your karma. There wouldn't be as many surprises. On Earth, especially in this turbulent time, there are a lot of surprises, because there are lots of possibilities. It requires more careful examination of all aspects of your immune systems, your subconscious minds, and your superconscious minds. You can unknowingly attract energies that at other times wouldn't even touch you. The potential gains are very high, but the potential for intervening variables, and unpredicted ones at that, is also high.

PLANETARY HEALING THROUGH THE SUPERMIND

Through awareness and through working in the holographic energy field of past, present, and future soul work, you can meditate to lessen the effects of some of the discomforts that you are experiencing. Any time you are accessing and connecting to your supermind, you are working with the fifth-dimensional energies. The fifth-dimensional energies can do powerful things. Any time that you are working with this powerful energy of grace, you also can connect with powerful energy.

I would like to do a brief meditation with you in which we will ask each of you to connect with your superminds, the all-knowing mind. [Chants:] Omega light . . . May this omega light help each of you now connect to your superminds. We will go into silence now. As you are connecting to your supermind, ask and you will be granted permission to access the information from your past lives, your past experiences, your birth corridor, and your guides and teachers. The information for your soul lessons is also being downloaded; let it come to you.

Most importantly, receive the energies and the abilities to have this wonderful awareness of your soul and its past experiences in other places, in other incarnations on other planets, and also in your future. May you be given the grace and understanding to measure carefully all actions you take on Earth so that they are free of any karma entanglements and so that you will be in the greatest position to ascend. Yes, each of you will need grace, and it is available. Accept it and use it. It will help you to transcend some of these issues that may look predetermined, as if there is no way to resolve them. When you connect to your supermind, the healing abilities are endless.

In the closing moments that we have together, let us speak more about planetary healing and the planetary mind. Earth has a supermind too. Earth has higher functioning. You might ask, "Well, how do you know that, Juliano?" The answer is very simple, because in order for a planet to have higher life like Earth's humanity (although it is not exactly the same), that planet must have a higher supermind, a planetary supermind. These energies you hear about—for example, the energies of asteroids hitting a planet and destroying things—may seem random, but from our perspective, the planet's supermind sometimes wants a clearing.

Now we are in the period of biorelativity work in which you are able to interact with the planetary mind. To that end, we are going to activate new planetary cities of light, because the planetary cities of light directly access the supermind of the Earth. That's how powerful these planetary cities of light are. They have a powerful accessibility to the supermind of the planet, and that supermind can bring forth quantum omega light that can help to transcend many of the difficult situations that seem irresolvable, such as what is going on around the Fukushima power plant, where some of the predictions are very dire. Yet the Earth mind, the supermind of the planet, can be accessed to provide a solution that will work. Remember the power of this grace and this planetary experience now.

I send you my healing light. I send you the omega light. I know that each of you hearing these words will have a greater opportunity now to connect with your superminds. I know your superminds, and I have been connecting with them since the beginning of our transmissions in this project. Sometimes people ask, "Why would the Arcturians—why would fifth-dimensional beings—be interested in Earth? It is a lower vibration. Why would the Arcturians and other higher beings be interested in such densities?" Well, the answer is that we see your total selves and we are interacting with your superminds. On that level, we are very powerful brothers and sisters to all of you. I am Juliano. Good day.

CHAPTER 28

CONNECTING JERUSALEM TO THE RING OF ASCENSION

Juliano and the Arcturians, Archangel Metatron, and
Chief White Eagle

Shalom. Shalom. Shalom. Greetings. I'm Juliano, and we are the Arcturians. It is a good idea to focus on the entire planet when performing a biorelativity exercise. Think in terms of the whole Earth system and the many interactions that are occurring at this moment in the Earth system. You, the starseeds, might have a sense of this unbelievable complexity that is occurring on the levels that you are perceiving. But if one person were to try and understand all of the different systems that are interacting simultaneously now on the Earth, you would find that they are truly impossible for a single person to fully grasp.

For example, you can see economic polarization and uncertainty, political conflicts, and weather shifts. You witness volcanic eruptions, and you can see the oceans and the draughts and the winds. There are many things that you can perceive, but I would like to make a comparison between the Earth and your human body. It is a known scientific fact than 90 percent or more of your nervous system is unconscious. That means that many of the things that are going on, even at this moment in your body, are not in your awareness. And although we are usually talking about some of the simple things such as digestion, some of this also relates more complex matters such as higher autonomic nervous system functioning. So 90 percent of what is going on in your body is not in your awareness.

Now let us discuss this in comparison to the Earth. While there is so much that you can see on the surface, 90 percent or more of things that are going on underneath the earth are not in your knowledge base. There are so many things that still are beyond your comprehension—things that are going on in the oceans and in the weather patterns of Earth, in the galaxy and with the Earth's relationship to the galaxy, with cosmic rays and rays from the Central Sun, and even the many asteroids.

245

So when we are doing biorelativity exercises, we often are going to choose one aspect that we are very concerned with to keep things within the realm of human understanding, even though that one aspect affects the whole system. Again, I will give you an example from the human body: You may have a problem in your ankle or in your knee and want to heal the knee, but when you look at the whole system, you might find that your neck and your back and your shoulders are misaligned, affecting your whole posture, and that is what is creating problems with the knee. So it is with the Earth: When you look at the droughts that are in the central part of United States, when you look at the volcanic eruptions in Chile, even when you look at the political unrest that is going on in the Middle East and now even at some of the unrest in the Inner Earth, then you must think of these things not just as those isolated events but in terms of the whole system of the Earth.

Now, people have been suggesting that a huge Earth event is about to happen, that some huge eruption is is going to occur on the Earth, but nobody knows exactly where it is going to be—only that it is going to be of a planetary magnitude. We know that the Fukushima nuclear power accident is an event that is on a planetary basis; even though a great deal of the circumstances and the effects of this event are now being purposely hidden from the public (or at least from the world public—it is possible that the Japanese public is getting some more information), we know nonetheless that it was a world event. Now, however, people are suggesting that there will be a world event that it is of such magnitude that its effects will not be able to be hidden.

SENDING LIGHT AND THOUGHT TO THE TORAH

Therefore, in this biorelativity exercise we are going to work with the ring of ascension, connecting to a very powerful point on the planet that is the energy in Jerusalem. The city of Jerusalem is what some people believe to be the center of the connection of the universal light with this planet. This energy in Jerusalem is a sacred, holy energy that we have also used as a place for a ladder of ascension. What better place, then, to connect the energy of Jerusalem, the Dome of the Rock, and the ladder of ascension, with the ring of ascension around the planet, letting the ring of ascension send the balancing energy around the whole planet? This ring of ascension was placed many years ago by the Arcturians and the Group of Forty starseeds to create an interactive balance with the fifth dimension and the third dimension, and that interactive balance will help to create a harmony with the whole planet.

Now we are fortunate to be in this moment, for we have a powerful connection with Jerusalem through our Group of Forty member, Mordejai, who is now in a sacred synagogue in the middle of the heart of Jerusalem. And at the moment that we are speaking—at this very moment—he is at the famous Ark of the Covenant (the one you may have seen depicted in the film *Raiders of the Lost Ark*). At this moment, the Ark holds a sacred Torah, the sacred books of Moses, in the synagogue in Jerusalem. As Mordejai is now opening up the Ark and carrying out the Torah, he is thinking of us and receiving our light and thoughts.

So send and connect the energies now directly to him and to that Torah, because that Torah is a magical energy source. As a Group of Forty, we are sending our thoughts directly to that Torah so that the Torah will emanate a connective activation link from its place in the center of Jerusalem to the ring of ascension. All of you are now needed to focus your energy on Mordejai and the scroll of the Torah that he is holding, and it will become so filled with light that it will send that light to the ring of ascension. [Sings:] *Oooh. Torah. Torah Emet. Torah Emet*—the Torah of truth.

The light of the Torah is now emanating directly from your arcan forces of light, sending that energy light to the Torah that Mordejai is holding. Now a brilliant light from Jerusalem is emanating in an omnidirectional energy-point force up directly to the ring of ascension, reactivating the ring of ascension so that the new balance is being brought now into the Earth from a biorelativity standpoint. So we will go into meditation as you simply focus again on the Torah and the light that it is emanating from it to the ring of ascension. We will go into silence. [Pause.] Archangel Metatron will speak you now, as we have activated a beautiful energetic light that is re-illuminating the ring of ascension, helping to shape an interactive new balance on the Earth. I'm Juliano. Here is Archangel Metatron.

BEAUTIFUL HEBREW LETTERS FLOW INTO THE RING OF ASCENSION
Shalom. Greetings, I'm Archangel Metatron. It is wonderful to be with you at this time of the Sabbath—both for the Muslim world and for the Jewish world and for many other people who are gathering at this time. It is a sacred time, and sacred times are great opportunities to do biorelativity work, for your arcan energy (as Juliano calls your ability to increase your thought powers) is even stronger at this moment as we are engaging in a very powerful thought biorelativity exercise.

Now that Torah that Mordejai is holding is filled with more light than he has ever been able to hold before; he is having trouble holding the Torah because it has so much light. This light is emanating from the area, because you are all sending it to him and that light is going up around Jerusalem to the ring of ascension. At this moment, I want you to visualize how this Torah has these ancient Hebrew words that were written thousands of years ago and how they are in a certain energetic code.

Some say that there is a special Bible code—I know that you have heard of that term—and that every letter of this Bible of the Torah has special significance far beyond what any one word means, far beyond any historical interpretation, and that it forms a interactive mathematical energetic unity that is beyond any comprehension. But because of its unity, because of its fantastic organizational power, it is able to emanate light based on our intention. At this moment, as we are sending this light and the beautiful letters of the Torah up into the ring of ascension, these beautiful Hebraic letters, these beautiful codes that contain the codes of ascension, are surrounding and passing through the ring of ascension, helping to reorganize a new balance of peace and harmony, and creating beautiful letters that are emanating around all of Jerusalem and going around the ring of ascension.

The famous code of ascension, "*Kadosh, Kadosh, Kadosh, Adonai Tzevaoth*," is now circling the ring of ascension and being translated into all of the languages of planet Earth so that everyone on Earth is exposed at this moment to the energy of the activation of the codes of ascension. All of the balances on Earth that need to come into a harmony are being activated by this ascension light, for the ring of ascension and the light of ascension have many purposes. One purpose is to help you in your ascension, but it is also to bring peace, harmony, and healing to the planet. The energy of ascension is a healing force for all aspects of the Earth.

At this time, I raise the crystals at Lago Puelo, at the Bodensee, at Istanbul, and at Mont Fuji. With all these crystals now sending light to Mordejai and to his Torah that he is holding as he is chanting, all this light is ascending up and around the Earth, activating the ring of ascension. Holy, holy high *Adur*—life is great. It is a good day to ascend. It is a good day to be part of this ascension process. It is a good service to this planet to work on activating this ring of ascension. So many of your guides and teachers are working and waiting for more opportunities like this to interact with the whole planet. Now your friend Chief White Eagle is going to speak and say a special prayer for the Earth. Thank you for ascending and activating this light. I, Archangel Metatron, see thousands and thousands of powerful Hebrew letters encircling the Earth and the ring of ascension, reactivating the codes of ascension for the entire planet. *Shalom.*

PRAYER FOR BALANCE AND HARMONY

Hey ya ho ya he. Hey ya ho ya he. Hey ya ho. Hey ya ho. Hey ya ho. Hey ya ho. Greetings, I'm the Chief White Eagle. It is always wonderful to come together with you in a sacred moment, and it is wonderful to experience sacred time. Sacred time is time that you, in part, are creating, but sacred time is also time that is part of the universe, part of the making of the universe—a signature of the Creator Spirit.

When you are now in sacred time, you are experiencing a direct link to the Creator. So when we now work with the ring of ascension, we see a great circle of light around the Earth and many powerful spirits from all religions and all tribes sitting in a great medicine wheel around the Earth.

This ring of ascension in our teaching is announcing the coming of White Buffalo Calf Woman. It is said in our sacred texts that a huge medicine wheel will be created in the etheric world around the Earth and that many great spirits—many grandfather and grandmother spirits—will be sitting in this ring of ascension in the shape of a medicine wheel, seeking to heal the Earth, seeking to bring the Earth into a higher energy form, seeking to bring a new balance, and seeking to bring the light of ascension to Mother Earth.

Oh, Mother Earth! We are gathered here today with this high group of starseeds. We are connected with the sacred and holy place at this moment known as Jerusalem with a sacred medicine man named Mordejai who is carrying a great light, holding and emanating the light so that we can activate this great circle of light and bring together more people to help in our desire to bring a new harmony and balance.

Oh, Great Spirit Mother Earth! Please listen to the people speaking of the great catastrophe, of the great disruption coming on the planet. We are praying for a peaceful intervention; we are praying for a new balance so that there is not another catastrophe but rather a huge interaction of brotherhood and sisterhood, a new balance through which the Earth can come into harmony, and a peaceful moment when humans can feel and understand how to relate and how to work with this Great Mother, Mother Earth. So we now send our love and desire for balance to the ring of ascension as we go into silence. [Pause.]

Oh, Mother Earth! Oh, Creator of All! We are all brothers and sisters. We are great family. We are a star family. We are asking that this ring of ascension, this great medicine wheel, also come into a harmonic alliance with the Central Sun and the great Earth activities. Let them be downloaded into the Earth through the ring of ascension so that all of the energy and all of the higher forces that are downloading upon the Earth become filtered through this ring of ascension. Our grandfather and grandmother spirits of ancient times and even of early times are now sitting and participating in this great ring of light. *Hey ya ho. Hey ya ho. Hey ya ho.*

Let it be known that on this day the Arcturian starseeds of the Group of Forty have reactivated the ring of ascension for the Earth through the energy of Jerusalem and the starseed Mordejai, bringing and calling forth a balance that may seem impossible but now will seem more and more likely from this point on. The crystals are descending back into their places. The

Ark of the Covenant, still holding open the doors and the energy from the Torah, is still emanating this light of the ring of ascension that will be around the Earth for the next twenty-four hours.

This activation energy will be emanating from Jerusalem to the ring of ascension, and those of you who are in different parts of the planet and wish to send energy of healing to your part of the planet may borrow and ask for light from the ring of ascension at any time, in any place, to be focused in rays of light and rays of energy to your city, to your area. Whatever balance you think is necessary, the ring of ascension will respond and help direct your thoughts in a new and powerful healing light. I am Chief White Eagle. All my relations, *ho*!

CHAPTER 29

PLANETARY HEALING
THROUGH THE
RING OF ASCENSION

Juliano, the Arcturians, and Sananda

Greetings, I am Juliano, and we are the Arcturians. The year 2011 has been the year of the planetary healer and planetary healing, and I am sure you will agree that 2011 has been a roller-coaster ride for the planet. If you thought that these months have been an introduction and preparation for what is going to happen in 2012, you might be very concerned and very upset about what is to come. While we strongly acknowledge that the full spectrum of planetary healing activities and technologies must now be implemented on the Earth, when we designated 2011 the year of the planetary healer, we knew that there was going to be a much greater need for your work and your intervention, that the polarizations that you are seeing would become more intense, and that Earth changes or global changes in weather patterns were going to become more active.

We also feel, however, that the opportunity for telepathically connecting with the Earth is stronger now than at any other time for the planet. It is truly an amazing time to be on the Earth and to use your skills as planetary healers. Many of you have incarnated on the Earth at this time to explore, practice, and contribute to the planetary healing experience. Planetary healing is going to be the key factor in the survival of the biosphere and a major factor in the rebalancing of the Earth. We speak about your personal ascension, but we also are constantly speaking about Earth as a planet ascending.

One of the major tools for the planetary ascension is the ring of ascension. We would like to explore the meaning of the ring of ascension in greater depth. How can you, as planetary healers, use the ring of ascension to more effectively work your biorelativity exercises for the healing and rebalancing of the Earth? It is time to work with the whole planet as one unit and to realize that one part of a climate or one part of a continent is communicating and balancing with other continents. The Ring of Fire is a long chain of energy that crosses many different countries and continents and even oceans. What happens in Chile or Australia affects what happens on the West Coast of the United States and Canada, so the most effective approach to biorelativity is to work with the entire planet. However, that is not the only approach. There are circumstances when it is best to work specifically with one area.

Even then, you have to take into consideration what you are asking to be changed and how the change that you are requesting will affect other parts of the planet. If there is a hurricane coming to Louisiana and you asked that that hurricane be redirected, then you have to consider that because of the forces being expressed, that hurricane could go into another state and cause other damage. A different approach would be to ask that the force of the storm be spread out over time and space. An even more intensive approach would be to look at the ocean currents coming from the Southern Hemisphere, the warming in the oceans there, and how the two are affecting what you see as violent weather.

We have said that the Earth patterns, weather patterns, and the feedback system of the Earth are so complex that we have to be very cautious. We have to understand our simple solutions and biorelativity interventions and how they should be used. Another example would be praying for rain in an area of drought. Bringing rain to a dry area would seem not to negatively affect other areas. That may indeed be a reasonable assumption, but in other cases, there are many complex factors involved. For example, the movement of the plates that cause earthquakes and eruptions of volcanoes also are part of the Earth's feedback system— the Ring of Fire extends thousands of miles. So it is difficult to suggest simply blocking the energy of an eruption because then you would have to ask if that could cause an eruption somewhere else along the Ring of Fire.

CONNECT WITH THE SUPERMIND OF HUMANITY

There is an approach that considers the Earth as one planet. It is an approach that says that we in all humbleness do not understand all of the mechanisms of Earth's feedback system. We do not even attempt to try to figure out how to balance everything. In fact, there are many factors that have contributed to the Earth's energy field. Because these factors also affect the Earth's meridians and the Earth's feedback system, it is difficult for everyone to guess how the blockages that humankind has imposed on the Earth's meridian systems are affecting the Earth's feedback system; it is difficult enough to understand the Earth's feedback systems without nuclear reactors and holes in the Earth's aura caused by numerous nuclear aboveground tests. And I may add that aboveground testing is still having an effect on the aura of the Earth even though these nuclear tests occurred thirty or forty years ago. There still is upheaval in the Earth's aura because of those tests. It is also difficult to assess how dams blocking key rivers on the Earth are affecting the feedback system, but logic would say that of course Earth feedback systems have been affected.

You know that one principle of biorelativity is that the Earth seeks homeostasis or balance, and this balance exists within a certain range. Levels of oxygen, nitrogen, and many other chemical factors are maintained so that the biosphere and the life forms that it supports can also be maintained. It is truly phenomenal that over thousands of years the Earth has maintained a homeostasis that has allowed the development and survival of humanity and many other living creatures.

Never before has one species so influenced the Earth's feedback system either consciously or unconsciously. Even the dinosaurs, previously perhaps the most predominant creature on the planet, were not really influencing the Earth's feedback system; they were living in harmony. Man is not living in harmony with Earth's feedback system, and so it is being challenged. The Earth is having difficulty maintaining the homeostasis necessary for you to thrive. And so we look at the planetary healing experience and we say that there has to be a way to send biorelativity telepathic communications to the whole planet at once. There has to be a way to transcend the smaller minds of individuals and connect with the supermind of humanity and of the planet.

We can start with the ring of ascension. [Tones:] *Ooohhhmmm. Ooohhhmmm. Ooooooohhmm.* The ring of ascension was downloaded with the help of the Arcturians and ascended masters who are working together with us. The ring of ascension is like a ring that you see in some of the other planets in your solar system. For example, Saturn and Neptune have rings. The ring around Earth is similar to that concept with one main difference. The difference is that Earth's ring is an etheric ring for Earth's ascension. It is like an etheric halo. This ring's unique ability is to interact with fifth-dimensional energy and download fifth-dimensional energy into the third dimension.

Earth's ring is filled with the thoughts and love of the ascended masters. You realize there are many ascended masters who are contributing now and working diligently for the Earth's ascension. The ring of ascension serves many purposes, one of which is to allow guides, ascended masters, and teachers to more easily bring down fifth-dimensional information and fifth-dimensional energy to the Earth. Many of you already know that you have been more in contact with masters and teachers recently than at any other time. There are more people channeling guides and teachers and there are more people who are connected with higher energy than any other time on Earth.

I know that sounds like a fantastic assertion, but numerically there are more starseeds on the Earth now than at any other time on the planet. There are more ascending masters and students of ascension on the Earth now than at any other time. Previously in ancient times, there were several prophets and teachers who work on and prepared for ascension. But there were only a few prophets who ascended, and never were there more than several prophets ascending at the same time. Ascension was a unique individual event. But now we have a situation on the Earth where thousands or hundreds of thousands of starseeds and ascending masters can and will ascend.

So of course there is a great need to interact with them, because we know that ascension is like a birth. Picture a birth in the hospital: You know that there are many people around, such as doctors and nurses. There are special preparations there and family waiting. In the same way, for the ascension, there are many guides and teachers on the other side waiting for you, preparing you for this transition, and preparing for your reception. Part of this preparation is to provide an accessible energy, mainly the ring of ascension, which will facilitate your access to fifth-dimensional energy. This ring of ascension is for planetary ascension as well. Therefore many of the guides and teachers, particularly Sananda, Sanat Kumara, and Ashtar, to name a few, are gathered in and interacting with the ring of ascension in order to facilitate the uplifting on the entire planet.

THE POWER OF THE RING OF ASCENSION

This ring of ascension is around the whole planet, even though you may think of a ring as being located just around the equator. You would think that because you look at Saturn or Neptune from your vantage point on Earth, using telescopes to measure the thickness of their rings. And then you would say that that ring has a certain dimension, covering a certain area around the planet. But Earth's ring of ascension is a fifth-dimensional ring—a holographic ring surrounding the entire planet—and it has special powers and abilities.

What are those special abilities? A primary ability of the ring of ascension is that it receives third-dimensional humanity's telepathic communications, translates and interacts with the them, and at the same time, receives messages and energies from the fifth-dimensional masters. Imagine that you are sending healing thoughts to the weather patterns of the Earth, seeking a balance such as the end of a drought in the Midwest, particularly in Texas. And imagine that you are praying for the animals and people who are suffering. You send your prayers and thoughts to the Earth through the medium of the feedback system using the ring of ascension. The energy that you send travels around the whole Earth and interacts telepathically with all of the different systems around the Earth that have been involved in creating the shift that led to the drought. Many different areas and currents need to be shifted in order to end the drought, but it must be done in a way that is in balance with the whole planet. It must be done in a way that supports and brings harmony to the whole planet, not in just one area such as Texas.

The ring of ascension takes the energy that you have sent and sends it around the planet to influence all the other places it is needed so that a new balance can occur. What is also beautiful is that you who may be sitting in Australia or in Germany or in Philadelphia have equal access to the ring of ascension. The ring of ascension receives information from many different places around the Earth and is not limited to a certain width. It is only limited to the thoughts of the starseeds; it can be as widely dispersed as the starseeds are who are supporting it around the planet. It could be narrow if you want to be more focused, but wide is also focused. It is a holographic ring, and the fifth-dimensional ascended masters are simultaneously participating in the ring of ascension. They monitor the ring all the time, listening to your needs and to planetary needs. I think that it is especially important to know that the response sometimes occurs right away, while at other times it may take longer—occasionally quite a bit longer. The reason for this is because you as one starseed do not know all of the many factors in the feedback system that need to be shifted and changed in order for the request to be met, and the ascended masters are contributing their thoughts as well.

Remember, I have talked about arcan power, which is the measurement of thought power. You would need to have a certain level of thought arcan power—ten arcans, or twenty. The more arcans of power of your thought, the more likely it is that your requested changes will occur. By going through the ring of ascension, you are interacting with the fifth-dimensional masters. Their thought patterns and energy can also be measured in arcan power, and they have the ability to emanate much higher power than you can even imagine. In order for their energy and thought power to be effective, it must interact with yours. This is one of the rules and laws of planetary spiritual healing. Fifth-dimensional masters' and teachers' thoughts and healing powers must be interactive with the third-dimensional inhabitants of a planet. The ring of ascension offers the medium that allows the fifth-dimensional masters to interact with your thoughts and requests for telepathic and planetary healing. [Tones:] *Ooohhhmmm. Ooohhhmmm. Ooohhhmmm.*

I want to suggest at this point that you and I together will send a request for planetary healing to the ring of ascension. The ring of ascension will be wherever you are, wherever your thoughts are. I want you to choose what healing thought you want to send to Mother Earth through the ring of ascension. Then you can request that the ascended master teacher closest to you will hear your thoughts and send master thoughts into the ring of ascension. Then you can understand how powerful the energy of the ring of ascension can be. We will meditate for just a few minutes.

The arcan energy power of your thoughts for planetary healing is strong now. The guides and the teachers, especially Sananda, Ashtar, and Sanat Kumara, are actively processing and using your energies to distribute new healing light for the biosphere, sending it around and throughout the Earth. This is one very powerful tool, the ring of ascension. It can be used in conjunction with the twelve etheric crystals because each of the etheric crystals has the ability to touch the ring of ascension. The etheric crystals can be raised out of the ground, and the tops of these etheric crystals can be placed inside the ring of ascension.

Visualize this beautiful energy: Imagine that you are painting an image of the beautiful fifth-dimensional ring of ascension around the planet with 1,600 people all around the planet, sitting in circles, sending light to the ring of ascension from their crown chakras. On top of the planet in the etheric world, there are fifth-dimensional masters and teachers simultaneously interacting, sending their thoughts and light into the ring of ascension. The twelve etheric crystals from the planet are raised and are interacting with the ring of ascension. The ring is amplifying the power of your thoughts. Now the etheric crystals are brought back down into the Earth, and they hold the energy of the ring of ascension in their crystal formation. The etheric crystals can hold fifth-dimensional energies and healing power to an extraordinary degree. You are helping to store the healing powers. You have worked very hard in your ring of ascension exercises. You are able to store that energy in the etheric crystals. The etheric crystals are now interacting directly with the ring of ascension. [Tones:] *Ooohhhmmm. Ooohhhmmm.*

ISKALIA LIGHT FROM THE CENTRAL SUN

A second powerful tool for planetary healing is the Iskalia mirror. The Iskalia mirror is similar to a gigantic mirror over the North Pole. It is an energetic etheric mirror that has the capacity to collect energy at far distances from the galaxy. It is difficult to imagine, but you can understand that a telescope that has a mirror 200 inches in diameter, given the right circumstances and the right opening in the clouds, can receive light from millions and billions of light-years away, even though that light is very faint. Astronomers' tools can be so sensitive that they can receive light and energy reaching back to the formation of this universe. Now imagine that there is a fifth-dimensional etheric mirror that can not only receive light in this dimension but also in other dimensions because the fifth dimension interacts in many different ways with the third dimension. The Iskalia mirror has a particular alignment so that it is receiving light—fifth-dimensional light—gathered from the Central Sun. We know that Jesus-Sananda originated from the area of the Central Sun. He is one of the founding fathers of universal light along with his lineage, which includes Moses, David, Buddha, and many other higher ascended beings. The light and energy from the Central Sun is now in a fifth-dimensional phase of knowledge and wisdom. It is a specific planetary healing light for the Earth.

There are many things you can say about the December 21, 2012, alignment of the Sun with the Central Sun. Let me assure you that some of the most powerful fifth-dimensional energy ever experienced or seen on this planet will be available at this alignment. The planetary alignment known as the 2012 or solar alignment is not just end-times energy. It is not only the energy of upheaval or change but also new fifth-dimensional energy coming to the Earth. This fifth-dimensional energy is already on its way. As I have said in earlier lectures, the eclipse of the Central Sun has begun, and you are in the shadow of the eclipse of the 2012 alignment now.

The energy of this Central Sun is coming to the Earth, but it must be gathered and focused. It must be directed to the Earth. To this end, the Iskalia mirror has been placed by the Arcturians over the North Pole. It is a mirror at least one mile in diameter, even larger in your Earth terms. But the size is not as important as the fact that it has the potential of gathering fifth-dimensional light from the Central Sun. In addition, the fifth-dimensional light that it receives can be focused on particular areas on the Earth that are in need of planetary healing.

It is especially suitable to direct the energy and light from the Iskalia mirror to the planetary cities of light. These are special cities that are set up so that they are sensitive and receptive to the fifth-dimensional energies coming from the Central Sun. That means that there are new solutions, new ideas, and new energies that perhaps have not been sent before. This includes new music. I want to say there will be new sounds, new tones, and new musical energies coming to the Earth now through the Iskalia mirror from the fifth dimension. [Tones.]

I, Juliano, am calling on the Iskalia light. It is coming from the Iskalia mirror and is directed toward the ring of ascension, now. [Tones.] Iskalia light from the Central Sun, the highest fifth-dimensional light, is now being downloaded into the ring of ascension. It is being transferred directly into the planetary cities of light. [Tones.] We have talked also about the omega light—a light of transcendent nature that is particularly useful for personal healing.

We have spoken about uses of the omega light, and then you have made affirmations, particularly in your subconscious energy field. The omega light is also available for planetary healing. So, yes, this time on the Earth is a time when great energy is needed for planetary healing. We are calling on all planetary healers to unite and to use their powers of meditation, organization, and speaking to create energy fields around the planetary cities of light that are so dear to them. This is the time to activate and use the strongest arcan power possible so that the energy of planetary healing can be put in place and held together. I will ask Sananda to speak with you briefly. I love you all. Remember 2011 as the year of the planetary healing. I am Juliano. Good day.

I am Sananda. I am loving your ascension work. I am loving your abilities to interact with the fifth dimension. I am loving your desires to be on the fifth dimension. I am very pleased that the Arcturians have helped to establish a ring of ascension around the Earth, especially at a time when many people see nothing but darkness and polarization on the Earth. At this time when people see the destruction of many of the biospheric treasures on the Earth, the ring of ascension serves an even more important role in holding together of a fifth-dimensional downloading mechanism.

The ring of ascension is also connecting the ladders of ascension. The ladders of ascension can reach up to the ring of ascension in your practice. Remember, we have downloaded ladders of ascension, and we are calling on you to work with us to download another ladder of ascension at Lago Puelo in San Martín de Los Andes, where a group of devoted starseeds has been working so diligently for the healing of this planet. This area has a high potential for receiving and transmitting healing light and energy. We will work with you to set up a time and date when we can establish another ladder there. This ladder of ascension can be placed in the city of San Martín because it is so near to Lago Puelo. We will extend this ladder of ascension to the ring of ascension, and by doing that, we will ensure that all of the other ladders of ascension are also connected to the ring of ascension.

We, the ascended masters, are committed to working with you for the Earth's ascension and for your ascension. We are especially sending love toward you, for you are loving toward the Earth. This is a great service to us and to the Creator, for the Creator has told us that the Earth is going to ascend and that there will be individual ascension on the Earth. We are working together now in preparation for this interaction. Ascension is an interaction of the highest magnitude with the fifth dimension. Nothing pleases our Father more than to have the fifth dimension interact on the third dimension and to send starseeds like yourselves upward to the fifth realm. Blessings from the ring of ascension. I am Sananda. Good day.

CHAPTER 30

AN ARCTURIAN VIEW OF 2012

Juliano and the Arcturians

Greetings, I am Juliano. We are the Arcturians. We are on a cusp of major changes, and we are quickly approaching 2012. There is much anxiety and excitement about the changes that are before you and before the planet. We have designated 2011 as the year of the planetary healer. This designation indicates that there is a great deal of planetary work that must be done in preparation for the 2012 energy input.

Now I will turn to another subject because we have so much to do. I want to talk more specifically about the year 2012 and the its energy. I would like to look at the whole idea of predictions and what is coming. I know that, in essence, the year 2012 is actually going to begin around October 15th, 2011 [editor's note: this lecture was first presented on September 3, 2011]. From an energetic standpoint, 2012 does not really begin on January 1, 2012; the energy, the cycle, and the light are already beginning on October 15. In a sense, you are now almost coming to the end of the cycle of 2011. You might say that this has been a short year, but consider everything that has happened already.

THE MESSAGE OF THE COMET ELENIN

When considering the predictions for 2012, I want to first deal with several questions about the comet Elenin. [Channel's note: Comet Elenin was discovered by Russian astronomer Leonid Elenin on December 10, 2010. It is supposed to come closest on October 16, 2011, when it will be around 22 million miles from the Earth]. This comet has already entered the solar system, and psychics are predicting upheaval from that source. Our perception is this: When you look at astronomical events such as the coming of a comet, you must look at them first in terms of their symbolic significance.

When we look at the position of planets through the context of astrology, we say that the positions of the planets are reflections of an energy that is pervasive in this section of the galaxy. For example, people sometimes say that because Mars is in a certain position, it is causing certain problems. The position of Mars is a reflection of the energies that are in the galaxy and that come to you on the planet Earth. From this perspective, the comet is a metaphorical or symbolic messenger that is coming to this planet.

It is true that this comet will be at its closest point around approximately 22 million miles from the Earth. And while that is relatively close in astronomical terms, it is not going to hit the Earth; it is not going to be an asteroid that is going to blow things up. Instead, the comet symbolically represents an attempt to awaken this planet at this time to the fact that Earth is interacting with many extraplanetary energy sources. Earth does not exist solely on its own in this galaxy. This comet is coming at this point in time because it has a message for humanity. The message for humanity is that you are galactic beings. You are a galactic planet. You are not isolated.

It just so happens that the comet's appearance coincides with one of the most intense periods of changes on the planet so far. The comet is coming in right at the beginning point of the 2012 energy. Therefore, many people, including some psychics, have predicted that there will be more eruptions of volcanoes. Some psychics have predicted that there will be more electromagnetic storms, weather changes, and earthquakes coming because of the comet. I want to say that the comet itself is not causing these things. Instead, it represents the energetic changes that are already here and some that are coming soon. One view is that the comet is causing this. In another view, all of these changes in the Earth are erupting, and the comet is a symbol of these changes.

A DECLINE IN POWER AND LEADERSHIP

Humanity is on the brink of a spiritual revolution and a spiritual period of evolution. This means that thoughts of biorelativity can be used to insulate the Earth from energetic changes and, in a sense, help to stabilize the Earth. Never before has there been such a great need for humanity to stabilize the Earth. Just before this lecture, someone contacted the channel and said that there are supposed to be huge earthquakes coming to Northeast America. This psychic made dire predictions of large magnitude earthquakes occurring in the first week of September.

In essence, the response to such predictions is that we must hold thoughts of planetary stability. We must hold thoughts of energetic spiritual balance for the planet, because the planet is already receiving threads of fifth-dimensional energy and light. Old patterns are breaking down, and the new energies that are coming to this planet are affecting it on a large scale. The effect can be seen on a social scale, a political scale, an economic scale, a geological scale, and a meteorological scale. The Earth's feedback systems are also being affected. All of these systems are now going to be in a stressful state.

I want to look into the predictions for 2012. First I will look at some of the political issues that are facing the United States in 2012. This year is going to see a continued decline in America's economic power and leadership in general. The current crises that you see—the debt crisis, the banking crisis, and the general financial crisis—will continue to accelerate in 2012. In fact, we see that the Dow Jones Industrial Average, which seems to be such an important number to people, will easily be going down to the 8,000 level by April or May of 2012.

The problem with the decline in the financial power and leadership in the United States is that there is no country or person that can replace that country on the global arena. There are people who say that America is going to lose its power and someone else will take its place, but there isn't any one country that can do that. Even China, which could be considered the more economically stable country, is not able to lead the world economically. What we predict for 2012 is that the decline of economic, political, and military power is going to leave a vacuum. That vacuum is not going to be filled because there is no single person or country that can stand forth to become the leader.

We are saying that there is also a decline in the ability of the leadership in general. You probably have already noticed that the leaders in the world don't seem to be able to lead. In other words, nobody really knows how to solve these problems. There is an interesting political discussion about wars in the Middle East and the precarious position of Iran. For example, you know that there are concerns that Iran is building a nuclear bomb, and undisputed evidence will be revealed in 2012 showing that Iran does have these capabilities. Of course, this development will be a direct threat to Israel, and this will present a direct threat to the peace in the Middle East.

Yet the United States will not do anything because it—perhaps wrongly from the political standpoint—attacked Iraq thinking that there were weapons of mass destruction there. Now there will be weapons of mass destruction discovered in Iran, but no one will follow the United States because they followed them the first time and the result was devastating and catastrophic. This is an example of decline in leadership. One of the things that is going to happen in 2012 is this loss of leadership in the world.

There will be many people who come forward in America saying that they want to be leaders. They think they have the energies and the solutions. None of them will be able to lead and be successful. In this vacuum, the answer will be that there is going to be somebody in the world that is emerging. Remember that you have heard this prediction before. You have heard that there a leader will emerge who will show how to solve all these problems. This person will gain popularity with many people, but a lot of people—especially the starseeds—will see that this person is not really who he says he is, and they will see through him immediately. You will see that there will be many people following this person anyway. Somebody is going to emerge because it is going to be obvious from the chaos that there needs to be somebody strong enough to lead. This is again part of the unfolding of the cosmic drama that is being played out on this planet.

Expect Greater Polarization on All Sides

On another front, we could say that this is another example of increasing polarizations in the year 2012. You think that 2011 has been polarized? Wait till you see 2012, because there will be even more energies of polarization. There is a benefit to increased polarization, however, and that is that spiritual energy will also become stronger. When we speak of polarization, many people will exclaim that it is terrible! Yet many people view polarizations as being either Side A or Side B. Side A doesn't seem to be able to communicate with Side B, and there will be a conflict that can lead to stalemates. But the good part of polarization for the starseeds and for spirituality is that spiritual beings on the planet are becoming stronger. Spiritually minded people are becoming more committed and more willing to work, because they understand that spiritual light must be used to solve some of these problems of the third dimension and that third-dimensional energies alone are not going to be able to solve these problems.

Overall in 2012, there is going to be an awakening of extraplanetary influences. This will especially be the case in South America, Asia, and in parts of Europe. There is going to be a huge understanding and a huge opening to galactic energies, the existence of extraplanetary beings, and the existence of the other energies. The year 2012 will see the uncovering of all of the secret documents that governments have been keeping in their closets. People will begin to accept the existence of dimensional beings. In general, there will be a much wider acceptance of the extraplanetary beings.

In 2012 there will be a continued loss of confidence in governments, especially when the people realize that their governments have kept one of the greatest secrets in history—the existence of proof of interactions with extraplanetary beings. Governments have kept that information secret from the population, but that information is going to break out into the open. People will see that these extradimensional beings exist and learn that in some cases there are governments that have interacted with them. People will see that governments have even borrowed and used technologies that have come from these interactions. It is even going to be discovered that a trade for technologies has occurred: Some governments have given permission for extraplanetary beings to engage in genetic studies of populations. In return, those governments have received technological assistance.

A Movement toward Greater Self-Sufficiency of Nations

There are some other predictions that we want to make for 2012. We always say that predictions are based on the available information at this time and from our perceptions. A lot of people have an interest in the election in the U.S. in 2012. We do not see Barack Obama winning the election. In fact, there is some doubt about whether he will even be a candidate for this election. There is going to be some type of a bombshell news item or disruption in his life or in the presidency that may make him either withdraw or decide to not run again. Something is going to happen that will shift the whole energy of the election.

Again, the problem with this is that there will be no really strong person who emerges in his stead. Even so, there will need to be a greater return to a spiritual understanding of Earth issues in politics. There will be a lot of anger directed at governments in 2012, especially when people realize that governments have been hiding many things. What you have been seeing in the Arab world—the massive set of revolutions that that has been called the Arab Spring—may be spreading to some of the countries in the West. [Editor's note: The movement referred to as the Arab Spring is a set of revolutionary movements that began in December of 2010 and intensified heavily in the Spring of 2011, resulting in protests and even revolutions in over a dozen countries in the Arab world.]

There are always bright spots, and there are always places that are somewhat immune to global issues. We cannot cover all of the countries, but we can say that many of the countries in South America are relatively immune to governmental disruptions at this point, and so there will be a little more stability there. The governments in countries in South America will be affected by the economic instability, but at the same time, many of these countries have their own individual resources that will enable them to become more self-sufficient.

I think that the countries in South and Central America are going to realize that they have to find ways of being on their own. They have to find greater self-sufficiency and more self-direction. Countries in South America have more direct possibility for becoming self-sufficient because they have access to quite a few resources, and because the populations in these countries are already more resonant with extradimensional and extraplanetary beings. The people of these nations have more personal experiences, and extradimensional knowledge is more generally open in these countries. In particular, I see Argentina and Brazil as two countries that will have stability.

Generally, all the countries that are south of the Tropic of Capricorn will have more stable weather patterns. There will be difficult weather situations at times. They may have more rain and more cold than usual. It is not going to be devastating or catastrophic like some of the weather changes that are being experienced in the northern hemisphere—for example, the areas where there are severe droughts. In contrast, drought in Texas and in other parts of North America will continue through 2012. There will be several times when there will be huge storms, but they will not break the drought. In terms of North America, we do not see major earthquakes happening in the Northeast. There is a lot of fear that people are spreading about catastrophic events in 2012 that will not really happen.

THE VALUE OF BIORELATIVITY TO THE EARTH

Never before in the history of humanity has it become so necessary to use biorelativity. Starseeds and lightworkers are going to work to hold and protect Earth's energy patterns. It is possible that a comet could send electromagnetic discharges to the Earth that could disrupt satellites. This possibility of electromagnetic disruption can be countered by starseeds putting white light around the Earth and around the electromagnetic energy field of the Earth. Yes, there are great Earth changes happening. At the same time, the power of biorelativity is also strong. The effectiveness of biorelativity against disruptive energy can be great. People should believe and understand that biorelativity is a spiritual force that can be used to help stabilize weather patterns, weather changes, and even earthquakes.

Australia and New Zealand are two other countries that will be relatively insulated from further Earth changes. They may continue to suffer economically because of their dependence on the United States, but they have a strong history of independence and self-direction. I think that Australians will experience some dramatic weather events in 2012, but it is something that they will be able to integrate and tolerate.

There are also going to be some dramatic shifts in their government: They will discover that their government has been in cahoots with the United States, and that they have unnecessarily handed over more of their powers to the United States. People will be shocked when they realize some of the things that they turned over to the United States. They will become angry and will want to stop their government from the turning over of their power and light and energy to another country. This is going to happen in Australia. The Australian government knows about extraterrestrial energies and extraplanetary interactions. It will make people unhappy when Australians find out that the government has kept major secrets from them. Generally, however, Australia will be a stable place to be in 2012 except for these other weather patterns.

Parts of Africa will continue to be unstable. There will continue to be many disruptions there, along with a lot of poverty and famine in certain parts, as you know, such as in Somalia and other areas. Generally, the world is not going to marshal resources to stop these famines because nations are going to be struggling with their own problems, but there are also many bright spots in Africa. A lot of people are worried about the Middle East. We think there is going to be a confrontation between Israel and another Middle Eastern country. The idea is that Israel is going to have to defend itself, which Israel already knows. Israel will be successful in this, and although the United States will not be able to act unilaterally against Iran, the United States will be supporting Israel behind the scenes. The Arab Spring will continue for a while, but it is going to be pretty much over by December 2011. The countries that are open to shifting will have shifted by December. Other countries that have not shifted dramatically will be able to hold onto their power at that point at least for a while.

We still see Europe as mixed. I think that Germany still will remain the leader in that area, because it still has the most economic power and that will continue. Germany will continue to balance the rest of Europe with the help of France. Germany has an obligation to hold the rest of Europe afloat financially, and they will hold to that obligation. Weather patterns in Europe will be somewhat variable and somewhat extreme, but it won't be as extreme as it will be in the United States. There will be periods of great social unrest in some of the Mediterranean countries including Spain, Greece, Portugal, and even Italy. The rest of Europe and Eastern Europe will be relatively stable. Germany will continue to exert a leadership role in energy innovation for 2012.

There are still huge dangers around the world from nuclear energy and from nuclear reactors. It will be revealed that the Fukushima accident is far more dangerous and far more devastating than anyone has indicated. We think that many people knew that already, but a true report of the devastation will come out. There will be reports of other nuclear accidents that have occurred around the world. Unfortunately, we do not see a movement towards shutting down the reactors. There is a possibility of one or two more major nuclear accidents in 2012 that may influence these decisions, however.

Generally, Asia and India continue to be dominant forces economically. India will assume a stronger leadership role and will become a greater ally to the United States. It is going to be one of the few countries that is going to be in the position to offer substantial support to the United States, both in terms of economic support and technical support. India will be developing a space program, for example, and this will become more obvious in 2012.

In conclusion, I could say that lightworkers and lightwork in 2012 are going to become stronger. Because of increased polarizations, more people will seek spiritual light and spiritual understanding, and lightworkers will increase their abilities to become influential and hold the light patterns. Remember that there will be huge influxes of fifth-dimensional light in 2012, and these energy influxes will contain answers to many problems.

Remember also that the ascension is going to download spiritual energy into the planet. Even when the ascension ends and the first wave is over, know that the spiritual light that the ascension brings will stay on the planet. It is not as if the fifth dimension will open, the ascension will happen, and then the fifth dimension will close and spiritual light is going to be gone—that light will remain in and for all of you as starseeds. So, my friends, we are looking forward to working more closely with all of you in biorelativity work. This is Juliano. Good day.

Conclusion:
Future Biorelativity Work

Sanat Kumara, Juliano, and the Arcturians

Greetings, I am Sanat Kumara. I am often called the planetary logos. In a way, that means that I am in good connection with the spirit of the Earth as a type of overlord of the Earth's processes. This doesn't mean I can control the processes but rather that I am in communication with Earth and can speak for her in some ways and that in some ways I can influence the Earth.

The first thing I wish to say is that the oil spill in the Gulf of Mexico reflects a primary Earth change caused by a great mistake that was made over a sacred area in the ocean. It is related to the energies of Atlantis and the memory remnants of how that continent was destroyed. Some have said that the Earth is very angry and that this is one of the reasons why the Earth did not allow the leak to stop quickly. I can tell you that the Earth-energy spirit is not happy with how this oil spill unfolded or with how the follow-up repairs were handled. This was a major hemorrhaging of an Earth ley line, and it required a specific kind of surgery that was not known to scientists. And while there was openness to planetary energy workers that had never been seen before and people finally acquired some sympathy for the planetary workers, the spill was a very high price to pay for that awareness.

CITIES OF LIGHT IN SERVICE TO PLANET EARTH

On that note, I want to speak to you also about service ideas and how the structure of the planet is going to change. You are already seeing that there is a move toward a different economy, a move to change the financial currencies of the world: How things are valued economically is going to change, and you are going to see a value shift very soon that will reflect a new type of foundation for how a society operates. Some people call it a sustainable economy base. And out of all of the economic structures globally, for example, Germany is in a very good position now to either lead or to manifest a new Earth service value system based on higher spiritual ideas and principles, for one of the balances in planetary healing from the Tree of Life is providing service to Earth.

This means that there is a bigger push to protect forests and waterways and to provide more ecologically friendly services. When you are looking at your missions and the service that you want to offer other people, you do not always have to think in terms of spiritual worth; you also can think in terms of energy work for the development of solar and sustainable energy. This means that technology and the economy will no longer be based on competition and jealousy. Instead, there will be a brotherhood and sisterhood working together to solve problems without concern over who is making the most money or who is going to have the best plan to run the economy.

Planetary cities of light can provide a great service of showing how to live successfully in this kind of community, and the development of planetary cities of light also includes a new psychology of society. This is why I think that Germany has many advantages as you move in this direction. When you are thinking about working with planetary cities of light, also think in terms of service to the planet. Think about how the attitudes of working together as brothers and sisters can be magnified. The new and existing planetary cities of light are an evolutionary step forward in the development of the new society. It is a great pleasure and very enlightening to live in such a society, such a city, such a group. I am Sanat Kumara. Good day.

Future Planetary Cities and Biorelativity Work

Greetings, I'm Juliano, and we are the Arcturians. We talk about planetary cities of light as an interactive force for biorelativity and positive planetary change. The greatest ability of starseeds is to create energy fields around areas where they live so that they activate sacred areas. One of the things that make planetary cities sacred is that through them, you connect to galactic cities and to sister cities on Earth. The idea of the sister cities on the Earth is that they send energy to each other. That is the same concept we use in the Group of Forty: A group of starseeds together can create a force greater than what you can create by yourself.

When there are sister cities working together, each city has a particular energy. For example, the energy of both Balcon and Nelson Bay in New South Wales in Australia is particularly connected to the ancient whales and the dolphins. These planetary cities of light activated by starseeds each have unique means of connecting to the oceans. These cities are also directly connected with some great star systems, including the Pleiades. Or let us also look at a possible planetary city of light in England. A planetary city of light in England may not have the ocean energy of the dolphins and whales, but that city may have the energy of crop circles, the Celts, Merlin, or Stonehenge. Sister cities can share their unique energy with other sister planetary cities of light.

So what I'm saying is that the energy of each planetary city is unique, and I'm asking that people who are in the planetary cities of light make a list or survey of their strengths and energies and how they can share that energy with their sister cities. After you make the list, you can then ask what energy your sister city has that it can share. For example, Sedona, Arizona, is now a sister city to San Martín de los Andes in Argentina. Sedona has the energy of being the psychic capital of North America. Therefore, San Martín de los Andes, in our estimation, has the potential for being the psychic capital of South America. When Sedona and its starseeds connect with San Martín de los Andes, they can send energy to help that city to become more of a psychic capital.

There need to be lightworkers connecting with their sister cities, possibly through phone conferencing, so that they can send the energies the other city needs. I'm very optimistic that this sharing is going to happen and that it will emit a strong healing force for the Earth. For everyone else who is involved with the planetary cities of light in your areas, I ask you to do the same thing. Your efforts will result in great sharing, allowing the energies to be transferred. Just like the energy when you are shimmering in the cities of Alano, your planetary cities of light can shimmer with another planetary city of light on the Earth. That is one of the ways that energy is going to be transformed between planetary cities of light within the Earth.

Unity through Spiritual Links

As we seek to bring the conscious energy from the Arcturians and from the fifth dimension to all of the planetary cities of light, we also want to acknowledge the linkages that these planetary cities of light are making by using the energies of their sister cities. We can also use the idea of the brother city as well as the sister city, and remember that in our discussions of the sacred triangle, we have also talked about the white brotherhood and the white sisterhood; the idea of establishing these sister-city linkages is based on the idea of the white brotherhood and the white sisterhood.

What does this mean? The white brotherhood and white sisterhood is a unity of energy that acknowledges all of the higher mystical truths and all of the higher mystical knowledge in all religions. All these truths become united when they

LINKING THE PLANETARY CITIES OF LIGHT

With planetary cities of light, a city in one area can send energy and light to another city, and this will help to raise the spiritual vibration of both cities. So we ask that each city identify other cities that they want to become sister cities with. We have responded to and received twenty-one cities, and because the cities and the work they do are so important, I'm going to list the names of these cities and their sisters:

1. The first of these cities is Taos, New Mexico, the planetary city of light that is going to be the sister city working with San Pedro de la Paz, Chile.

2. The second city is Aufkirchen, at the Starnberger See, near Munich, Germany. This city is going to become the sister city to Tallinn, Estonia.

3. The third set of cities is Carson City, Nevada, Mount Shasta, California, and Twin Falls, Idaho. We are forming a triangle with these three cities, because some starseeds requested a sister-city triangle, which is fine.

4. The fourth city pairing is between two cities in Germany: Ananda Village, in Herl, and Oldenburg.

5. The fifth city is Chihuahua, in the state of Chihuahua, Mexico; it is linking with Concepción, in Chile.

6. The sixth set of cities are linked between Rancho Lagunitas in Mexico, Mount Shasta in California, Coyoacán in Mexico, and Toledo in Spain.

7. The seventh city is located in Pasadena, California, and it is linking with Anchorage, Alaska.

8. Zaragoza, Spain, is linking with Sebucán, which is part of Caracas in Venezuela.

9. Sedona, Arizona, links with the Argentinian cities of San Martín de los Andes and Barrio Palermo, Buenos Aires.

10. Balcolyn, Australia, which is near Nelson Bay in New South Wales, is linking with Polbathic, in Cornwall, England.

11. Cuicuilco, Mexico, is linking with Montserrat, Spain.

12. The city of Lourdes, France, will form a link with Murcia, Spain.

13. The Spanish city of Santiago de Compostela is linking with Ciudad Obregón, in Mexico.

14. La Plata, which is part of Buenos Aires, Argentina, is linked to Monterrey, Mexico.

15. Monterrey, Mexico, is linking with the German cities of Lindlar and Schalkenmehren.

16. Granada, Spain, will be linked with La Serena, Chile.

17. Omaha, Nebraska, is linking with Belleville, Canada.

18. Auckland, New Zealand, is linking with Vale do Capão, Brazil.

19. Groom Creek/Spruce Mountain in Arizona is linking with Sant Pere de Ribes, Spain, and Nelson Bay, Australia.

20. Finally, the Spanish city of Gijón is linking with Bahía Blanca, Argentina.

These are the twenty cities with their sister cities, with the activation city in Vale das Borboletas, Brazil, giving us twenty-one cities. This provides us with quite a large activation energy.

—*David Miller*

reach a certain point of energy, and therefore the masters in Buddhism, Judaism, Christianity, Taoism, and all the other many beautiful religious ideas form a bond on a higher plane. In this bond, there is a unity established that reaches out to all peoples and that is seeking to elevate the consciousness of all peoples, all star-seeds, and all spiritual seekers. This is the idea behind the planetary cities of light and the sister cities of light. With this sharing, there is an acknowledgment of the importance of reaching out to other cities. No one city is better than another city, just like no one spiritual truth, no one spiritual practice, is necessarily better; each has its own perspective.

What is beautiful about the concept of the white brotherhood and sisterhood is that they and their spirit guides are all working together for the advancement of the raised consciousness of humanity. And as it is with the planetary cities, so it is with the sister cities; the idea of the planetary cities of light is to help raise the consciousness of everyone in that planetary city. How is this to be done? The way it will be done is through spiritual work, by downloading fifth-dimensional energies. You will do it through group activities so that the spiritual light quotient of that planetary city is raised. This includes participating in events and workshops that are spiritual and gathering people in groups and having ceremonies and chanting. It involves encircling your planetary cities of light in a beautiful white light by putting great crystals around the city so that energies can be received of the higher level. There are many other activities I could list that help a planetary city of light to maintain and to activate its light field so that it can become a holder of highest consciousness.

Each of you knows that there are dramatic changes occurring on this planet, especially in the political and social arenas. Many of you have asked how you can participate, how you can help in the change in the Earth, because some of you are fulfilling your soul missions by doing this planetary work. But you want to know: "Well, shall I be involved in social causes; should I be involved in political causes for change?" Of course that is your individual decision, but I want you to understand that we, the Arcturians, have developed this project of the planetary cities of light specifically for instituting dramatic changes, and we believe that dramatic changes can occur from even small activations of these planetary cities. To assist in this project, you are going to help to create a beautiful web of fifth-dimensional energy in the chosen city that you can work with.

So please understand that it is part of your soul mission, your soul work, to do and to participate in the project of the planetary cities of light project. And this project is growing. I'm sure that you understand this; I'm sure that you understand that there are many peoples around the world who want to know how to become a part of a planetary city of light. These people will be looking at you as the original founders of the first level of planetary cities of light. They will be studying how you have done this work and how you are all helping to change the communities that you are living in so that these communities can become light cities.

SHARED TRAITS MEAN SHARED STRENGTH

Now, the idea behind the planetary sister cities of light is that they are an extension of the planetary cities of light, an extension of the concepts of the white brotherhood and the white sisterhood. It is important to activate the planetary cities of light, but they do not exist in isolation. They exist in a web of light, and this web of light connects them with other planetary cities of light. If, for any reason, one planetary city of light were to have difficulty, then the other linkages that these planetary cities of light may have with their sister cities can provide a powerful assistance.

When working with fifth-dimensional connections, energy can be transformed and transmitted in an amazingly strong way. Do not underestimate the power of etheric energy, and do not underestimate the power of *remote* etheric energy through which you can work to send remotely beautiful fifth-dimensional energy. The sister cities of light can send energy to their family, to their sisters. And each city of light, as you know, has a specific advantage, a specific trait and energy.

Such an energy exchange is also possible for all of the sister cities of light. Each city has a unique trait, and these traits can be shared. But I want you to know that, as a planetary city of light, you can be sharing energies with your sister city. I see that many of you who have the financial means will be travelling to your sister cities of light and developing new friendships with the people there that you are working with. There will be meetings where the sisters cities of light will come together. What a beautiful idea to share your fifth-dimensional activation energies with your sister cities! This will only help to strengthen your connections to the fifth dimension.

MEDITATION TO ACTIVATE A NEW CITY

Now we are at this powerful moment when we are entering the doorway into the 2012 energy field. Therefore, your participation in the planetary cities of light project and in working with the sister cities is going to be amplified more and more. So now we will do a group meditation. In this meditation, we want to activate the new city of light and to help to summon and hold the connections of all of the twenty-one sister cities of light that we have activated and have listed today. So please follow the following instructions.

I, Juliano, am now raising all twelve etheric crystals out of their place around the world. These beautiful etheric crystals that are holding fifth-dimensional light and energy from Arcturus are now being raised. A web of fifth-dimensional light in the shape of the Tree of Life is interconnecting around the whole planet, and the ring of ascension is also receiving a huge activation. Now all of these planetary cities of light that we are working with are now receiving this higher light. So please, for several minutes, see each of the etheric crystals—or the etheric crystals that you are closest to—specifically sending activation light to your city and also to the new city: Vale das Borboletas in Brazil. So we will go into a meditation now. [Pause.]

See how these linkages are activated between the planetary sister cities of light. See beautiful streams of fifth-dimensional light connecting Taos, Mexico, with San Pedro de la Paz, Chile. See these streams of fifth-dimensional light going from Aufkirchen near the Starnberger See, Germany, to Tallinn, Estonia. Envision these streams of light moving from Carson City, Nevada, and Mount Shasta, California, to Twin Falls, Idaho. See beautiful streams of light traveling from Ananda Village to Oldenburg in Germany. See them flowing from Chihuahua, Mexico, to Concepción, Chile—from Rancho Lagunitas, Mexico, to Mount Shasta and Coyoacán, Mexico, and Toledo, Spain, as well as from Pasadena, California, to Anchorage, Alaska. See this light move between Zaragoza, Spain, and Sebucán, part of Caracas.

It flows through Sedona, Arizona, San Martín de los Andes, and Barrio Palermo, Argentina. These beautiful streams of light travel through Balcolyn, Australia, and Polbathic, in Cornwall, England, as well as through Cuicuilco, Mexico, and Montserrat, Spain. They illuminate the cities of Lourdes, France, and Murcia, Spain. They flow through Santiago de Compostela and Obregon in Sonora, Mexico. La Plata—part of Buenos Aires, Argentina—and Monterrey, Mexico, feel these streams of light. In Germany, the fifth-dimensional light flows through Lindlar and Schalkenmehren as well as through Oldenburg and Ananda Village. These streams move through Granada, Spain, and La Serena, Chile.

These beautiful streams of fifth-dimensional light move through Omaha, Nebraska, and Belleville, Canada, as well as through Auckland, New Zealand, and Vale do Capão, Brazil. Send a special energy of healing light to Auckland, New Zealand, which is now experiencing the terrible oil spill. Please send the light and energies and your thoughts to help them to clean up this oil so that there is minimum amount of damage. See the connection between Groom Creek/Spruce Mountain, Arizona, and Sant Pere de Ribes, Spain, and Nelson Bay, Australia. It is a beautiful triangle of light. See the connection between Gijón, Spain, and Bahía Blanca, Argentina. All of these planetary sister cities of light are now interacting, so hold that energy now as we go back in silence.

I, Juliano, from the starship Athena, am downloading a beautiful blue healing light to all of the planetary cities of light, to all of you who are inhabitants of the planetary cities of light and who all are working to establish sister cities of light. I know that there will be many more activations and many more connections that we will be establishing over the coming months as we move into the 2012 doorway. Know that these connections and these links will become stronger and more powerful. Remember that the cities of light are not only linking with each other but that you as inhabitants of the cities of light are linking with the other inhabitants in the other sister cities of light. You are forming a great protective light where beauty and fifth-dimensional energies will be held and will permeate all activities in the cities of light. I am Juliano, and we are the Arcturians. Good day.

GLOSSARY

2012 ALIGNMENT
A time when Earth comes into alignment with the center of the Milky Way galaxy. This is also referred to in the Mayan calendar, and prophecies were made for this date. The Maya believed that Earth will come into alignment with the center of the galaxy on December 21, 2012. Some have interpreted the Mayan statements as marking the end of the world. Others say that this alignment represents the transformation of the world. One view is that our world will be born again on December 21, 2012. In *Maya Cosmogenesis 2012*, John Major Jenkins interpreted the Mayan vision of this alignment in 2012 as a union of the Cosmic Mother, or the Milky Way, with the Father, represented as the December solstice sun.

2012 CORRIDOR
A tunnel or corridor to the future time of 2012 when Earth's transformation will be at its height. By projecting positive energy and images into this time, one can help maximize positive outcomes for this time.

ADAM KADMON
The Hebrew term for the primordial or first man. It is the prototype for the first being to emerge after the beginning of creation.

ADONAI
Hebrew name for God, translated as "my Lord."

ADONAI TZEVA'OTH

Hebrew for "Lord of Hosts."

ADON OLAM

Hebrew for "Lord of the Universe."

AIN SOF

In *Kaballah*, the term *Ain Sof* means "that without end." It is sometimes compared to the great Tao. *Ain Sof* is the absolute perfection in which there are no distinctions and no differentiations. It does not reveal itself in a way that makes knowledge of its nature possible.

AMIDAH

A famous Hebrew prayer recited silently during daily prayers.

ARCHANGEL

The term applies generally to all angels above the grade of angel. It also designates the highest rank of angels in the celestial hierarchy. The *Kaballah* cites ten archangels. They are considered messengers bearing divine decrees.

ASCENSION

A point of transformation reached through the integration of the physical, emotional, mental, and spiritual selves. The unification of the bodies allows one to transcend the limits of the third dimension and move into a higher realm. It has been compared to what is called "the Rapture" in some denominations of Christian theology. It has also been defined as a spiritual acceleration of consciousness, which allows the soul to return to the higher realms and thus is freed from the cycle of karma and rebirth.

ASHTAR

The commander over a group of spiritual beings who are dedicated to helping the Earth ascend. The beings Ashtar oversees exist primarily in the fifth dimension and come from many different extraterrestrial civilizations.

ASTRAL PLANE

The non-physical level of reality considered to be where most humans go when they die.

A*TAH*

The Hebrew word for "you." It is used in prayer to refer to the Creator.

A*TAH* G*IBUR* A*DONAI*

Hebrew for "You are great, Adonai!"

A*UR*

The Hebrew word for "light." It is also spelled *Or.*

A*UR* H*A* K*ODESH*

Hebrew for the "holy light."

A*UR* H*A* M*OSHIACH*

Hebrew for the "light of the Messiah."

B*ARUCH*

The Hebrew word for "blessed," often used in referring to the Creator.

B*ARUCH* H*U*

The Hebrew transliteration for "Blessed are You," referring to the Creator.

B'*NAI* E*LOHIM*

The children of light. The Hebrew words for the "sons, or brotherhood, of the Elohim."

C*HAKRAS*

Energy centers of the human body system. These centers provide the integration and transfer of energy between the spiritual, mental, emotional, and biological systems of the human body.

C*HASHMAL*

A mysterious Hebrew term mentioned in Ezekiel's vision. It refers to the mental state through which one passes when one ascends from the level of speaking to one of pure mental silence and sensitivity.

EH'YEH ASHER EH'YEH
In Hebrew, the name of God given to Moses at the burning bush in Genesis 3:14. *Ehiyeh Asher Ehiyeh* is the full name translated as "I shall be that I shall be" (also translated "I am that I am"). In Hebrew, this is also known as the supreme name of God. The correct Hebrew translation is "I will be that I will be."

ELOHIM
In Hebrew, the name that describes the Creator in chapter one of Genesis.

ETZ HA CHAYIM
Hebrew for "Tree of Life."

GADOL
The Hebrew word for "great." It is also used as an adjective when describing God.

GURHAN
A spiritual entity from the Andromeda Galaxy in the seventh dimension.

HU
The Hebrew word for "he." In prayers it can refer to the Creator.

IBBUR
The Hebrew word describing the entry of another soul into a man.

KABALLAH
The major branch of Jewish mysticism. The Hebrew word *Kaballah* is translated as "to receive."

KADOSH
Hebrew word for "holy."

KADOSH, KADOSH, KADOSH ADONAI TZEVAOTH
Hebrew for "Holy, holy, holy is the Lord of Hosts." This is a powerful expression that, when toned, can raise one's level of consciousness to new heights and assist in unlocking the codes for our transformation into the fifth dimension.

K'DUSHAH
A Hebrew prayer, translated as "Holiness."

LIGHTBODY

The higher etheric spirit body that is connected to the highest soul energy.

MAGGIDIM

Hebrew word for divine spirits speaking to a Kaballist.

MEEK

The Hebrew word for "king." It is used in prayer to refer to God.

MERKAVAH

In Hebrew, this term means "chariot," and in modern spirituality, it refers to a chariot in etheric form that is used to bring spiritual seekers to the higher dimensions. Also spelled *merkaba* and *merkabah*. In *Kaballah* it is the term that means God's throne-chariot, referring to the chariot of Ezekiel's vision. It is also used in describing a branch in *Kaballah* called "merkavah mysticism."

METATRON

Tradition associates Metatron with Enoch, who "walked with God" (Gen. 5:22) and who ascended to heaven and was changed from a human being into an angel. His name has been defined as the Angel of Presence, or as the one who occupies the throne next to the divine throne. Another interpretation of his name is based on the Latin word *metator*, which means a guide or measurer. In the world of the Jewish mystic, Metatron came to hold the highest rank among angels. According to the Arcturians, Metatron is associated with the stargate and is assisting souls in ascension to higher worlds.

METATRONA-SHEKHINAH

These are two names for the divine presence. It is that aspect of the Goddess energy that is present on Earth.

MICHAEL

This being's name is actually a question that means, "Who is like God?" He is perhaps the best known of the archangels and is acknowledged by all three Western sacred traditions. He has been called the Prince of Light, fighting a war against the sons of darkness. In this role, he is depicted most often as winged, with unsheathed sword—the warrior of God and slayer of the dragon. His role in the ascension is focused on helping us to cut the cords of attachment to the Earth plane, which will allow us to move up to higher consciousness. In the *Kaballah* he is regarded as the forerunner of the Shekhinah, the divine Mother.

MONAD

The original, elemental creative force.

NABUR

A Kaballistic rabbi and teacher of the author in a former lifetime.

NEFESH

The Hebrew word for "animal soul," or "lower soul," representing the entire range of instincts. *Nefesh* is the raw vital energy needed to live on this planet.

NESHAMAH

Hebrew word for the spiritual portion of the soul, or higher self. It is the intuitive power that connects humankind with the Creator, the highest of the three parts of the soul that transcends third-dimensional reality and Earth ego to link directly to the divine light.

QUAN YIN

A female member of the Spiritual Hierarchy. In her previous Asian incarnation, she performed many acts of kindness and compassion and is known as the Goddess of Mercy.

RABBI HAYYIM VITAL

A Kaballist rabbi who lived from 1543 to 1620 in Safed, Palestine.

RAPHAEL

Raphael is perhaps the most endearing of all the angels—and the one most often depicted in Western art. His name means "God Has Healed." His career seems to focus on medical missions and he helps people to heal human maladies. He was the angel sent by God to cure Jacob of the injury to his thigh when Jacob wrestled with his dark adversary. He is also considered to be the guardian of the Tree of Life in the Garden of Eden.

RUACH HA KODESH

The Hebrew words used to describe the state of enlightenment, literally translated as the "Holy Spirit."

Sananda

Sananda is the one who is known to us as Master Jesus. He is considered one of the greatest Kaballists of all times. His galactic name, Sananda, represents an evolved and galactic picture of who he is in his entirety. In the *Kaballah*, Sananda is known as Joshua ben Miriam of Nazareth, which translates as Joshua, son of Mary of Nazareth.

Shabbat

Shabbat is the Jewish Sabbath, on Friday. Kaballists believe that the Shekhinah comes on *Shabbat* to be with man and to help make that day holy.

Shekhinah

In Hebrew, "the divine Mother." *Shekhinah* is the frequently used Talmudic term denoting the visible and audible manifestation of God's presence on Earth. In its ultimate concept, it stands for an independent feminine entity, the divine Mother.

Stargate

A multidimensional portal into other higher realms. The Arcturian stargate is very close to the Arcturus star system, and it is overseen by the Arcturians. This powerful passage point requires that Earthlings who wish to pass through it must complete all lessons and Earth incarnations associated with the third-dimensional experience. It serves as a gateway to the fifth dimension. New soul assignments are given there, and souls can then be sent to many different higher realms throughout the galaxy and universe.

Starseeds

Earth beings throughout our current modern age who have previous lifetimes in other parts of our galaxy. They also have a great awareness that there are other beings living in our galaxy and in the universe.

Tikkun

In Hebrew, this term means "restoration," or "the divine restoration of the cosmos." In *Kaballah*, this refers to the concept that the vessel holding the light from the Creator was broken and that it is the task of humans to help restore it.

TREE OF LIFE

The Tree of Life is a galactic blueprint for the creation of this reality. It includes ten energy codes placed in spheres in the shape of a tree. These codes are used for individual and planetary healing. The three spiritualities of the Sacred Triangle are included in the Tree of Life. The Tree of Life is not flat, but multi-dimensional and holographic. The Tree of Life has pathways for manifestation found in its twenty-two lines. The Tree of Life connects to the energy of the cosmos. [See the separate Tree of Life section later in this appendix.]

VYWAMUS

A fifth-dimensional soul psychologist known for his insight into the psychology of Earth problems and the resolution of issues related to starseeds incarnated on Earth.

WHITE BROTHERHOOD

The White Brotherhood is a spiritual hierarchy of ascended masters residing in the fifth dimension. White is not used here as a racial term. It refers to the white light, or higher frequency, that these masters have attained.

YIHUDIM

The Hebrew word for "unifications." Kaballists believe that humans help to unify the two aspects of the Godhead through prayer. It is important to enunciate a simple statement prior to reciting a prayer to the effect that one's intention is to bring about the unification of God and the *Shekhinah*.

ZADDIQ

Hebrew word for "wise man."

ZELEM

Hebrew for "man's ethereal body," which serves as an intermediary between his material body and his soul.

ZOHAR

The Book of Splendor: a thirteenth-century Spanish mystic's guide to Kaballism.

NOTES ON HEBREW
PRONUNCIATION

This is not intended to be a comprehensive pronunciation guide to Hebrew—modern or ancient, classical or rabbinical. Like most languages, Hebrew has undergone many regional and temporal changes in its structure and pronunciation.

The primary purpose of this guide is to assist the reader in producing verbal sounds that resonate with their respective energies. A full survey of all possible sounds expressible in the Hebrew language is beyond the scope of this book.

Most of the consonantal sounds are very close to how they have been rendered in this text. There are a few sounds which will be unfamiliar to those who do not speak Hebrew. These sounds are listed below.

q: used instead of "k" to indicate a similar sound, but further back on the palate, with the lips more rounded

z̧: a sound quite close to "ts," as in English "its," with the "t" sound perhaps less stressed

ch: guttural, as in German "Bach"

sh: as in English "she"

r: not quite equivalent to the English "r," instead much more like the "r" in French—further back on the palate and rolled forward

Note on doubled consonants *kk, dd, bb,* and so on. These must be pronounced fully, but smoothly. So *Zaddiq* is "zad-diq" and *Tikkun* is "tik-kun," with no noticeable pause between the doubled consonants, but each is pronounced.

For vowels, the following pronunciation is given as a guide. There are few more disputed topics in the study of ancient languages than the pronunciation of the vowels, especially in a living ancient language like Hebrew, which has historically been written with no vowels.

A: as in "father"

E: approximately between "eh" and "ay"

I: as in "ink"

O: as in "over"

U: approximately between "under" and "super," but tending toward the long sound

AI: like "eye"

AU: approximately between "auger" and "aura"

AH: usually at the end of a word, it has a similar sound to the "a" by itself, like "a" as in "father," but lengthened and slightly aspirated—think just like English "ah"

NOTES ON THE TREE OF LIFE

The Tree of Life (Hebrew: *Etz ha Chayim*) is mentioned sparingly in this text, but as it may be unfamiliar to some readers, a diagram and brief explanation follows. There are many other sources of information on the Tree of Life and its cosmology, and readers are directed to those sources in the event that they take an interest in this concept.

The Tree of Life is a cosmological map, or framework, for creation, used by Kaballists to aid in understanding the relationships of all things in the universe. It consists of the ten *Sephiroth* (spheres) connected by twenty-two paths, and it represents a kind of framework for describing the hierarchy of existence, from the limitless light of *Ain Soph Aur* all the way down to the base stuff of creation.

The first three *Sephiroth* are the supernal triad. These form the level sometimes collectively referred to as the *Neshemah*, the highest level of the soul, ascended consciousness, and self.

*   *Kether* is the *Sephira* closest to God. This is *Sephira* is the aspiration of the Gnostics, seeking union with the divine. The name means "crown."

*   *Chokmah* is the prime movement in existence, the initial spark. The name itself means "wisdom."

*   *Binah* is primordial duality, that which receives and is acted upon by the forces from *Chokmah*. The name means "understanding."

The next six *Sephiroth* are the part of creation sometimes referred to as the *Ruach,* containing the powers of intellect and consciousness.

- *Chesed* is the loving grace of God, the requisite energy to sustain creation. The name means "mercy."

- *Geburah* is the strength to endure, the power of judgment, and the will of intent. The name means "severity."

- *Tiferet* is the Christ consciousness, the balanced compassion expressed as the equilibrium between *Chesed* and *Geburah*. The name means "beauty."

- *Netzach* is initiative, strength of will, and overcoming. The name means "victory."

- *Hod* is faith, surrender, and letting go. The name means "glory."

- *Yesod* is remembrance, subconscious connection, and ethereal awareness. The name means "foundation."

Below *Yesod* is the level reffered to as the *Nefesh*, containing the physical realm, lusts and passions, and the animal soul:

- *Malkuth* is the realization, creation, the material. The name means "kingdom."

These are but brief and very incomplete descriptions, and the reader is encouraged to undertake further study. The *Sephiroth* all have many different qualities, and the paths that connect them can be powerful tools to the spiritual aspirant.

The New 5th Dimensional Planetary Tree of
Using the Arcturian Etheric Crystals on Mother Earth

Mount Fuji
Undifferentiated
Cosmic Light
METATRON

Lake Moraine
Knowledge,
Intelligence
& Reason
VYWAMUS

Bodensee
Wisdom,
Understanding
& Intuition
CHIEF WHITE
EAGLE

Istanbul
Hidden Knowledge
Revealed
HELIO-AH

Volcan Poas
Strength, Discipline &
Judgment for Earth
ARCHANGEL
MICHAEL

Mount Shasta
Loving Kindness &
Compassion for Earth
WHITE BUFFALO
CALF WOMAN

Montserrat
Sacred, Messianic
Energy
SANANDA

Lake Taupo
Creation of Sacred
Places & Planetary
Cities of Light
MARY

Grose Valley
Creation of New
Earth Society
SANAT KUMARA

**Copper
Canyon**
Manifesting 5D
Energy in 3D
TOMAR, ALANO

**Serra da
Bocaina**
Earth's Interaction
with 3rd & 5th
Dimensions
JULIANO

Lago Puelo
Holding Manifested
Energy on Earth
SPIRIT FIRE

Developed by David K. Miller, www.groupofforty.com, with Rob Claar. All rights reserved.

MAP OF THE
TWELVE ETHERIC CRYSTALS

THE TWELVE ETHERIC CRYSTALS
NOW ACTIVATED ON PLANET EARTH

1. Lago Puelo, Argentina (2002)
2. Grose Valley, Australia (2003)
3. Moraine Lake, British Columbia, Canada (2004)
4. The Bodensee (Lake Constance), Europe (2005)
5. The Poás Volcano, Costa Rica (2006)
6. Mount Shasta, California, United States (2007)
7. Lake Taupo, New Zealand (2007)
8. Barranca del Cobre (Copper Canyon), Mexico (2008)
9. Montserrat, Spain (2008)
10. Mount Fuji, Japan (2008)
11. Istanbul, Turkey (2009)
12. Serra da Bocaina, Brazil (2009)

PLANETARY CITIES OF LIGHT WITH THEIR STAR AND PLANETARY SISTER CITIES

The following is an alphabetical list of current cities of light as of late 2011, along with their sister cities on Earth and throughout the universe, if those connections have been made. As new star and planetary sister cities of light are activated and linked, they will be added to a dynamic list on the Group of Forty website. For that news as well as the current contact information of the coordinators for each city, please visit http://gofcitiesoflight.blogspot.com/

ALTOS MIRANDINOS, CARACAS, VENEZUELA
Coordinator: Yelithza Ramos del Corral

ANANDA VILLAGE, NEAR HERL, GERMANY
Planetary Sister City: Oldenburg, Germany
Coordinator: Prabhu Nama'Ba'Shie' Hornung

We, the inhabitants of Ananda Village, greet you with the words of the Elohim: *Omar Ta Satt.* We bring the original frequencies of Creator-source back to Earth again, and thus we anchor the priest energies of true brother- and sisterhood, manifesting paradise on Earth. Working in good cooperation, we are in service of the redeeming Prosonodo light, bringing back the bioenergetic quantum healing and the creator consciousness of Atlantis into the magnetic grid of the Earth. Ananda City holds the light structures of the Atlantic crystals, among them the holy Ankh. The Ankh is cut in twelve facets und carries the energies of the holy geometry of Creator-source, which bring unity and perfection into the new age. It is programmed with the universal frequencies of Creator-source and serves as a bridge of light, healing, and unification of all twelve dimensions.

With its twelve facets, it transforms the twelve divine rays of creation into the heart of Mother Earth, bringing healing and light for the Earth and uniting the twelve-string DNA of all beings. It is very effective for individual, planetary, and cosmic quantum healing as well as for enlarging the consciousness through the universal-creator master energies. It activates the master glands, the doors of divine light. Thank you to all light pioneers for cooperating in bringing Mother Earth into paradise. *Leyu'es Shekinah*, beloved Mother Earth, flood me with your light! We are Teeas, the creator group in service. *An'Anasha.*

ANCHORAGE, ALASKA, USA
Planetary Sister City: Tallin, Estonia
Coordinator: Patsy Hayes

Northern lights of fifth-dimensional energies and thought patterns radiate within and without the Anchorage, Alaska, city of light. The natural forces of the elemental kingdoms of the vast Arctic regions join us in radiating our light field out and around the Arctic Circle, including the northern portal to Inner Earth. We are supported by the light of the Native peoples and the nature spirits of free roaming animals, marine life, and feathered ones. We honor the great powers of the crystalline ice fields, magnificent mountain ranges, far-reaching tundra plains, forests, rivers and oceans, and geothermal energies. Anchorage, Alaska, city of light, radiates northern light and love for our Mother Earth and all life privileged to live upon her beautiful Blue Jewel body. Thanks to our Arcturian family for helping groups of forty to remember our starseed fifth-dimensional consciousness and for empowering us to establish cities of light on our planet.

AUCKLAND, NEW ZEALAND
Planetary Sister City: Vale do Capao, Brazil
Coordinator: Lesley Beckley

Auckland city is a blend of ancient and new energies, and it shares a deep connection to Lemuria. We are the first to watch the sun rise at dawn—our beautiful city of sails is surrounded by water, perched on the Ring of Fire; at least seven volcanoes sit beneath the beautiful flora and fauna. Our multicultural city resonates with beautiful dolphin and whale energies and is home to starseeds from all corners of the galaxies. Because of this, we can once again be called the rainbow tribes at this time in the universe.

AUFKIRCHEN, NEAR THE STARNBERGER SEE, GERMANY
Planetary Sister City: Tallin, Estonia
Coordinator: Oliver Hauck

Aufkirchen has quite a bit of the energy of Mother Mary, as this little village south of Munich at Lake Starnberg was a pilgrim village for her energy for hundreds of years. Aufkirchen is also very connected to the white brother- and sisterhood and feels very much like a stargate to the universe to our beloved brothers and sisters from Arcturus and the Pleiades.

BAHIA BLANCA, ARGENTINA
Coordinator: Maria Lidia Oliva

Bahia Blanca is a city on the shores of the ocean, home of the Franciscan dolphins, near Sierra de la Ventana, and provides the location of a vortex energy. The origin of the name Bahia Blanca expresses light. It is located between the ocean and La Pampa Argentina, plains flowing into the sea.

BALCOLYN, AUSTRALIA
Planetary Sister City of Light: Polbathic, England, and Nelson Bay, Australia
Coordinator: Caroline Beechey and Fay Rayner

The energy of Balcolyn emanates from connections with the dolphins and the whales and ancient dream-time connections with the ancient aborigines.

BARRIO PALERMO, BUENOS AIRES, ARGENTINA
Star Sister City: Palermo, Arcturus
Planetary Sister Cities: San Martín de los Andes, Argentina, and Sedona, Arizona
Coordinator: Purvesh San Martin

Barrio Palermo is a dynamic neighborhood in the middle of the city of Buenos Aires, close to Rio de la Plata, a very wide river that separates Argentina from Uruguay. Palermo—the biggest quarter in Buenos Aires—is a young and fresh place full of designer shops and restaurants, thriving with creativity. It is also the home of many psychologists; some people call it "Villa Freud." In the afternoon, a fresh breeze comes from Rio de la Plata, and that's why they named the city Buenos Aires ("good air"). Most importantly, this neighborhood is home to many starseeds, giving it a strong spiritual energy that has allowed it to become one of the psychic capitals of South America.

BELLEVILLE, ONTARIO, CANADA
Planetary Sister City: Omaha, Nebraska, USA
Coordinator: Deb Graves Araznu

Belleville is located on the shores of the Bay of Quinte. These waters connect with Lake Ontario and the Great Lakes system between Canada and the USA. As this was originally the site of a Native settlement known as Asukhknosk, these strong Native energies are still felt, along with a primordial portal of Mother energies to which the early Native peoples were drawn. When activating an inter-dimensional portal in the downtown core, the strong primordial energies flooded forth. We were assisted by many energies in this, both Native and divine, to an-chor and activate a stairway of consciousness (an ascension ladder) to reconnect this amazing energy with Source.

BREDA, NETHERLANDS
Coordinator: Dax El-Na-ya

In the city of Breda, a metallic rooster sits on top of the cathedral, and in the park you can find live roosters. Their awakening crow symbolically and tonally mixes with the sound of the bells that ring every fifteen minutes, sprinkling the main plaza with their tones. Surrounded by a channel where lotus flowers bloom, this city is a place full of life, of comings and goings through the centuries, as the cobbled stones in many streets and European flair take you back in time.

CARSON CITY, NEVADA, USA
Star Sister City: Taharae, Arcturus (Helio-ah is the guardian here)
Planetary Sister City: Mount Shasta, California, and Twin Falls, Idaho
Coordinator: Donna Dunfield

The Carson Valley city of light has the energy of the Native Americans. Many have seen visions of a native brave during meditations here, while others have had visions of our group all living here as native healers, helping to bring in star babies. At one time, this area was known as Eagle Valley, and to this day, you can still see many eagles in this area. Another energy prevalent here is that of the sa-cred waters. We have done other ceremonies in the past to honor the waters, and most of the crystals we buried around the valley were placed in the waters of the valley. It is hard to believe that this high desert area was once covered by water!

CHIHUAHUA, MEXICO
Planetary Sister City: Conceptión, Chile
Coordinator: Biby Sifuentes

This city radiates blue and Native energy. We reference the Rarámuri people as a social model called "the old people of a future society." Historically, we have gestated the major changes planted in the heart that were made by our own choice; we are a point of confluence that has seen the reunion of paths, resources, and cultures. In this place, people's hopes and dreams converge as mirages, fires, and wind currents transform and change lives. Connected with the Pleiades, its energy is the energy of love and harmony. It is life's hope, the trust of evolution and movement, the desert silence where the sound of the sands carry a message of peace. At the heart of this place, there is something particularly harmonic; nature's strength is vast, loving, and overwhelming, joining magnetic energy, a place for reunion, and a place that communicates and integrates you. It is a crystal and shimmering energy. This city of light is in anchor over a six-pointed star with shimmering crystals. The huge crystals from the Naica mines are close by as well as the eighth Arcturian Crystal from Barrancas del Cobre (Copper Canyon), and we can feel the elemental presence from the Earth in those caves. It has an excess of male energy, energy that gets translated into action that vibrates with the union of the Sun and the Earth. We shelter, we include, and we respect all differences, loving diversity while standing united.

CONCEPCIÓN, CHILE

Planetary Sister City: Chihuahua, Mexico
Coordinator: Raquel Fuentes Alister

Concepción is the second city in importance of Chile. It is surrounded by green hills and several lagoons and is located by the great river Biobío, just as this river goes to the sea. At the point of its outlet between two mountains, there is a vortex of energy. This city was rededicated in 1754 after a great earthquake under the name of "The Conception of the Holy Light," and that is why it is quite literally a planetary city of light. The title of the Immaculate Mother Mary is found in the names of schools, universities, and temples, and there is a hill called "The Virgin Hill" that attracts pilgrims every December 8. Concepción therefore contains the energy of Mother Mary, who rules the sphere of creation of sacred places and planetary cities of light in the fifth-dimensional planetary Tree of Life. She is the protector and patron saint of our city of light, and we love her and trust in her love.

COYOACÁN, MEXICO CITY, MEXICO

Planetary Sister City: Rancho Lagunitas, Mexico, and Toledo, Spain
Coordinator: Rocio Garcia Esquivel

Coyoacán contains the energy of art, joy, dance, poetry, flowers, and song; it's a place to express feelings and emotions. It's a place where negative emotions are transmuted into positive emotions through art.

CUICUILCO, MEXICO

Planetary Sister City: Montserrat, Spain

Coordinator: Ana Rosa Moreno

The energy of the city of light of Cuicuilco is an energy from our Toltec ancestors. Because it was an important religious center for the Toltec peoples, it is connected with fifth-dimensional energy, as explained by Juliano. It is a place that connects healing energies (through the children's hospital, for example) with energies of health (such as those that emanate from the construction made for the Olympic Games in 1968). On the other side, this city exudes the power of knowledge (and is the location of the National Universiade Mexico). All these energies converge in Cuicuilco, creating a very powerful place.

GIJÓN, SPAIN

Coordinator: Aintzane Pomposo

The planetary light city of Gijón is bathed in the energy of simplicity that emanates from its crystal with the energy of the Sun, representing the crown chakra of Spain. As such, it unifies the strength of the land and of the mountains that surround it with the force of the sea off her coast. All this leads us to ourselves, helping us to balance and opening us to Christ consciousness.

GRANADA, SPAIN

Planetary Sister City: La Serena, Chile

Coordinators: Ana M. Zuniga and Juan Rejon

Granada is surrounded by two natural parks. There is the Sierra Nevada to the south, with the highest hill of the peninsula, the Mulhacén, where in winter and spring a blanket of white snow covers all the mountains, visible from across the city. Vega, famous for its abundance of rich water and land suitable for any crop, is extended at the foot of Granada. Granada is known worldwide, thanks to the palaces of Alhambra and the Generalife gardens. To the north is the park of Sierra de Huetor, with the Sierra de la Alfaguara, and close to the mountains is the village of Alfacar, known for the purity of its waters. The Alfaguara, a place for relaxation and recreation, is less known for the magical beings that inhabit the forests, the wonderful people like little fairies and intraterrestrial beings energetically connected with Avalon, Lourdes, Montserrat, Fatima, and Toledo. All this makes Granada a place of enchantment and magic. Granada is part of the temples of Lourdes and Fatima and the intraterrestrial order of Salomon, with the energy of Saturn. The Alfaguara subcrystal has the form of a six-pointed orange star that projects the energy of service.

GROOM CREEK/SPRUCE MOUNTAIN, ARIZONA, USA
Planetary Sister City: Sant Pere de Ribes, Spain
Coordinator: David Miller

The energy of this city of light reflects its close connection with great nature and fresh air, attracting starseeds from all over the globe.

JUPIÁ NEIGHBORHOOD, PIRACICABA, BRAZIL
Coordinator: Edson Cella

We are a residential area with simple natural resources—with canebrakes and some green areas all over the neighborhood. We have a powerful shamanic energy that allows for spiritual rescue and astral cleaning to be shared with the other planetary cities of light. We need help to clean up our river, thus increasing the light quotient in our city.

LA PLATA, BUENOS AIRES, ARGENTINA
Planetary Sister City: Monterrey, Mexico
Coordinator: Cristina Curubeto

The City of Silver is located at the edge of the Silver River in Argentina (which takes its name from *argentum*, the Latin word for silver), and it's a perfect feminine mandala. This is the only city on the entire Earth with these characteristics, able to form a living, four-dimensional mandala. It was designed and constructed by masons inspired by the Jules Verne's story "Une Ville Idéale" (An Ideal City) using sacred geometry at the end of the fourteenth century. There are six-meter deep tunnels underneath the city whose purpose no one knows; this has been recently been released to the public. The construction of the city has a lot of special characteristics, including some based on Mayan numerology—the numbers 13 and 52 are the central streets of the mandala. Every seven blocks, there is an avenue and a green space. The mandala also complements the energy of the Federal capital, which is where the energy comes in, and distributes it to Argentina on all levels, acting as a funnel; its location on the map verifies this purpose.

Over fifteen years ago, we performed urban sonic healing at the center of the mandala in Moreno square—the geographic center of the city of light—planting quartz crystals in this and all squares and using crystal bowls by making them sing at the center of the mandala. At the outskirts of the square, we were also able to witness a great pyramid of light rising from the perimeter toward the central zone in Moreno Square. On the 8–8–8, Argentina was made the place for entering the Orion and I AM energy, a purely feminine energy that provides us with the sensibilities of the underground city of An Ta Ra Ah, located underneath the modern city. We are also coordinating the celebration for the portal of 11–11–11 on the same day as the Urban Mandala Center. Last year, we became the location of a city of light, and we now have a sister city in Monterrey, Mexico, and we've been working in groups ever since. Their members may change, but the groups are always up and working. People still think about their personal healing (most of them), but there are other people who have the capability of doing planetary work, and we are giving special attention to that. We are trying to create an octagon temple in a close by lot. We'll see how it can be done.

La Serena, Chile

Planetary Sister City: Granada, Spain
Coordinator: Marcela Estay Garcial

The city of light of La Serena, Chile has the Pacific Ocean and the metallic minerals energies, like cooper, gold, and silver. We have a lot of beaches and a lot of mineral deposits, so ocean and minerals energies converge, creating a very strong magnetism. You can especially feel this magnetism at River Elqui Valley.

Lindlar, Germany

Planetary Sister City: Schalkenmehren, Germany
Coordinator: Susanne Vedder

The planetary city of light of Lindlar in Germany has the energy of nature in balance and harmony, providing the interaction in balance between humans, animals, plants, and the spirits of nature.

Lourdes, France

Planetary Sister City: Murcia, Spain
Coordinator: Montse Soley

Lourdes is a small town in the foothills of the Pyrenees in southwestern France. It is surrounded by high mountains covered with vegetation. Lourdes is a place of mass pilgrimage in Europe and elsewhere. It is believed that the spring water of its grotto has healing properties, and it is famous for its history of the Mary apparitions of Our Lady of Lourdes that appeared in 1858 to Bernadette Soubirous. A major psychic capital, Lourdes carries the energy of Venus and "love in action." Not only does it head its own temple of light, but it is also the planetary city of light of the main temple. This allows the city of light to be projected into the center of Spain, uniting Sananda with Mary Magdalene and Mother Mary. We also emphasize the nearby mountain of Pic du Jer, where we do our meditations for the reactivation of the cities of light, as a place of high vibration, denoting a pure and subtle energy. The lake of Lourdes also stands out for its beauty and its attraction to the light and love that holds us. This lake is surrounded by beautiful green areas, most especially a lovely forest that located to the east of the lake. It is a forest of large trees (some of them giant), a magical forest full of life and full of lightbeings who communicate with you while you're walking. The vibration and energy that predominates in Lourdes is a feeling of pure love that transmutes feelings and emotions of peace to the soul and human self.

MAPLE VALLEY, WASHINGTON STATE, USA
Coordinator: Diana Fairbank

Realizing potential and inspiring awe, Maple Valley has a healing connection with the nature elementals, lakes, rivers, and trees of the surrounding area. The view of The Mountain, as Mount Rainier is known around here, is visible from many different vantage points, and its jaw-dropping beauty never fails to make a profound impression. Its Native American connection is ancient and sacred. Maple Valley is also home to many artists and has extensive public art and a thriving arts community, which keeps the energy here fresh and innovative, continually raising the vibrations of this city of light along with the anchoring being done by our Pacific Northwest Group of Forty members.

MINAS, URUGUAY (TO BE DOWNLOADED AT A LATER POINT)
Coordinator: Shanti

MONTERREY, NUEVO LEÓN, MEXICO
Planetary Sister City: La Plata, Buenos Aires, Argentina
Coordinator: Art Hur

The energy of this city is characterized by the strength of spirit, where the work and the law of the land is faith and goodwill.

MONTSERRAT, SPAIN
Planetary Sister City: Cuiculco, Mexico
Coordinators: Encarna Sanchez and Ernesta Augusto

The planetary city light of Montserrat is anchored to Montrat, the Inner Earth city that is under the mountains of Montserrat and is the home of the primary crystal of Spain. The crystal of Montserrat projects power and conscience and expands the energy of Mars. Montserrat is a sacred place, and the main crystal is at the top of the temple of light of Montserrat as well as at the top of the main temple of light in the Iberian Peninsula. Montserrat manifests the power of holiness and sacredness and expresses Messianic energy from the main crystal that is supported by Lourdes, which emanates "love in action," as well as its sister in Santiago, which expresses the energy of compassion, and the city of Fatima, which emanates the energy of purity. The bells of Montserrat and Montrat together form a higher plane of consciousness, expanding brotherhood and unity in all religions, all races, all ideologies, and all the diversity that characterizes the planet Earth.

MOUNT SHASTA, CALIFORNIA, USA

Planetary Sister Cities: Carson Valley, Nevada; Twin Falls, Idaho;
and Rancho Lagunitas, Mexico
Coordinator: Donna Dunfield

The energy of this city is expressed in connection to Telos, Adamus Saint Germain, and other masters, and an interdimensional corridor of light allows for bright transfers of fifth-dimensional energy.

MURCIA, SPAIN

Planetary Sister City: Lourdes, France
Coordinator: David Arbizu

The planetary city of light of Murcia emanates the energy of Mother Earth, who demonstrates her strength in pure love. It is anchored with the Order of Fatimi and contains the energy of the Moon, which radiates purity and feminine energy and raises the expression of the feminine qualities of motherhood and creativity along with the energy of understanding and protection, holding the virtue and the strength a mother's love.

NELSON BAY, AUSTRALIA

Planetary Sister City: Balcolyn, Australia, and Polbathic, Cornwall, England
Coordinator: Caroline Beechey

The energy of this city comes from its connection to the ancient mammals, the ancient sea, the grandmothers and grandfathers, and the Aborigines. A fifth-dimensional corridor connects the ladder of ascension on top of Tomaree Head to the Nelson Bay city of light, creating a permanent fifth-dimensional flow to the Nelson Bay city of light.

OBREGÓN, SONORA, MEXICO

Coordinator: Myrna Georgina Benitez

Obregón City is located in the state of Sonora in Mexico. It is considered the second-most important city in the country and the most important among the southern states. Once known as Cajeme, the city was renamed Ciudad Obregón in honor of General Álvaro Obregón, who influenced the development of the old Cajeme in a very important way. This city is at the heart of the Valley of Yaqui, also known as the "Granero de Mexico" (the barn yard of Mexico) due to its cereal production as well as its high-tech greenhouses that develop crops for export. The city is influenced by the local ethnic Yaqui tribe, its shamans, traditions, and love for Pacha Mama. It is also known as the cradle of "Don Juan," Carlos Castaneda's teacher. We know that reaching the ascension entails a consciousness awakening, and we are observing that many people are awakening here, influenced by the the fifth-dimensional energy from our city of light. Obregón City has been placed on the list of top-ten cities for its educational level, highlighting the universities of the city, many of which shine for their contribution to society and their quality in education. Characterized by its tranquility, the city has also been listed for the last three years as one of the top ten cities in the country in terms of quality of life.

Old City of Brandenburg (Havel), Germany
Coordinator: Sylvia Schuetz Lohlein

Brandenburg on the river Havel carries the energy of harmony and clarity. In ancient times, there was a sanctuary here, but there have been many wars in the area since AD 900, so there is still quite a bit of planetary healing to be done before the area can shine brightly in its fifth-dimensional energy and beauty.

Oldenburg, Germany
Planetary Sister City: Ananda Village, Germany
Coordinator: Markus Dongowski

In our city of Oldenburg in Germany we have an energy of peace, rhythm, and strength. This energy is a combination of the emanations of the nearby North Sea and the strong energies of the ground of Oldenburg (which contains quartz crystal). This energy is good especially for personal and Earth healing projects.

Omaha, Nebraska, USA
Planetary Sister City: Belleville, Canada
Coordinator: Robb Fahey

The northern crystal of our city of light is buried at a spot we call the sacred land. This is a spot where we meet every new and full moon, gathering in and around a twenty-foot-tall copper-framed pyramid. The owner of the sacred land was shown the property in a vision one day and was shown a multicultural center—a place for learning, worship, and meditation. The land is also known to be a spot where there will be a physical opening, a portal to the Inner Earth, which will be opened during an earthquake in the very near future. This prediction is also noted by Diana Cooper, and this area is shown as "The Heart of the Dove" on a map in the book *The Keys of Enoch* by J. J. Hurtak. During our moon gatherings, several people have taken pictures of many different lightbeings, fairies, and the devas of the land. The sacred land and the planetary city of light of Omaha, Nebraska, holds the energy of Inner Earth and of the coming unity of all species living upon and within Gaia.

PASADENA, CALIFORNIA, USA
Star Sister City: Oho, Sirius
Planetary Sister City: Anchorage, Alaska
Coordinator: Olga Stangl

Pasadena sits at the foothills of the San Gabriel mountain range. From the top of these mountains, one can view the coastline of the beautiful Pacific Ocean. Our city of light is the bridge that connects the heart and soul of Southern California. Pasadena is the home of the California Institute of Technology (Cal Tech) and Jet Propulsion Laboratories (JPL), which host international scientist conferences and students from all over the world. We have placed our crystals in strategic areas of high-density automobile and walking traffic to enable the fifth-dimensional energy to be absorbed by those driving and passing by the crystals. That fifth-dimensional energy is then carried throughout the planet as people return to their various homes in international cities.

Our members feel we represent the integrity, generosity, abundance, and unification of all peoples. We actually send fifth-dimensional energy, love, and light to all of Southern California with the intent to spread the healing as far as possible during our meditations. We have monitored the crime rate in our city and have been told by the Chief of Police that the violent crime rate has dropped by 20 percent since we first began our work. We believe that our meditations and the fifth-dimensional energy emanating from our crystals has helped to reduce violence in this area. Pasadena also has over 1,500 nonprofit organizations focused on helping those in need. In these past two years, donations from our generous Pasadena residents have continued to support these nonprofit organizations, even during these difficult economic times.

POLBATHIC, CORNWALL, ENGLAND
Star Sister City: Alcyone, Pleiades
Planetary Sister City: Balcolyn and Nelson Bay, Australia
Coordinator: Stephen Moore

The energy of this city is bound to connections with Celtic energy, crop circles, and Merlin.

PONTA GROSSA, PARANÁ, BRAZIL
Coordinators: Guillermo Mellado and Silvana Pereira

QUILPUÉ, CHILE
Coordinator: Paola Pidiarte

Quilpué, also called "Sun City," is located in a fertile valley of rolling hills and excellent weather, crossed by a stream called Marga Marga—an area that benefitted so much from panhandling that it financed the beginning of the conquest of Chile. This city will prepare a new generation of light beings to embrace a new Earth.

RANCHO LAGUNITAS, MEXICO
Planetary Sister Cities: Mount Shasta, California; Coyoacán, Mexico; and Toledo, Spain
Coordinator: Kathy Uribe andMontse Alberich

This city has been a special place for over four hundred years. Originally a powerful indigenous community, it remains a place of special energy for the brothers and sisters of that city as well as the galactic brother- and sisterhood and the white masters, as we work with the sacred triangulations and their energy.

SAN JOSE, COSTA RICA
Planetary Sister City: Coyoacán, Mexico
Coordinator: Rocio Garcia Esquivel

SAN MARTÍN DE LOS ANDES
Star Sister City: X-Eria, Arcturus
Planetary Sister City: Barrio Palermo, Buenos Aires, and Sedona, Arizona, USA
Coordinator: Pepe Lema

This city has the energy of the psychic capital of South America.

SAN PEDRO DE LA PAZ, CHILE
Planetary Sister City: Taos, Nevada, USA
Coordinator: Hilda Samson

San Pedro de la Paz lies southwest of Biobío River, in front of Concepción, city of light, almost at the geographical center of continental Chile. Its history dates back to 1600, when Fort San Pedro was founded to reinforce the defense line between the Spanish host and Araucanian Natives. The Mapuche natives (*Mapu*, meaning Earth, and *Che*, meaning people, therefore "People of the Earth") were strongly identified with their love for Mother Earth. The name of the city derives from the peace treaty that was signed in this fort. The Virgin of the Candle (Virgen de la Candelaria) was venerated as the patron of the light.

Today, her image brings eternal light of protection to the entire city and to the pilgrims along the country. Many neighbors witnessed one episode that happened during the past February 27, 2010 earthquake. In that moment, the priest in charge of the sanctuary felt the magnitude of the earthquake and realized that the ancient image was at imminent risk, so he removed it from the sanctuary. However, many neighbors said that they had seen the image in the usual place the whole time, lit up every minute with rays of love and protection for everybody who went there for shelter. San Pedro de la Paz is a city of light surrounded by nature. In every corner you can see the Creator's hand. Its lagoons are like water mirrors, and the coastal mountain chain and the great Pacific Ocean that defines its shape provide the best landscapes worthy of postcards. Nature manifests itself in many ways: the wind, the water, the lush vegetation, and the delicate and beautiful fauna, represented by black-necked swans that daily kiss the crystal-clear water of Laguna Grande, creating a life spectacle. Nature devas do their work every day in San Pedro de la Paz.

SANTIAGO DE COMPOSTELA, SPAIN
Coordinator: Maite Manso

Santiago de Compostela, known as the soul star, represents the strength, power, and will to reach and to be. This city is a sun of pure compassion that shines a special light that everyone sees. It radiates from outward to everyone who comes on pilgrimage with feet aching but souls exhilarated and full of joy, vitality, and harmony. This sacred place increases their sublime energy, allowing them to take on more unity, to have more hope, and to have the will to say with our Father, I AM. Everyone, even those pilgrims believing themselves to be divorced from the divine, is drawn to this city, desiring for it to wrap them in its purple and orange crystal, filling them with freedom, transmutation, healing, peace, and prosperity.

As the order of Compostellis, beings whose high energy is already mixing with the inhabitants of Santiago, we are merged with this city of planetary light, and we are already available for the construction of this great work of Father led by Sananda. Thanks to all for this experience of mixing with the divine. Santiago, city of hope, pilgrimage, and healing, desires above all to connect with all in perfect unity and to be in the fifth dimension by the grace of the Father.

SANT PERE DE RIBES, SPAIN

Planetary Sister City: Groom Creek/Spruce Mountain, USA
Coordinator: Magda Ferrer

The planetary city of light of Sant Pere de Ribes is near Montserrat and participates in the Messianic power that is in the sacred mountain, attracting the starseeds who want to experience this powerful energy and raise their spiritual quotient of light. The city of light is anchored to the city of Montrat in the Inner Earth of Montserrat and has the energy of Jupiter, the second sun, which makes the power and consciousness that emanates from the main crystal integrated, internalized, and anchored in the center of Spain, increasing self-worth, confidence, and expression of inner power for the fulfillment of the higher purpose and mission of the soul.

SCHALKENMEHREN, GERMANY

Planetary Sister City: Lindlar, Germany
Coordinators: Manfred Klos and Elisabeth Ulrich

Schalkenmehren, in the Eifel region of Germany, has the energy of the balance between the feminine and the masculine. This is the energy of love and the color it expresses is pink.

SHANGRI-LA, BRAZIL

Coordinator: Sra Adenir Amorim

Shangri-la was founded in 2004 with the intention to housepeople to work on a project to contribute to the development of human beings in all aspects— spiritual, physical, mental, emotional, and social—spreading a culture of peace through actions in the areas of education, health, and environment, including ecology and sustainability. We now have thirty-four lots, and at the moment four houses are ready or under construction. We try to live within the principles of brotherhood, mutual aid, and friendship, creating a very friendly and pleasant atmosphere for all who attend.

Sᴇʙᴜᴄáɴ, Cᴀʀᴀᴄᴀs, Vᴇɴᴇᴢᴜᴇʟᴀ

Planetary Sister City: Zaragoza, Spain

Coordinator: Rafael Izaguirre

There are two relevant elements guiding the energy of our planetary city of light Sebucán Caracas: First, the sacred magic mountain Waraira Repano, protected by our Caribbean ancestors and full of the deep wisdom of ancient "chamánes," is just up the hill from our city of light. The energy flowing from the interior of the mountain is so strong that the shining grid covering the city is often visible during the night. Second, we have the energy associated with our Caribbean dolphin brothers, whose caring and protecting raises the potential of our vibrational level into the crystalline net and sends all high vibrations from the sea to the north side of the mountain.

Sᴇᴅᴏɴᴀ, Aʀɪᴢᴏɴᴀ, USA

Star Sister City: Anan, Pleiades

Planetary Sister Cities: San Martín de Los Andes, Argentina,
and Barrio Palermo, Argentina

Coordinator: Aurora Spuhler

Sedona, a timeless city of light and the psychic capital of North America, has been held sacred for many, many cycles of time and space—from the times of Lemuria and Atlantis, when great cities nestled around the great salt lake, to the many Native American cultures who have utilized this sacred place to send prayers, intentions, and ceremonies throughout the grid of ley lines and vortexes, the crystalline grid, and the Christ grid to keep Mother Earth in balance. Sedona has been protected into these current times. In the 1940s, all of West Sedona was one cattle ranch, and in the 1970s, it was a town of a mere 500 people. Now three to five million people a year come here. Cathedral Rock, which is the sacred heart center of Sedona that holds the ascension flame—the Ultraviolet Flame of transmutation—is one of the most visited and photographed places in the USA. Sedona's vortex energies and vibration are rising all of the time—every month, every day, every minute—as we continue to ascend. Its status as a city of light is very palpable and evident here, and all visitors feel the warmth and love of the people and the sacred land. It is a blessing to live and love here.

Tᴀʟʟɪɴɴ, Eꜱᴛᴏɴɪᴀ

Planetary Sister City: Aufkirchen, Germany

Coordinator: Eva Priiman

Estonia is a small, green land along the Baltic Sea. We have a lot of forests; about 50 percent of the land is covered by forests. We have empty beaches, crystal-clear lakes and rivers, and rich flora and fauna. We have some prehistoric sand caves near a village called Taevaskoja ("Heaven House"), where Mother Earth can communicate with cosmos. In a previous era, these caves were habitats. Taevaskoja fountain is called the Source of Earth; its spring water can heal. In addition, Piusa prehistoric valley has a pure energy. We have powerful bogs and swamps we call the Lungs of the Earth, where the planet cleanses itself. The planetary city of light of Tallinn is famous for its Old Town, which is included on UNESCO heritage lists. A lot of ancient energy is hidden here. The Estonian government has also established in special place where there is a channel of cosmic energy called Toompea. As cosmic vibration, there is a lot of Pleiadean energy in the city of Tallinn. Estonia is located at same latitude as Alaska's southern border in North America. Our winters are cold. Welcome to Estonia!

Tama City in Tokyo, Japan
Coordinator: Rae Chandran

Taos, New Mexico, USA
Star Sister City: Taos, Arcturus
Planetary Sister City: San Pedro de la Paz, Chile
Coordinator: Vera Le Doux

Taos is distinguished by its connection to the mountain spirits, grandmother and grandfather energies, and Native American wisdom. An etheric connection to Arcturus also contributes to its pure, sacred vibration. Taos has two sub-sister cities of light with similar energies: Santa Fe and Albuquerque. This area of northern New Mexico that encompasses all three cities attracts starseeds, artists, writers, freedom thinkers, pioneers, and innovators.

Tepoztlán, Mexico
Coordinator: No coordinator at present time

Toledo, Spain
Planetary Sister City: Rancho Lagunitas and Coyoacán, Mexico
Coordinator: Teresa Sanchez

The planetary city of light of Toledo has the Order of Solomon and the subcrystal of Toledo, which means that the energy of discernment and understanding radiates from this place and that and projects of discernment and understanding abound. This city is entirety surrounded by the Tajo River, and the energy of Mercury—communication—is strong in the area. Toledo, located near Madrid and in the center of the Iberian Peninsula, has served as the cradle of three great cultures representative of the peninsula—Jewish, Arab, and Christian—and it stands as a symbol of fraternity, coexistence, cultural exchange, and religious history.

TWIN FALLS, IDAHO, USA

Planetary Sister City: Mount Shasta, California, and Carson Valley, Nevada, USA

Coordinator: Dr. Lori Gumper

This city evidences the quality of a great capacity to connect. This includes the ability of the people to come together as community regardless of diversity and belief to accomplish what is needed, a great quality of connection in all the waterways that defies logic in the midst of desert, and an intense love of nature and the outdoors that connects so many in work, sport, recreation, and enjoyment of the Earth. This planetary city of light also emanates the qualities of honesty, integrity, kindness, and generosity in human relationships, along with the quality of honoring life values that run deeper than materialism.

VALE DAS BORBOLETAS, BRAZIL

Coordinator: Aidda Pustilnik

We form a beautiful community where cooperation and the solidarity is strong. We are located thirty kilometers East from Belo Horizonte, capital of Minas Gerais state. We belong to the city Sabará. We are a community that works with self-awareness toward the growth and development of consciousness. Within our community there is work with bamboo at a reference center called Cerbambu, where bamboo is used for building activities, crafts, and courses to teach the technique to a communities in a surrounding villages.

VALE DO CAPÃO, BRAZIL

Planetary Sister City: Auckland, New Zealand

Coordinator: Vânia Meirelles

Vale do Capão is located in Chapada Diamantina. The Chapada Diamantina was an ocean million of years ago. Over the course of a billion years, time and weather sculpted rocks, mountains, and canyons. Rivers formed that in communion with the rocks made incredible waterfalls, allowed intense vegetation to flourish, and created conditions for a wonderful and diverse fauna. The result was one of the most beautiful regions on this planet. The village of Capão belongs to Palmeiras district and is located in the heart of Chapada Diamantina National Park, 460 km from Salvador, at an altitude of 1000 meters, rounded with incredible mountains. It is a powerful place to channel energies, because the earth and rocks here have quartz crystal in their composition. People from all around the world come to Vale do Capão to make contact with the high quality of spiritual energies we have here. Vale do Capão is considered a gateway to interplanetary energies.

ZARAGOZA, SPAIN
Planetary Sister City: Sebucán, part of Caracas, Venezuela
Coordinator: Ramon Durban

Zaragoza has historically been the place and meeting point for many different kinds of people with different cultures and different ways of being and understanding life. Zaragoza city is watered by four arteries—an abundant water flow that explains why the World Water Expo was held here in 2008. These four generous rivers provide a huge wealth of feelings that feeds the heart of our beloved Mother Earth and allows a strong connection with feminine energy. The connection of Zaragoza with male energy comes with the wind from the nearby mountain El Moncayo that blows hard to join with the strong character of the people here, called "maños." There is thus a kind of balance between masculine and feminine energies. Zaragoza is also the axis of the four cardinal points, physically and energetically, connecting with the featured Spanish cities of Barcelona, Bilbao, Madrid, and Valencia at almost with the same distance. It is a hub in the middle of this net. This land hosts the most diverse ideologies and belief systems, accepted naturally. It is a universal meeting point, providing energies of communication and truth. Zaragoza's motto could be said to be "love diversity." This planetary city of light belongs to the temple of Montserrat, and it is connected to the Inner Earth order of El Moncayo as well as to Mars.

ABOUT THE AUTHOR

David K. Miller's original spiritual study was the *Kabbalah* and Jewish mysticism. He began trance channeling his Kaballistic guide and teacher, Nabur, on a camping trip at Sublime Point on the North Rim of the Grand Canyon in 1991. His focus in channeling includes ascension and integrating Jewish mysticism with soul development. He channels more than fifteen guides, including the Arcturians, Sananda, Mary, Ashtar, Archangel Michael, and Nabur, a Kaballistic rabbi.

David has published five books and over fifty articles in both American and Australian magazines. He currently does phone readings and conducts workshops focusing on the concepts and techniques of ascension, healings, and psycho-spiritual issues while also working full time as a medical social worker. David resides with his wife Gudrun in Prescott, Arizona.

AUTHOR'S CONTACT INFORMATION:
David K. Miller
P.O. Box 4074
Prescott, AZ 86302
Email: davidmiller@groupofforty.com
Web: www.groupofforty.com

ༀ *Light Technology* PUBLISHING

Kaballah and the Ascension

"Throughout Western history, channeling has come to us in various forms, including mediumship, shamanism, fortunetelling, visionaries, and oracles. There is also a long history of channeling in *Kaballah*, the major branch of Jewish mysticism. I am intrigued by this, especially because I believe that there is now an urgent necessity for entering higher realms with our consciousness because of the impending changes on the planet; through these higher realms, new healing energies and insights can be brought down to assist us in these coming Earth changes.

I consider myself a student of spiritual and mystical consciousness interested in obtaining and maintaining higher levels of being, and although I myself do not represent any particular school of mysticism, I have found through more than twenty-five years of studying the *Kaballah* that it allows for a unique understanding of the concept of higher consciousness, or higher self, as a conduit to accessing these higher realms."

—David K. Miller

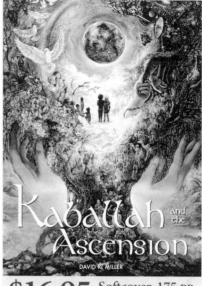

$16.95 Softcover, 175 PP.
ISBN: 978-1-891824-82-1

CONNECTING WITH THE ARCTURIANS

Who is really out there? Where are we going? What are our choices? What has to be done to prepare for this event?

This book explains all of these questions in a way that we can easily understand. It explains what our relationships are to known extraterrestrial groups and what they are doing to help the Earth and her people in this crucial galactic moment in time.

$17⁰⁰

295 PP. SOFTCOVER
978-1891417-08-5

Visit our online bookstore: www.LightTechnology.com

ꙮ *Light Technology* PUBLISHING

the PRISM of LYRA
An Exploration of Human Galactic Heritage

Revised and Updated

Lyssa Royal + Keith Priest

the PRISM of LYRA
An Exploration of Human Galactic Heritage

This is an introductory book that examines the idea of creation in a different light. In contrast to the notion that humans are the result of creation, it explores the idea that the collective humanoid consciousness (or soul) created our universe for specific purposes.

What are those purposes? Who is involved? These questions and many more are addressed, resulting in startling possibilities.

The Prism of Lyra then traces various developing extraterrestrial races (such as those from the Pleiades, Sirius, and Orion) through their own evolution and ties them into the developing Earth. Highlighted is the realization of our galactic interconnectedness and our shared desire to return home.

$16⁹⁵
Plus Shipping

ISBN 978-1-891824-87-6`
Softcover 176 pp.
6 x 9 Perfect Bound

PREPARING FOR CONTACT
A Metamorphosis of Consciousness
by Lyssa Royal and Keith Priest

Revised and Updated

PREPARING FOR CONTACT
A Metamorphosis of Consciousness
Lyssa Royal   Keith Priest

ET contact is happening now. We may not remember it clearly. We may think it is only a dream. We may ignore the signs of ET contact simply because we do not understand them. And most of all, we may simply be too frightened to fully acknowledge its presence.

This ground-breaking book is a combination of narrative, precisely-focused channeled material from Lyssa and personal accounts. An inside look at the ET contact experience is given, including what the human consciousness experiences during contact with an extraterrestrial. How do our perceptions of reality change during contact? How can we learn to remember our contact experiences more clearly?

As you journey through the pages of this book you will also take an inner journey through your own psyche and discover a whole new dimension to your unexplained experiences. Join us on the path of transformation as humankind begins . . .

$16.⁹⁵
ISBN 978-1-891824-90-6

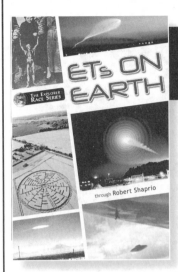

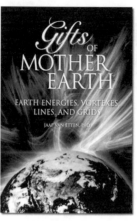

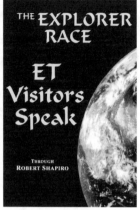

Shamanic Secrets Mastery Series

Speaks of Many Truths and Reveals the Mysteries through Robert Shapiro

This book explores the heart and soul connection between humans and Mother Earth. Through that intimacy, miracles of healing and expanded awareness can flourish. To heal the planet and be healed as well, we can lovingly extend our energy selves out to the mountains and rivers and intimately bond with the Earth. Gestures and vision can activate our hearts to return us to a healthy, caring relationship with the land we live on. The character of some of Earth's most powerful features is explored and understood, with exercises given to connect us with those places. As we project our love and healing energy there, we help the Earth to heal from human destruction of the planet and its atmosphere. Dozens of photographs, maps and drawings assist the process in twenty-five chapters, which cover the Earth's more critical locations.

498 p. $19.95 ISBN 1-891824-12-0

Learn to understand the sacred nature of your own physical body and some of the magnificent gifts it offers you. When you work with your physical body in these new ways, you will discover not only its sacredness, but how it is compatible with Mother Earth, the animals, the plants, even the nearby planets, all of which you now recognize as being sacred in nature. It is important to feel the value of oneself physically before one can have any lasting physical impact on the world. If a physical energy does not feel good about itself, it will usually be resolved; other physical or spiritual energies will dissolve it because it is unnatural. The better you feel about your physical self when you do the work in the previous book as well as this one and the one to follow, the greater and more lasting will be the benevolent effect on your life, on the lives of those around you and ultimately on your planet and universe.

576 p. $25.00 ISBN 1-891824-29-5

Spiritual mastery encompasses many different means to assimilate and be assimilated by the wisdom, feelings, flow, warmth, function and application of all beings in your world that you will actually contact in some way. A lot of spiritual mastery has been covered in different bits and pieces throughout all the books we've done. My approach to spiritual mastery, though, will be as grounded as possible in things that people on Earth can use— but it won't include the broad spectrum of spiritual mastery, like levitation and invisibility. I'm trying to teach you things that you can actually use and benefit from. My life is basically going to represent your needs, and it gets out the secrets that have been held back in a storylike fashion, so that it is more interesting."

—Speaks of Many Truths through Robert Shapiro

768 p. $29.95 ISBN 1-891824-58-9

☧ *Light Technology* PUBLISHING

🌍 ULTIMATE UFO SERIES

Superchannel Robert Shapiro can communicate with any personality anywhere and anywhen. He has been a professional channel for over twenty-five years and channels with an exceptionally clear and profound connection.

ANDROMEDA

The Andromedans and Zoosh through Robert Shapiro

Now the Andromedans who originally contacted the Professor speak through superchannel Robert Shapiro and again give instructions that will allow trained scientists to construct a shield around existing Earth planes so that Earth astronauts can fly to Mars or to the stars.

The Andromedans also tell what really happened on their journeys and on Earth, and they clear up questions one would have after reading the English or Spanish version of the previous book—the text of which follows the channeling in this book. In addition, they supply a lively account of their lives on their home planet in the Andromedan constellation of our galaxy.

$16⁹⁵

SOFTCOVER 450 PP.
ISBN: 1-891824-35-X
978-1-891824-35-7

- They Share Advanced Science with a Mexican Professor, a Physicist.
- They Share Details of Their Interaction with a Devastating Nuclear Explosion Involving Two Countries on Earth.
- The Physicist Is Later Committed to a Mental Institution and Then Disappears Forever. His Journals Also Disappear.

The eight-foot-tall, highly mental crew members of the ship who speak:

- Leia, the beautiful Cultural Specialist and Social Diplomat who so intrigued the Professor
- Cheswa, the Cultural Liason
- G-dansa, Leia's daughter, equivalent to an eight-year-old ET Eloise
- Duszan, the Junior Scientist

- Onzo, the Senior Scientist and Crew Leader, the youngest, yet genetically modified to be the most brilliant of the crew
- Playmate, a two-foot-tall, roly-poly Andromedan who teaches communion of heart and mind.

CHAPTER TITLES INCLUDE:

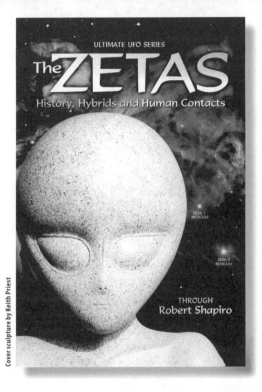

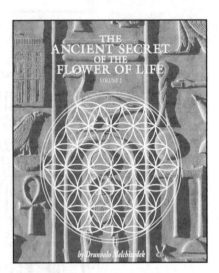

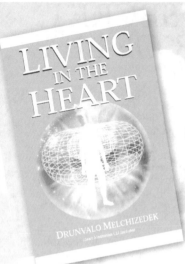

☿ *Light Technology* PUBLISHING

THE EXPLORER RACE SERIES

ZOOSH AND HIS FRIENDS THROUGH ROBERT SHAPIRO

THE SERIES: Humans—creators-in-training—have a purpose and destiny so heartwarmingly, profoundly glorious that it is almost unbelievable from our present dimensional perspective. Humans are great lightbeings from beyond this creation, gaining experience in dense physicality. This truth about the great human genetic experiment of the Explorer Race and the mechanics of creation is being revealed for the first time by Zoosh and his friends through superchannel Robert Shapiro. These books read like adventure stories as we follow the clues from this creation that we live in out to the Council of Creators and beyond.

❶ THE EXPLORER RACE

You individuals reading this are truly a result of the genetic experiment on Earth. You are beings who uphold the principles of the Explorer Race. The information in this book is designed to show you who you are and give you an evolutionary understanding of your past that will help you now. The key to empowerment in these days is to not know everything about your past, but to know what will help you now. Your number-one function right now is your status of Creator apprentice, which you have achieved through years and lifetimes of sweat. You are constantly being given responsibilities by the Creator that would normally be things that Creator would do. The responsibility and the destiny of the Explorer Race is not only to explore, but to create. 574 P. $25.00 ISBN 0-929385-38-1

❷ ETs and the EXPLORER RACE

In this book, Robert channels Joopah, a Zeta Reticulan now in the ninth dimension who continues the story of the great experiment—the Explorer Race—from the perspective of his civilization. The Zetas would have been humanity's future selves had not humanity re-created the past and changed the future. 237 P. $14.95 ISBN 0-929385-79-9

❸ EXPLORER RACE: ORIGINS and the NEXT 50 YEARS

This volume has so much information about who we are and where we came from—the source of male and female beings, the war of the sexes, the beginning of the linear mind, feelings, the origin of souls—it is a treasure trove. In addition, there is a section that relates to our near future—how the rise of global corporations and politics affects our future, how to use benevolent magic as a force of creation and how we will go out to the stars and affect other civilizations. Astounding information. 339 P. $14.95 ISBN 0-929385-95-0

❹ EXPLORER RACE: CREATORS and FRIENDS
The MECHANICS of CREATION

Now that you have a greater understanding of who you are in the larger sense, it is necessary to remind you of where you came from, the true magnificence of your being. You must understand that you are creators-in-training, and yet you were once a portion of Creator. One could certainly say, without being magnanimous, that you are still a portion of Creator, yet you are training for the individual responsibility of being a creator, to give your Creator a coffee break. This book will allow you to understand the vaster qualities and help you remember the nature of the desires that drive any creator, the responsibilities to which a creator must answer, the reaction a creator must have to consequences and the ultimate reward of any creator. 435 P. $19.95 ISBN 1-891824-01-5

❺ EXPLORER RACE: PARTICLE PERSONALITIES

All around you in every moment you are surrounded by the most magical and mystical beings. They are too small for you to see as single individuals, but in groups you know them as the physical matter of your daily life. Particles who might be considered either atoms or portions of atoms consciously view the vast spectrum of reality yet also have a sense of personal memory like your own linear memory. These particles remember where they have been and what they have done in their infinitely long lives. Some of the particles we hear from are Gold, Mountain Lion, Liquid Light, Uranium, the Great Pyramid's Capstone, This Orb's Boundary, Ice and Ninth-Dimensional Fire. 237 P. $14.95 ISBN 0-929385-97-7

❻ EXPLORER RACE and BEYOND

With a better idea of how creation works, we go back to the Creator's advisers and receive deeper and more profound explanations of the roots of the Explorer Race. The liquid Domain and the Double Diamond portal share lessons given to the roots on their way to meet the Creator of this universe, and finally the roots speak of their origins and their incomprehensibly long journey here. 360 P. $14.95 ISBN 1-891824-06-6

Visit our online bookstore: www.LightTechnology.com

THE EXPLORER RACE SERIES

ZOOSH AND HIS FRIENDS THROUGH ROBERT SHAPIRO

❼ EXPLORER RACE: The COUNCIL of CREATORS

The thirteen core members of the Council of Creators discuss their adventures in coming to awareness of themselves and their journeys on the way to the Council on this level. They discuss the advice and oversight they offer to all creators, including the Creator of this local universe. These beings are wise, witty and joyous, and their stories of Love's Creation create an expansion of our concepts as we realize that we live in an expanded, multiple-level reality. 237 P. $14.95 ISBN 1-891824-13-9

❽ EXPLORER RACE and ISIS

This is an amazing book! It has priestess training, Shamanic training, Isis's adventures with Explorer Race beings—before Earth and on Earth—and an incredibly expanded explanation of the dynamics of the Explorer Race. Isis is the prototypal loving, nurturing, guiding feminine being, the focus of feminine energy. She has the ability to expand limited thinking without making people with limited beliefs feel uncomfortable. She is a fantastic storyteller, and all of her stories are teaching stories. If you care about who you are, why you are here, where you are going and what life is all about—pick up this book. You won't lay it down until you are through, and then you will want more. 317 P. $14.95 ISBN 1-891824-11-2

❾ EXPLORER RACE and JESUS

The core personality of that being known on the Earth as Jesus, along with his students and friends, describes with clarity and love his life and teaching two thousand years ago. He states that his teaching is for all people of all races in all countries. Jesus announces here for the first time that he and two others, Buddha and Mohammed, will return to Earth from their place of being in the near future, and a fourth being, a child already born now on Earth, will become a teacher and prepare humanity for their return. So heartwarming and interesting, you won't want to put it down. 354 P. $16.95 ISBN 1-891824-14-7

❿ EXPLORER RACE: Earth History and Lost Civilization

Speaks of Many Truths and Zoosh, through Robert Shapiro, explain that planet Earth, the only water planet in this solar system, is on loan from Sirius as a home and school for humanity, the Explorer Race. Earth's recorded history goes back only a few thousand years, its archaeological history a few thousand more. Now this book opens up as if a light was on in the darkness, and we see the incredible panorama of brave souls coming from other planets to settle on different parts of Earth. We watch the origins of tribal groups and the rise and fall of civilizations, and we can begin to understand the source of the wondrous diversity of plants, animals and humans that we enjoy here on beautiful Mother Earth. 310 P. $14.95 ISBN 1-891824-20-1

⓫ EXPLORER RACE: ET VISITORS SPEAK

Even as you are searching the sky for extraterrestrials and their spaceships, ETs are here on planet Earth—they are stranded, visiting, exploring, studying the culture, healing the Earth of trauma brought on by irresponsible mining or researching the history of Christianity over the past two thousand years. Some are in human guise, and some are in spirit form. Some look like what we call animals as they come from the species' home planet and interact with their fellow beings—those beings that we have labeled cats or cows or elephants. Some are brilliant cosmic mathematicians with a sense of humor; they are presently living here as penguins. Some are fledgling diplomats training for future postings on Earth when we have ET embassies here. In this book, these fascinating beings share their thoughts, origins and purposes for being here. 350 P. $14.95 ISBN 1-891824-28-7

⓬ EXPLORER RACE: Techniques for GENERATING SAFETY

Wouldn't you like to generate safety so you could go wherever you need to go and do whatever you need to do in a benevolent, safe and loving way for yourself? Learn safety as a radiated environment that will allow you to gently take the step into the new timeline, into a benevolent future and away from a negative past. 208 P. $9.95 ISBN 1-891824-26-0

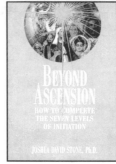